Pelican Books
English Progressive Schools

Robert Skidelsky was born in 1939 in Harbin, Manchuria,
of Russian-born parents who were naturalized British
citizens. He went to school at Brighton College, then won
an open scholarship in history to Jesus College, Oxford,
from which he graduated in 1961. After postgraduate
work he was made a Research Fellow of Nuffield
College, Oxford, and in 1968 he became a Research
Fellow of the British Academy.

He has mainly worked on twentieth-century British
history, and his book *Politicians and the Slump* (1967)
was an account of the Labour Government of 1929–31.
His biography of Sir Oswald Mosley is to be published
shortly in England and America.

ROBERT SKIDELSKY

English
Progressive
Schools

PENGUIN BOOKS

Penguin Books Ltd, Harmondsworth,
Middlesex, England
Penguin Books Inc., 7110 Ambassador Road,
Baltimore, Maryland 21207 U.S.A.
Penguin Books Australia Ltd, Ringwood,
Victoria, Australia

First published 1969
Reprinted 1970
Copyright © Robert Skidelsky, 1969

Made and printed in Great Britain by
C. Nicholls & Company Ltd
Set in Linotype Times

Contents

To Packly –
Who didn't go to one

Preface

I would like to thank Mrs Jean Floud, who took great trouble over the manuscript, and did her best to preserve me from the twin snares of sociology and educational theory which lead the unwary into an ever deepening fog of mystification. Richard Hodgkin, headmaster of Abbotsholme, A. S. Neill and Kurt Hahn also read relevant sections of the manuscript and made valuable suggestions, many of which I have incorporated. Where I have disagreed I have given their comment in a footnote. I must also thank A. S. Neill for permission to quote from his unpublished autobiography, and Kurt Hahn, who has given me permission to quote from unpublished letters, as well as supplying me with a mass of material. Thanks are due also to Alan Humphries and Mrs Archer for giving me permission to quote from an unpublished history of King Alfred School.

It is a great pleasure to thank John Aitkenhead (Kilquhanity), F. R. G. Chew (Gordonstoun), Hugh and Lois Child (Dartington Hall), Michael Duane (Risinghill), Desmond Hoare (Atlantic College), Richard Hodgkin (Abbotsholme), Alan Humphries and Mrs Archer (King Alfred School), Timothy Slack (Bedales) and L. C. Taylor (Sevenoaks), all of whom extended me the hospitality of their schools and answered my various inquiries with patience and good humour. I am only sorry that I cannot always be nice about the things they so sincerely try to do. A word of thanks is due finally to John Slater (housemaster of Bedales), with whom I had many conversations late into the night, and to all those teachers and boys and girls who made my stays so enjoyable and informative.

PART ONE

The Progressive Schools Today

1 · The Schools and Their Pupils

What is progressive education? The term conjures up various phrases from history's scrap-book: learning-by-doing, Arts and Crafts, Dalcroze eurhythmics, self-expression, free discipline. And the progesssive school? To some it is a delinquent's paradise of smoking, swearing, window-breaking and free love; to others, a society of sages and youths clad in shorts and sandals communing with Nature and milking cows; to others still, the site of antiquarian orgies of basket-making, weaving and pottery, sustained by health foods and mystic visions. The picture that emerges is of a movement at once primitive and idealistic, down-to-earth and yet seemingly remote from ordinary life. What set of historical and social circumstances gave rise to it? What theories of life lay behind it? Is it possible to distinguish a common credo?

The answer to these questions lies in the history of the progressive school movement. About eighty years ago there arose in England and on the Continent an impulse in education to which the name The New School Movement was generally given. A second wave of New Schools followed the First World War; a third wave in the 1930s. They all stood for something vaguely described as the New Education. Most of them were members of the New Education Fellowship, and subscribed to its journal, the *New Era*. In what exactly did their novelty consist?

This book describes the lives and ideas of three major progressive pioneers: Cecil Reddie of Abbotsholme, Alexander Neill of Summerhill and Kurt Hahn of Gordonstoun. These men, two of them living and active, may justly be considered the creative minds of the English progressive school movement. In some sense they epitomize, respectively, the successive stages of progressive foundations. Each is a remarkable personality in his own right, which adds interest to their story.

But the progressive school movement is not just a historical phenomenon. It is a living concern. It is right, therefore, to open this account with a brief description of the progressive schools today, seeking out characteristic contemporary features, before attempting to trace their inspiration in the past.

I have visited eight progressive schools, which make up a fair cross-section of the movement, spending about a week at each one. What follows are mainly impressions gained from these visits, reinforced by written records – school magazines and so on. They do not attempt to be scientific or comprehensive. For example, most of the schools had junior departments which I have largely ignored. No one would dispute the claim that the progressive ideal has triumphed, or is triumphing, at the primary and junior level. The question which interested me was: what are its chances of success at the senior level? – and this has given the whole study its focus. Again, I have concentrated upon what seem to me the distinctive features of the schools, rather than with features which they share in common with any school, or which have been largely incorporated into conventional school practice. Thus there will be comparatively little said about the poetic, dramatic and artistic manifestations of progressive education. Nothing is more irritating than reading enthusiastic reports of the wonderful 'art' or drama seen at progressive schools, uninformed by the knowledge that similarly wonderful 'art' or drama is being produced at all good schools throughout the country.

Abbotsholme School, situated on the banks of the River Dove in Staffordshire, was included in the itinerary mainly for historical reasons. The first of the English progressive schools, it was started by Cecil Reddie in 1889. Today, after many vicissitudes, it is securely established, if no longer particularly progressive, with 200 pupils of public-school age. Its most famous offshoot was Bedales, founded in 1893 and moved to its present site in Petersfield, Hampshire, a few years later. J. H. Badley, its first headmaster, died only last year at the great age of 102, a striking instance of the longevity of most progressive headmasters. 'Reddie,' he said 'taught me what to do and how not to do it.' Badley was responsible for one important innovation: coeducation, apparently forced on him by his fiancée as a condition of their marriage. Today the senior school has 250 pupils divided evenly between boys and girls, and a big expansion programme is under way.

Also dating from this 'first wave' of progressive foundations is King Alfred School, Hampstead. A coeducational day school, it began in 1897 when the seven founder members issued a circular on a 'proposed Rational School'. The first headmaster, C. E. Rice, had already taught science at Bedales for a number of years, thereby inaugurating that tendency for progressive schoolmasters to move from one progressive school to another. Today K.A.S. has 170 pupils of both sexes, aged from ten to seventeen.

From the 'second wave' I have chosen two schools, Summerhill (1921) and Dartington Hall (1925), and also a third, Kilquhanity (1940), which, though founded later, acknowledges the inspiration of Summerhill. Summerhill was opened by A. S. Neill in Lyme Regis before moving to its present quarters in Leiston, Suffolk, in 1927. It represents the extreme libertarian wing of the progressive school movement, which accounts for its notoriety and its inability to establish itself on a stable footing: Neill's attractive books have won many converts for the Summerhill idea, but the practice still seems too extreme for most parents. Today, with Neill still in charge, the school has sixty children of both sexes, most of them Americans.

Summerhill has indeed become something of a Mecca to American visitors to these shores; and A. S. Neill, the prophet of a minor, but growing, transatlantic cult. Forty or fifty of these visitors come every summer week-end to the small and rather ugly East Anglian town of Leiston, in their Cadillacs and coaches, to see for themselves the freedom and happiness they have read about, to take photographs of the children, to attend the meetings of the Summerhill Parliament, and to shake hands with the headmaster. For Neill, now eighty-six, this is welcome, if belated homage, bestowed characteristically, not by his own country, but by the traditional home of enthusiasms, the New World.

Dartington Hall was part of a much more grandiose project of rural revival, financed by wealthy landowners. The school was to be one element in a large community devoted to agriculture, the arts and traditional crafts. Today, it is part of a huge estate, with a farm, a textile mill, shops and a college of arts. There is much expensive equipment and new buildings: great, zigzagging hexagonal slabs of glass and concrete. But the pupils are not much interested in the farm, and the beautiful gardens are more admired by tourists and visitors than by the children. The first headmaster, William Curry, who retired in 1956, was heavily influenced, as was Neill, by Freudian psychology, a tradition that continues with the present heads, Mr and Mrs Child.* Today, the senior school, Foxhole, numbers 140 boys and girls.

Kilquhanity, set in the magnificent country side of Galloway, Scotland, with its delicate, differing summer shades of green, brown and purple, is the smallest of all the schools, numbering forty pupils of both sexes. Its founder and present head, John Aitkenhead, is a fervent Scottish Nationalist.

Finally, I visited Gordonstoun (1934) and Atlantic College (1962). The inclusion of these schools in a book on progressive education may occasion some surprise; yet Gordonstoun's links with Abbotsholme, and more generally with the German New School Movement which was partly inspired by Abbotsholme, are clear; and Atlantic College is closely linked to Gordonstoun. Moreover, in the concept of Outward Bound, a special Gordonstoun contribution, a number of progressive teachers see an important growth point in the modern progressive school movement. Gordonstoun itself was started in Morayshire, Scotland, by a German émigré, Kurt Hahn, and was a continuation of Hahn's German school, Salem. The surrounding country in early spring was austere and windswept, with grey grass and heather. The school is surrounded by scattered small-holdings; ten miles away, Elgin's spiky buildings look like something out of Grimm's Fairy Tales. In the school's rather drab main building hang pictures by Erich Meissner, Hahn's trusted friend and colleague, slightly mad-

*They have been succeeded by Dr. Royston Lambert.

looking, Germanic, symbolic. An extraordinary and pagan-looking Valhalla, then under construction, was to be the new school chapel. Gordonstoun's association with royalty, among other things, has made it very successful, and today there are 400 boys.

Atlantic College was the realization of Kurt Hahn's dream of a sixth-form international school based on Gordonstoun principles. The international membership is largely limited to countries in N.A.T.O., although the trustees hope eventually to establish similar schools all over the world. The school is in the process of becoming coeducational. It is situated on the Bristol Channel a few miles from Cardiff. St Donat's castle is certainly a most impressive home for a school. Basically it is a Tudor country house of the fifteenth to seventeenth centuries, contained within a castle of the early fourteenth century, parts of which have been enlarged to include medieval roofs, fire-places and bits of other houses. These enlargements were carried out by William Randolph Hearst, the American news-paper tycoon, who owned it from 1928 to 1938. In addition, Hearst installed central heating and increased the number of bathrooms from three to thirty-five. Chefs and butlers came from Claridges and the Savoy, rare wines were obtained, and altogether the many guests 'indulged in a certain amount of riotous living', in notable contrast to the somewhat Spartan regime in force today.*

Of these eight schools, seven are boarding, charging fees which place them well beyond the reach of most parents. (K.A.S. is a day school.) A qualification is necessary in the cases of Atlantic College and Kilquhanity. At the former, most English boys come on special scholarships provided by Local Education Authorities and firms. At Kilquhanity, an unusually high percentage – almost a quarter – are also supported by L.E.A.s on the more conventional ground that they come from disturbed homes. The fees range from £500 plus for Abbotsholme, Atlantic College, Bedales, Dartington Hall and Gordonstoun to £300 plus for Kilquhanity and Summer-

*This account is based on *St Donat's Castle: A Guide and Brief History*, by Esther Blackburn and Rita Williams.

	Professional			Business	Science	Farming	Other	Total
	Ordinary	Creative	Total					
ARDINGLY* (1958)	25	—	25	49	8	4	14	100 (294)
BEDALES (1967)	49	12	61	21	10	6	2	100 (240)
DARTINGTON (1967)	50	9	59	19	5	10	7	100 (140)
K.A.S. (1963)	24	25	49	31	7	—	13	100 (246)

*Ardingly's figures taken from G. Snow, *The Public School in the New Age*, p.20; other information supplied by the schools. The figures in brackets on the extreme right-hand column denote total population. The K.A.S. figures include both senior and junior schools. The 'other' category for Ardingly and K.A.S. consists largely of widows; for Dartington, it is unclassified.

hill. On the whole, therefore, the progressive school clientèle comes from the same income bracket and social class as that of the public school – from the professional and managerial classes.

Nevertheless, there are important differences between the two types of parent. The table opposite compares the parental occupations of pupils in an ordinary public school with those of pupils in three progressive schools.

The main conclusion from these figures is that the progressive schools attract a much higher proportion of professional parents than the public school and a corresponding lower proportion of 'business' parents. The term 'creative' denotes parents working in the arts – musicians, writers, painters, television and film producers, entertainers and so on. This category is entirely missing from Ardingly. K.A.S. is clearly something of a special case, the 'creative' group being swelled by a Hampstead clientèle extensively connected with the world of entertainment and broadcasting. In London too it is no surprise to find the 'business' proportion rather higher than in the other progressive schools. At both Bedales and Dartington, the main professional groups seem to be psychiatrists and academics, especially Oxford and Cambridge academics. Dartington, in addition, has nineteen parents (out of 140) who are architects. Figures supplied by Abbotsholme suggest that the pattern there resembles that of the public school rather than the others, which is what one would expect from a school whose progessivism is largely historical. Indeed, the headmaster, Richard Hodgkin, reckoned that for most parents Abbotsholme was simply the nearest available public school. Kilquhanity and Summerhill are roughly similar to Bedales and Dartington, though in Summerhill's case 70 per cent of parents are Americans. No figures have been furnished by Gordonstoun.

The explanation of these results must be tentative. Parents engaged in commerce are more likely to have a utilitarian idea of education, measuring success in terms of examinations and opportunities to 'get on'. Professional and creative parents are likely to assign a higher value to self-discovery and fulfilment in work. Creative parents tend to have creative children and would be attracted by the Progressive emphasis on developing the imagination; and at the same time be less put off by unconventionality in opinions and clothes. Psychiatrists would be interested as much in mental health as in mental training and would approve of the greater permissiveness of the progressive schools as well as their coeducation. Many parents in the liberal professions are opposed to characteristic public-school features: sex segregation, the prefect system, beating, fagging and so on. They may, like the poet Robert Graves, who sends his son to Bedales, have had unpleasant experiences at public schools themselves. On the other hand it remains conventional for them to send their children away to boarding schools: socially and educationally they still reject the state system. Progressive schools fill an obvious gap.

Another way of looking at the progressive school intake is to consider whether parents might send their children to these schools for special psychological reasons, of which the most obvious is a disturbed home background, leading to 'maladjustment' on the part of the child. Schools like Summerhill claim therapeutic results which might easily attract the parents of 'problem' children. Of Summerhill's sixty children, thirty-nine come from 'broken' homes. At Kilquhanity there are a number of disturbed or retarded children. From the figures supplied it would appear that about 15–20 per cent of the children at Bedales and Dartington come from 'broken' homes – using that term widely to include one or more parents dead, desertion or divorce, invalid mother and so on. But it is not easy to interpret these figures. Perhaps such children would have been sent to progressive schools in any case: it may simply be that 'creative' persons are more likely to get divorced than others. And is the percentage higher than at a public school? We do not know. My guess would be that a disturbed home background does not in itself constitute a sufficient reason for sending children to a progressive school, except possibly in the case of schools like Summerhill which emphasize therapy. In any case, it does not follow that children coming from disturbed homes are themselves disturbed, though they may be. A much more important group of parents are those who live abroad or move around in their jobs. Thirty per cent of Gordonstoun parents live overseas. The headmaster of Bedales writes: 'It is my strong impression that a considerable number of our parents are people who would not be choosing to send their children to a boarding school if they were living in a fixed geographical point in this country.' With the growth of international organizations and a possible British entry into the Common Market this trend will probably continue boosting the figures at both progressive and public schools. Where the progressive schools might especially hope to benefit is in their internationalist outlook, attractive to the cosmopolitan parent, and in the desire of peripatetic parents to keep brothers and sisters together: most progressive schools are coeducational.

Finally, parents may select particular progressive schools for particular reasons. Many parents send their children to public schools because they went to public schools themselves, and often try for the school which they themselves attended. This is now true of the older and better progressive schools: 20 per cent of present Bedalians have Old Bedalian parents. Or there may be a particular aspect or tradition that appeals: music at Bedales, art at Dartington, Outward Bound at Gordonstoun. About 20 per cent of Gordonstoun's annual places are reserved for 'slower boys'. On the whole though most progressive schools cannot afford to be too choosy in whom they take. An exception is Bedales, which is highly selective academically. Of course, the schools repel one type of parent as much as they attract another. One would not expect a father to send a son with an I.Q. of 140 to Gordonstoun; sporting enthusiasts would tend to give all progressive schools a wide berth.

The progressive schools took over one central idea from the public schools: that education is concerned with much more than classwork. But they altered the four traditional pillars of public-school education – Classics, games, chapel and prefect system – out of all recognition, hoping that by doing so they would bring them into some kind of relationship with each other as elements in a coherent process. Lessons were given a more practical and 'modern' bias so as to connect them more closely to the pupils' own interests and contemporary life. But more importantly, the early progressives believed that the everyday experiences of life – nature in all its manifestations, manual work – could do more to arouse interest and furnish instructive lessons than either books or competitive games. Then there was the whole province of the imagination largely uncharted by ordinary schoolwork concerned with memorizing facts, dates and formulae, and by such religious experiences as afforded by the chapel. Finally, the school itself was a community, with important social lessons to be gleaned from shared problems and experiences, largely obscured by removing one sex altogether and by handing over power to a pampered prefectorial athletocracy.

The next wave of progressive schools added a strong libertarian dose to this mixture. It recognized that communal life imposed obligations and restraints but sought to make the communal experience egalitarian and democratic. Seeing education as a process of 'drawing out' rather than 'putting in' it concluded that the pupil's 'natural' instincts should be given maximum scope. He was to be interfered with as little as possible: permissive legislation rather than direct rule was the order of the day.

The third wave added something new again. It sought to take the pupil not only outside the classroom but outside the school community itself, into the world of real problems. Education was to become the experience of serving others in a way that would appeal to the pupil's imagination and his sense of duty and compassion. Gordonstoun has no truck with the 'softness' of the permissive progressives, which it regards as a deviation. The Gordonstoun ideal, in its own eyes, is the Abbotsholme ideal grown up.

2 · Work

Progressive attitudes to classwork have been so confused and contradictory that it is scarcely possible to construct a coherent theory from them. The most we can do is to pick out certain dominant themes and illustrate them by contemporary progressive practice.

The earliest progressives wanted to broaden the syllabus from its narrow Classical base. Reddie, for example, anticipated the future importance of science and modern languages; he was a pioneer in sex instruction (though in a rather eccentric way). The idea behind this change was to make the syllabus more relevant to the pupils'. immediate interests and to modern life. The traditional idea was that of a syllabus determined not by mundane or temporary requirements but by the eternal concerns of the human mind; in other words, by moral concerns. The criticism of Reddie and Badley was partly empirical: whatever the high-blown claims of the old syllabus, the simple fact was that it failed to 'connect' at most points with the 'average' pupil, who was, after all, the object of education. This connexion could more easily be established if the subjects studied could be shown to be useful. Both pioneers also felt that hypocrisy and prudery had deliberately excluded or hopelessly distorted the whole question of sex education, leaving pupils ignorant and therefore vulnerable in this most important and delicate area of human and moral concern.

Subsequent psychological findings seemed to reinforce these early observations. John Dewey and Susan Isaacs drew attention to what now seems obvious: that young children are self-educating to an astonishing degree. If formal education could somehow build upon the child's natural curiosity in the world around him then the age-old problem of securing the pupil's interest would be on the way to solution. But this entailed jettisoning a large part of the traditional curriculum, which, far from arousing curiosity in the average child, created a hostility to learning which all too often proved permanent. Again, scientific studies cast increasing doubt on the 'transfer of training' theory. Hitherto, the curriculum had been dominated by general and abstract subjects which were thought to 'train the mind'. Thus a child studied Latin not to learn the language but to teach him 'how to think'. The work of Thorndike in particular suggested that Latin trained the mind to think no more than plumbing – and was a lot less useful. Hence the general subjects badly lost prestige – and particular subjects with a strong vocational or immediate appeal came crowding on to the syllabus.

Another line of inquiry suggested that children's learning capacities were closely related to stages of their intellectual, social and emotional development. This implied that the content and method of education should be varied according to age and by the needs and aptitudes of individual pupils. These ideas gradually discredited the notion of the common syllabus valid for all children of all ages. Every pupil, declared Edward Thring of Uppingham, had some talent, something that he could do well. Modern timetables, with their options and bewildering combinations of subjects, are increasingly designed to tap these talents, whatever they are, and give them opportunity to 'grow'.

There is an obvious conflict between these rather promiscuous ideas of intellectual self-development and the rigid demands of an external examination system based on traditional university courses or some conception of society's 'needs'. In the 1920s, the educationist Sir John Adams hoped that schools would soon be freed from the tyranny of external examinations: since then that tyranny has brought ever larger numbers of children under its sway.

One way out of this dilemma has been to include in the timetable many non-examinable subjects, traditionally relegated to the status of hobbies. Dartington Hall, for example, incorporates music and art in the regular syllabus. Most progressive schools now have what they call Project Mornings, offering a large choice of compulsory individual or group activities outside the normal curriculum. A Dartington Hall selection includes photography, stage lighting, poetry and jazz, butterfly collecting, and engine repair. Kurt Hahn of Gordonstoun has tried to boost the prestige of these Projects by making them eligible for certain awards – the Trevelyan Scholarship is an example. On the whole, it can hardly be claimed that the Project Morning is a very lively innovation. Most pupils fail to tackle their projects with that zest which Thring's dictum would have led one to expect. At Dartington Hall the most popular projects appear to be those that demand the least effort. Most progressive schoolmasters, one suspects, secretly welcome external examinations as giving them an excuse to impose a discipline which their own theories would lead them to reject, and as providing their pupils with a motive for hard work which would otherwise be absent.

However, although the external examination is apparently more in control than ever before, it has itself become much more flexible, allowing for a great variety of options and permutations. This in turn enables teachers to fit the work programme much more closely than before to the needs and aptitudes of the pupils. A distinguishing mark of the progressive school is the trouble taken to achieve this fit. Pressure is increased or eased according to the pupil's emotional condition. If his work is going badly the staff try to find out what is wrong, for at schools like Bedales and Dartington, with their highly selective entry, stupidity or boredom cannot be accepted as explanations for failure. At Dartington the staff wanted to bring back the post-O-level pupils three days before the start of term so that 'difficult decisions affecting their whole future do not have to be hurried through against the clock'. This degree of individual attention is of course made possible by the very favourable staff-pupil ratio; it also seems to vindicate the progressive emphasis on relaxed and informal relations between staff and pupils, leading to frank and fearless consultations. On the other hand, a number of pupils I talked to expressed the wish that the teachers would spend less time and energy sorting out their problems and more in making them get on with their work.

Progressive teachers in fact never seem to have examined their motives or objectives with the clarity and honesty required. They have been torn between a desire to make learning more efficient and a desire to make it easier and more pleasant. But it could be that guilt, resentment, unhappiness, provide the cutting edge for all substantial achievement; conversely, their elimination becomes a recipe for a well-adjusted mediocrity. Progressives of the libertarian persuasion have assumed without much warrant that their methods will create the truly astonishing new man: the well-adjusted genius.

In addition to changing the content of the syllabus, the progressives pioneered important changes in teaching methods, especially for young children. They rejected memorizing and rote-learning: they emphasized participation and 'activity'. This of course sprang from their original assumption that the child was a self-educating organism, not a passive recipient of information. Historical pageants were recreated in the classroom; igloos were constructed to teach the life of Eskimos; budding mathematicians were sent forth to measure the lengths, heights and angles of buildings; biological lessons were learnt from milking the school cow and watching the farrowing of the school sow. Learning-by-doing was the great motto.

Strangely, there were few comparable experiments for more senior pupils. An exception was the Dalton Plan, whereby each child carried out an individual plan of work in an appropriate subject room: this has now generally been abandoned. Many progressives would sympathize with Neill's bold assertion: 'I am not really interested in making subjects more interesting by modern methods; rather am I desirous of scrapping the lot of useless, boring subjects.'* In general progressives never showed much interest in the direct stimulation of their older pupils' intellectual appetites, concentrating chiefly on removing emotional impediments, real or imagined. They were concerned not so much to employ teachers who knew their subjects as those with friendly dispositions whom pupils could call Bob or Bert and who aroused no 'authority complexes'. Consequently senior progressive classrooms remained rather conventional,

*Talking of Summerhill, p. 63.

albeit more friendly, places. Bert might be puffing a cigarette, but the textbook in his hand would be one in use in thousands of distinctly unprogressive schools all over the country. More recently the progressives have by no means been the leaders of such modern classroom experiments as the new maths, language laboratories and programmed learning. These were initiated at the universities and tried out in ordinary schools. At Sevenoaks, a direct-grant grammar school in Kent, where the teachers wear gowns and are called 'sir', Gerd Sommerhoff has started a Technical Activities Centre which is far more interesting as an experiment in teaching and learning than anything to be seen in the modern progressive school.

This time the progressives were caught in another emotional contradiction: between the desire to make learning more efficient and the desire to make it more democratic. Their most characteristic innovations in method derived much more from libertarian social theory than from any study of the learning process. For example, they abolished rewards and punishments, prizes, marks and form orders, not primarily to improve the quality of work – though they hoped this would also result – but because they disliked the appeal to the competitive and acquisitive instinct. They regarded learning as a cooperative endeavour undertaken for its own sake and bringing its own rewards – rather as Socialists regarded adult work. Again, they tried to break down the divisions between teacher and pupil, mainly because they disliked authority. School practice for many of them was a prototype of social relations in a reformed society. Many of their innovations were based not on observed behaviour, but upon an optimistic philosophy of human nature, deriving from both liberalism and socialism. It must be said in their defence that many of the classroom practices they were rebelling against were derived from unbelievably pessimistic accounts of human nature, especially from the harsher versions of the original sin theory. The important point is that whereas the progressives have to some extent been pioneers of a 'scientific' approach to teaching and learning, science for them has always been subservient to metaphysics.

This has followed quite naturally from their anti-intellectual bias. One of Neill's books is called *Hearts Not Heads in the School*. This title sums up the progressive hostility to book-learning, to the mere assimilation of facts. Classwork, in the eyes of a former headmaster of Bedales, consisted in 'laying thin veneers of information on the surface of the mind'. The progressives were after more vivid and direct experiences; they yearned for the imaginative and intuitive, rather than the rational; and this inevitably took them outside the classroom. The public-school ideal was very similar, with its emphasis on character rather than brains, though the progressive 'character' was intended to be quite different from the traditional school one. In attitudes to learning, the real enemy was not the public school but the grammar school. The progressives believed that the most important education took place outside the classroom. Like the public schools they exploited the boarding environment in the interests of an all-round education. This anti-intellectualism, romanticism – call it what you will – sharply limited their 'scientific' approach to education itself. They felt strongly certain ideas and values to be right and were not unduly worried if the 'facts' pointed in a different direction. It is therefore a great mistake to think of the progressive schools as purely experimental ones, completely open to new ideas, constantly modifying their practice in the light of fresh facts. They stand for certain definite conceptions of education and life which will be revealed as this study progresses.

Many of their conflicting attitudes to classwork underlie Summerhill's practice of voluntary classes. (Dartington Hall, too, had such a system before the war, now replaced by the device of 'contracting out' of parts of the syllabus.) On the one hand it reflects the view that voluntary learning makes for better learning, because children only attend when they are interested, and teachers are forced to be stimulating in order to hold their audiences. This proposition is extremely dubious. Bertrand Russell, who was intellectually honest as well as idealistic, was forced to conclude that the voluntary principle at best only works with highly intelligent children.

The rest just stay away. And Neill implicitly relies on the external discipline of O-level rather than any natural curiosity to bring his children to class later on in their school careers. Again, voluntarism suffers from the crippling practical objection that very few teachers are good enough to work it. The wares they offer are just not attractive enough. At Summerhill some teachers get terribly depressed by empty classrooms and feel themselves inadequate: they soon leave.

Voluntarism is defended as a good in itself: the adult has no right to enforce his conceptions on the child. And indeed, carried to an extreme, the view of the child as self-educating does imply allowing him to do what he wants. Learning is assumed to be a purely private matter, of no concern to society. Even if this be granted, there is the further assumption that the child is the best judge of his own interests – an application of the well-known liberal argument which ignores the liberal proviso: only if he is rational. Mill explicitly excludes from consideration children and savages.

Finally, there is in voluntarism a concealed value judgement against learning. For children at Summerhill are *forced* to do other things, such as obey the community laws, which means that good behaviour is valued higher than good learning.

It is virtually impossible for the classroom to become an interesting and exciting place unless there is some public commitment to learning. This is why, perhaps, progressive classroom teaching at the senior level is rather conventional and flat: the emotional energies of pupils and staff are directed elsewhere; staff are chosen not for their teaching, but for their social and pastoral qualities. In practice, of course, no parents send their children to a school like Summerhill to get a good education in the conventional sense. They send them there to be 'sorted out' emotionally, and then whisk them off to 'proper' schools where they may learn something. Indeed, classwork at Summerhill sometimes seems to be a mere extension of group therapy, as the following scene depicted by a thirteen-year-old Summerhill girl suggests:

Cara enticed me to go to one of the lessons. It was current affairs and we all sat round the gasfire in the staff common room smoking while Harry [the teacher] sat on the table reading some items from the papers. Most of the girls sat with a boy's leg across her knee writing the names of all his lovers in Biro all over it. [sic]

At Gordonstoun, classwork is doubtless free from these amorous distractions. But here the anti-intellectual bias expresses itself in the prestige of the Outward Bound activities of mountaineering, sailing, life rescue, expeditions, etc. It is not so much that they take up the time which would otherwise be devoted to academic pursuits. It is rather that the emotional thrust of the school is centred upon them, leaving everything else in a subsidiary position. This tendency has probably increased since Kurt Hahn's retirement. Hahn himself approached much more closely to the all-round ideal than did his successor, Major Chew, who represented the character-building side of Gordonstoun. Although Hahn himself was no scholar, he did have an extraordinary capacity to attract to the school reflective and creative teachers who provided a counterweight to his own obsessive activism. It remains to be seen how far Chew's successor is able to tilt the balance once more to the other side.

Atlantic College provides a more complicated picture. The school is an international sixth-form college, its boys coming mainly from Great Britain, West Germany, Scandinavia, North America and Greece, but including a sprinkling from Asia and Africa. Broadly speaking, it has been easier to get together pupils from countries which are politically friendly to each other. The Indian Ambassador objected to pupils from China; the Jordanian Ambassador threatened to withdraw Jordanian pupils if any Israelis were admitted.

This international character of the school has raised a number of teaching problems calling for bold solutions. It was felt impossible, as well as undesirable, to provide national courses of study for the various groups, as some of the more lavish cosmopolitan Swiss boarding schools attempt to do. As no truly international course existed, the only solution was to plump for a proper A-level course on the English model, together with subsidiary courses weighted somewhat towards particular national groups. At the completion of a two-year stint at the College, each pupil will have taken three A-levels and have studied six other subjects – a far heavier work load than that borne by the average grammar-school pupil (its completion was thought to require one marathon term every year, stretching from January to June). So far the results have been very impressive: the failure rate of even the non-English pupils, studying their main course in a second language, is less than the national English grammar-school failure rate, though this may well be due to the high quality of recruitment rather than to the particular methods used at the school.

All the foreign pupils have to bring their English rapidly up to a high standard; equally, all English pupils are expected to master one foreign language. The quick learning of languages is therefore a top priority, and accounts for the school's extensive use of language laboratories. Finally, Atlantic College aims to get all its pupils into national universities. It has had to get its basic course accepted as a qualification for university entry in the countries from which the pupils come. But its long-term aim is an International Baccalaureat, acceptable everywhere. This is genuine pioneering work which opens up once more the exciting prospect of the roving scholar in the great medieval European tradition; a prospect which may well be realized if and when Britain joins the European community.

Are the egalitarians right to object to Atlantic College? To them the training of national élites in the public and grammar schools is bad enough; the training of an international élite to rule the world seems infinitely worse. The fact remains however that the nearest the world has approached to an international order was when small élites united by marriage and kinship (monarchies) or even by religion (Catholics and Jews) exerted a preponderant influence in the conduct of international affairs. The Atlantic College concept is an attempt to find a meritocratic substitute for the internationally-minded élites of the nineteenth century whose influence was largely destroyed by the rise of democracy and the popular passions which engulfed humanity in two world wars. And just as the most advanced nations have been endeavouring to discover, through education, a new basis for authority in their own societies, so it seems logical that the attempt should be made, through education, in the international or European sphere.

Although, as we have seen, the academic course is taken extremely seriously at Atlantic College, it is not the school's *raison d'être*. The élite envisaged by Admiral Hoare, the headmaster with a background of naval and youth work, is certainly not an intellectual élite. Nor is it precisely an 'aristocracy of service' in the Outward Bound sense (though while I was there I did see a notice strongly reminiscent of Gordonstoun: 'The following will be required for Cliff Rescue. . . . This supersedes all other activities'). Atlantic College, like all progressive (and indeed public) schools, is more than a school as it is usually conceived – a place where children are sent to study certain subjects and acquire certain intellectual and vocational skills. It is intended to provide a general education for leadership in the contemporary world, or perhaps in the world just round the corner. Its *raison d'être,* in other words, is its social philosophy, to which all its activities are subordinated. Both Gordonstoun and Atlantic College can perhaps best be viewed as 'new model' public schools – meritocratic (wealth is no longer the main criterion for selection), tough-minded, rooted in what their founders conceive to be the social realities and problems of the modern age. Other progressive schools too made this attempt to provide a 'new model' education for upper-class children in response to certain imperatives of their age as they saw them – democracy, equality, increasing leisure, international brotherhood. Hahn, being a German, no doubt takes a darker, and many would argue more realistic, view of man's fate than most English progressives, nurtured in the golden summer of Edwardian England and the liberal optimism of the greatest satisfied world power in history.

The purposes for which a school exists, or is believed to exist, determine to a large extent the staff and pupils it attracts, and this in turn determines the quality of its academic achievements. Old reputations die hard, and even if a reforming headmaster wishes to raise the level of classwork he may find himself up against not only an anti-intellectual image which inhibits parents of bright children entrusting them to his care, but also against a certain tradition within the school which constantly challenges his new ideas. Thus at Dartington Hall a recent proposal by the headmaster to change the name 'free periods' to 'study periods' in order to improve the attitude to work was heavily defeated by the School Parliament or Moot. Adult preconceptions are even harder to overcome. Children are rarely sent to Summerhill unless there is thought to be something 'wrong' with them. Similarly, the school is unlikely to attract, say, a brilliant historian to its staff. Many teachers, in fact, come to be 'cured' themselves. An Oxford don of my acquaintance admitted sending a son to Gordonstoun because he was not 'academic': a more intelligent son had gone to Eton.

Bedales, by contrast, has always had a fairly good reputation for work. Its founder, Badley, was a considerable Classical scholar; and though Classics itself was demoted in deference to the progressive emphasis on modern subjects, a tradition of sound learning was somehow able to survive even the vicissitudes of inter-war libertarian experiment. Consequently the school did not put off all those professional parents who wanted an enlightened education for their children but who valued the intellect. It was Bedales' extraordinary sense of balance – its avoidance of the extremes of Reddie's eccentricity, Neill's do-as-you-please approach, Hahn's Germanic inflexibility – that won for it in the inter-war years the reputation of being one of the best schools in Europe. Today, what makes it a school to which even the most brilliant academics are prepared to send their precocious children is not any advanced method of instruction, but simply the high quality and varied interests of the staff and the knowledge that their children will be part of an intelligent and interesting community. Much of the teaching, no doubt, is less thorough than elsewhere; pupils are not pushed as hard; the textbooks and methods are by no means remarkable. Yet the whole atmosphere is highly intelligent and civilized; Bedalians are disconcertingly articulate and well-informed; and university interviewing bodies obviously go for them in a big way.

3 · Play

It is when we venture outside the classroom that we come closest to the heart of the progressive school movement. The early English pioneers, we must remember, were all public-school men; and what they were reacting against was public-school education. As the emotional centre of the late Victorian public school was the games field, dominated by the schoolboy aristocracy, it is scarcely surprising that it was against the cult of athletics that they directed their heaviest fire. It might seem absurd to the modern reader that so many battles were fought over this issue. But in the public schools, games were not just a leisure activity: they were an integral, indeed the most important, part of the education offered. The progressive criticism was that the standard diet of Classics and games appealed only to a minority of gifted scholars and athletes; most pupils were dissatisfied camp-followers, prone to the dangerous temptations of boredom and day-dreaming. Moreover, games were irrelevant to modern conditions. This linked up with another line of attack. Competitive games were unpalatable precisely because they were competitive. Progressives of every stamp had vague paternalist or socialist aspirations. Competitive games, as much as competitive form orders, were seen as a preparation for the competitive capitalist society which was anathema to them. The problem, then, as they saw it, was to devise some other form of outdoor activity which would both appeal to the 'average' boy and be useful and cooperative in nature.

The solution to the problem was manual work. The new progressive schools were generally decaying old houses set in wild fields and lacking altogether the amenities necessary for boarding education. In the construction of new buildings, the felling of trees, the levelling and tidying-up of the grounds and the building of swimming pools, as well as in more routine estate and maintenance work, the progressives discovered obvious and convenient outlets for manual work; convenient, because they entirely lacked the finances to have these tasks done by paid labour. There were many other motives. Most progressives hated industrial society. They saw their schools as models of a revived rural and agricultural community, growing its own food and cultivating traditional skills. Hence most schools acquired a school farm, which provided opportunities for more manual work. Farm life, moreover, gave an insight into 'facts of life' too embarrassing to be dealt with in the classroom. Following Wordsworth, the progressives regarded Nature as the only true educator, its mysteries evoking all the child's latent curiosity, as well as his sense of wonder and beauty. Nor were more utilitarian considerations ignored. Chopping wood, it was argued, was a better preparation for a life in the colonies than playing rugger. Whether or not the British Empire had been won on the playing fields of Eton, both Reddie and Badley insisted that it was being lost in the decadence of contemporary public-school life, and could only be preserved if the upper classes were once more fortified in their impressionable years by the experience of honest toil. Indeed, there was something positively Puritanical about the way in which the early progressives inveighed against the 'softness' and decadence which they saw engulfing the upper classes. Under cover of a concern for health, they waxed positively enthusiastic in inflicting such horrors as icy showers and morning runs upon their pupils, as well as in their insistence on extreme simplicity, indeed frugality, in diet, clothing and living accommodation. In this respect, at any rate, there was considerably more of Sparta than Athens in their educational theory.

Many of these theories are still very much in evidence at Kilquhanity. 'We have always tried to keep things real at Kilquhanity,' says the headmaster, John Aitkenhead. Reality for him is the life of the community, of the farm and its animals, the local countryside, its habits, customs and festivals. All too often 'the eyes of the fool are on the ends of the earth', blinding him to immediate experience; education concerned with 'learning parrot-wise the formalized laws of past learning'. In education through experience Aitkenhead sees the answer to many social problems. 'Most children cannot accept and conform to the intellectual demands of the senior secondary programme. They are the pupils in revolt. . . . They are the juvenile delinquents to be.' And on the seamen's strike of 1966: 'The chances are the stokers and deck-hands wouldn't be fighting the owners this way, at this time, if education were more real; if teachers addressed themselves more often to the condition of their pupils; if more kids sailed up the rivers of Scotland and went low flying round the county borders' – a curious echo of the early progressive idea that 'real' education could become the solvent of class conflict.

With these attitudes one would not expect classwork to be given much importance, even if the school did have a large number of 'academic' pupils – which it doesn't. In fact class-work plays a very small part in Kilquhanity's 'scheme of things', the staff regarding teaching as a minor adjunct to their main duties. Their qualifications are equally peripheral. The main lessons are centred round the farm and the upkeep of the estate.

In the morning at 7 o'clock [wrote Smiddy, aged thirteen] Mark Muirhead and I get the cows from the field and take them up to the byre. This morning it was lovely. There was no wind at all. I like getting up early, though I have to be woken up. We went down to their field and we stood there with the gate open and called 'Suzy, Grishkin, Polly'. They came walking towards the gate and out. Then I shut the gate and we walked the cows to the byre. Suzy is heavy with her unborn calf. Her teats are at her knees. She waddles slowly. We are careful not to hurry her.

The facts of life and death are brought home in direct fashion:

On Tuesday, one of the large white sows farrowed. She had ten piglets but one died. Andrew, Douglas, Mark and Jem have been looking after them and seeing that the mother doesn't squash any of them.

On Monday, Mark, Sean, David, Johnny, Gordon and I were watching Colin killing ten cockerels. We had to carry them to the kitchen. I carried one with its head nearly off. Blood was dripping all over the place. We were having chicken for dinner on Wednesday.

As a Kilquhanity master put it:

Canoe – sailing boat – pigs – cows – hens – pets – theatre – workshop – fort – makeshift games – council meeting – common rooms – washing up – paid jobs – useful work – pottery – painting – outings – fishing – climbing – walking – bridgepool – ballet – piano – huts – the pond – rope swings – bonfires, etc., etc., are more than words to a kid at Kilquhanity. They are symbols of a part of education all too often neglected.*

Most of the other progressive schools (with the exception of Gordonstoun and Atlantic College, which we will consider shortly) have long since abandoned the school farm, and indeed virtually the whole of the physical side of education, apart from some vestigial maintenance work and school chores. Games are played by a few enthusiasts but not with any great success: they are played, as one pupil at Dartington Hall informed me, for enjoyment and not to win. The attitude to physical education is well summed up in the following comment from the *Bedales Chronicle*: 'Block 5 males have again made history. They actually asked Bob Pullin for an extra gym period!' In the more libertarian phase after the First World War, free time largely encroached on the manual work periods: and indeed, once the schools assumed their recognizable modern shape, there was very little manual work left to do. Today the average progressive school child spends his time out of class either on his own private amusements, or on some kind of artistic, musical or electronic activity, rather than in chasing balls round the field or in chopping down trees and clearing away manure. It is an ironic comment on the progressive school ideal that two young secondary modern visitors to Bedales could write: 'They have one advantage which they don't use and that is the countryside.'

The exceptions to this general trend are Gordonstoun and Atlantic College. Kurt Hahn of Gordonstoun demoted competitive games to one or two afternoons a week, replacing

*These quotations are taken from the Kilquhanity *Broadsheet*, an excellent duplicated weekly magazine.

them by elementary gymnastics, physical training, camping, mountaineering, sailing and training for various forms of rescue. Physical fitness was, and is, sustained by cold showers and morning runs. But it was mainly in his rescue activities that Hahn diverged from the conventional progressive school practice. He tried to find a pattern of service, not just to the school, but to the wider community, which would at the same time satisfy the boy's love of adventure and achievement. This pattern he discovered in the Outward Bound concept of rescue work. Gordonstoun takes its rescue service to the community very seriously indeed, though the community itself seems largely unaware of its intentions. A house just by the school caught fire; its owner, instead of summoning Gordonstoun's own smart and polished fire brigade, perfectly trained just for such a contingency, called Lossiemouth's, ten miles away. The pupil who told me this sad tale felt aggrieved that the call to service had not materialized.

Atlantic College follows Gordonstoun's programme, but less ostentatiously. The school is plainly embarrassed at being too closely identified with Outward Boundism. Partly this is the ordinary English embarrassment at Hahn's Germanic overstatement. Gordon Brooke-Shepherd is perfectly right in his comment:

So, whereas at Salem, for example, one has the feeling that this Outward Bound moral fervour is nailed to the mast ... at Atlantic College idealism is trailed more discreetly and is never allowed to smother the academic or social life of the school. It is the contrast between the explicit Continental approach and the implicit British one.*

It is worth taking a closer look at the 'explicit' continental approach, as revealed in the school magazine, *Gordonstoun Record*. It is precisely because Gordonstoun does not suffer from any reticence about its deep commitments that this is such a valuable source. Indeed the dominant tone is one of painful earnestness, in marked contrast to the irony and flippancy to be found in, say, the *Bedales Chronicle* – the obvious

Weekend Telegraph, 22 April 1966.

embarrassment at any intrusion of those Higher Thoughts upon which the *Gordonstoun Record* flourishes.

The Gordonstoun magazine does not hesitate to venture where cautious men fear to tread:

> If then, as many suspect, modern western man has lost touch with the fundamental rhythm of life and with the grass roots of his being, the urgent question of what to do about it presses upon us.

The editor himself has no doubts about the answer:

> Our need is, partly, so to be gripped by creation in all her moods that we find ourselves emotionally and intellectually engaged, at the unselfconscious level, in the rhythm of life.

The translation of this 'need' into a practical programme of education was the achievement of Kurt Hahn:

> Dr Hahn [declared H. Brereton, Gordonstoun's Warden, in a sermon delivered in the school chapel] recognized how civilization can rob folk of hereditary skills, won by our forbears in the evolutionary struggle with fate, pitting their wits and technical mastery against the elements as sailors or mountaineers, or to fight fire. Dr Hahn deliberately restored all kinds of non-academic experience into the school programme, for with the skill of the Scout, the Stalker, or the Carpenter, or the Labourer in the fields, so he believes, go insight and calmness of mind.

The school magazine tries to hold fast to these central purposes, 'avoiding', in the editor's words, 'merely clever literary exercises, encouraging boys to write about the world as they know it, and keeping the magazine open for the propagation of ideas which seem to reflect the ideals of the school.' As one of those aphorisms beloved by Hahn and his followers put it: 'The guided intellect is more powerful than the guided missile.'

Certainly the *Gordonstoun Record* contains not a word of dissent from the 'ideals of the school'. Boys' contributions tend to fall into three groups. First, there are rather disapproving commentaries on certain aspects of modern life. 'An Age of Moral Decadence?' was the heading of one symposium of sixth-form essays. The television programme *That Was the Week That Was* came in for some scathing criticism in an essay which contrasted David Frost with Aristophanes.

Aristophanes had 'high motives', the 'definite object of political and moral criticism' while the modern satirists' sole aim 'is to ingratiate themselves with the dirty-minded pseudo-sophisticates who enjoy their programmes'.

The next group of contributions consists of what might be called miniature Ph.D. theses, consisting of officially approved projects – 'Harris Tweed', 'Collecting Plankton', 'Wine-Growing in the Moselle', 'Anglican Religious Communities', 'Island and Town'. Great care is taken in the preparation of these somewhat lengthy contributions: facts are amassed; the right authorities are consulted; analysis is kept to a minimum – this indeed is the inevitable result of the choice of subject-matter. The painstaking accumulation of facts and the reverence for written authority is a natural counterpart of the mistrust of the speculative intellect. But even the sizeable capacity of Gordonstoun boys for absorbing mere information is not limitless: a talk on modern developments in the gas industry had to be abandoned 'owing to poor attendance'.

The largest group of articles described trips of discovery and exploration: 'Round India on £26', 'Across Canada', 'A Week in the Atlas', 'Public Schools' Party to the USSR', 'On the Wallaby'; sea voyages are also popular topics. Old Gordonstoun boys write long accounts of setting up schools on Gordonstoun principles or Outward Bound courses in India and Africa. There was a charity 'run' to London to arouse a national interest in the problem of leprosy; someone wrote of Voluntary Service in West Africa. It is perhaps in activities such as these that Gordonstoun boys feel themselves closest to the 'fundamental rhythm of life'.

The pages of the magazine reveal a confusion of aim that lies at the heart of Gordonstoun, perhaps even of the progressive school movement. On the one hand there is an attempt to create an awareness of social problems: vigilant citizenship is Kurt Hahn's watchword. At the same time there is a reluctance to dirty one's hands with politics, social reform or the everyday life of modern civilization. 'Social reforms,' declared Mr Le Quesne, the Second Master, 'do not in themselves abolish evil, they merely deflect it into other channels.' Evil can be eliminated only at source – 'in the individual will'. In order to achieve this the individual must be brought up uncontaminated by the evils of the outside world. But is it then really surprising that he should wish to continue living in that kind of world – the Gordonstoun world of sea, and hills, and adventure, remote from the actual problems that call for 'vigilance'? A poem written by a boy during an exciting and dangerous voyage in a sailing ship sums up a longing for peace and innocence which can never be recaptured in a world of cities:

> God speed thee Tall Ship Tawau,
>> God bless thee, boys and men,
> May He sail with thee across the sea
>> And guide thee home again.
>
> God give thee strength and courage
>> In trouble, storm and gale:
> And may God make thee thankful,
>> When Gentle winds prevail.
>
> Far from the world of politics,
>> From Rocker and from Mod
> But nearer to reality
>> And nearer much to God.
>
> And nearer to each other,
>> Away from vice and strife,
> In reliance and companionship
>> You'll find what's best in life.

Neill agreed with Hahn that modern life, and the education designed to prepare for it, stunted children's vital capacities and needs. Their contrasting approaches to the problem can best be illustrated by their explanations of delinquency and the remedies they advance for it – for to both of them the juvenile delinquent is only an extreme example of the distortion which conventional education imposes on modern youth in general. In addition, the pattern of Summerhill education cannot properly be understood unless it is realized that it was in origin a school for deliquent and malajusted children. It is precisely because it dealt with 'extreme' cases that it carried certain progressive ideas to extreme lengths. While, in general, all progressive education was a kind of therapy against certain 'distorting' tendencies of modern life, Summerhill education was a therapy for particular children who had succumbed to pressures which most children were able, at least partly, to resist.

That cure is still the main purpose of contemporary Summerhill is charmingly revealed in two poems of self-revelation taken from the school wall-sheet, *Summerhill Chronicle*:

(Boy of eight)

This is the story of a bear. He lived in the part of the jungle where no elephants were allowed. This bear had been a naughty bear; he had poisoned and made the crane ill and had put holly in his sister's bed. If his mother scolded him he would pull a rude face at her. It was impossible to get him to live right. So his parents sent him to Summerhill and he was one of Jane's housekids.

(Boy of thirteen)

I once knew a boy called Chris
  Who had to have his every wish
Or else he'd sulk and throw a pout
  Or give some younger kid a clout.
He always had to be dead right
  And if by chance he picked a fight
Twas always with a kid much smaller
  He couldn't tackle someone taller.
If caught doing something wrong
  And charged: My God, what a song!
Excuses poured out by the score,
  'It's not my fault' he'd implore.
The truth he simply couldn't take
  And these excuses he would make
Because this fact he had to hide
  He was weak and frightened down inside.

Both Hahn and Neill believe that the delinquent is an example of good qualities suppressed by conventional education and upbringing. For Hahn delinquency is the result of 'high spirits', the will to achievement, being given insufficient outlets; the cure lies in the adventure courses of Outward Bound. For Neill, delinquency is the result of a moralizing adult assault on the sexual and playful instincts of childhood; the cure is to give the repressed instincts full rein by removal of adult coercion and disapproval. Hahn's theory led to a Boy Scoutish activism on the part of the schoolmaster; Neill's to libertarianism and quiescence. Hahn's schoolmaster is seen as the leader in daring exploits; Neill's as the therapist allowing the child to 'live out' his problems. In psychological terms, we may say that Hahn is an Adlerian, Neill a Freudian. For Hahn, the will to power is the dominant instinct of man. His problem is to satisfy it without harming others. Mountain climbing is ideally suited for this purpose. It provides 'an experience of conquest without the humiliation of the conquered'. For Neill, the basic drive is primarily sexual. (The Summerhill magazine for old pupils and friends of the school is called *Id*.) For him the main task is not so much to provide positive outlets for sexual freedom and achievement as to remove the whole system of repression which actively seeks to stamp them out. His role is not that of the leader but of the encouraging onlooker; negative rather than positive.

We can now see why there has never been an 'active' side to Summerhill's pattern of education. In Neill's theory, any attempt to force the child to do certain things, however desirable in themselves, is merely an extension of the coercive and moralizing pressures to which the child's delinquency is a response in the first place. Although Neill has his own aims and values – in many respects similar to the 'enlightened' ideas of most progressives – he always tried to keep these very much in the background. He was entirely free from that cultural evangelism which forced pupils to listen to half an hour of Bach before breakfast – or to chop trees for the 'good of the community'. Summerhill children are left very much to their own devices. Boredom is one inevitable consequence; a certain lack of resolution in later life may be another. The educationist David Holbrook writes: 'Neill's products often have creative gifts and warm-heartedness – but they can't get up in the morning to use them.' Even if Neill were to accept these criticisms, he would not regard them as very important, compared with the freedom from sexual fears and neuroses he believes his methods achieve. And indeed, I am quite prepared to believe that Summerhill's regimen is absolutely ideal for certain kinds of disturbed and maladjusted children who are brought back from the edge of madness and despair. But whether it provides a valid general plan of education is quite a different matter.

The difference between the active and non-active side of the progressive school ideal is symbolized in the clothes progressive school children wear. The old pioneers rebelled against the 'polite' clothes of the Victorian gentleman, symbol of the fact that he never used his hands, and devised school clothes functionally suited to a hardy outdoor life. Formal clothes stood for so many of the things they disliked: drawing-room small-talk, repressed emotions, stiff-lipped respectability. Clothes, they felt, should express the 'natural' child whom they were releasing from the chains of 'artificial' society. This was the heyday of open-necked shirts, shorts and sandals. The more permissive progressives of the inter-war years agreed with many of these views. But as they laid more stress on individual self-expression and less on communal toil, they felt that they could safely leave it to the child to choose the clothes most appropriate to his 'natural' self.

So much of Abbotsholme life was lived out of doors that it was inevitable that Reddie and his successors should devise an alternative to the grey-flannel trousers and stiff-collar shirts then *de rigueur*; and as this was before the day of jeans and pullovers they put their pupils into shorts and open-necked shirts. This was primarily for convenience, but it was also symbolic – signifying that the classroom was no longer at the centre of education. This costume was followed by Hahn of Gordonstoun, who may have taken it from the German Wandervogel.* At Abbotsholme at present the boys wear green pullovers, light brown shorts and brown socks; at Gordonstoun, grey shorts and light blue pullovers. Atlantic College, more contemporary, dresses its pupils in blue jeans, and blue shirts and pullovers. All three have abolished the tie for ordinary wear. Although jeans would seem to be the most

*See below, p. 190.

modern hardwearing item of clothing, Gordonstoun boys do not seem to mind their shorts, although admitting that they look 'a little foolish in Elgin'.

These three schools have uniforms, however unconventional. Bedales, torn between the old and the new, tries to get the best of both worlds. Girls are expected to wear green pullovers and grey skirts for class; boys, grey trousers and shirts and pullovers (though they may wear 'respectable' alternatives). For formal occasions, boys are expected to wear jackets and ties and girls to 'look decent' (mini-skirts were grudgingly allowed after initial objections). For the rest of the time, both boys and girls may wear informal clothes, though jeans are only permitted three afternoons a week, and 'fancy' clothes are strongly discouraged. In fact no one is quite sure what is allowed and what is not; it is up to the pupils' 'good sense' – a typical progressive concept. 'Our only uniform,' remarked one of the staff, 'is enlightenment.'

At Dartington Hall, there is complete freedom of choice. The result (1965) is a standard informal uniform of jeans and pullovers. Hair is quite often shoulder-length for pupils of both sexes. Like most modern teenagers, Dartington girls wear little or no make-up, but jewellery – especially rings and bracelets – is common to both boys and girls. Summerhill and Kilquhanity children, being somewhat younger, are less fashion-conscious. They also wear jeans and pullovers but do not emulate Dartingtonians in modishness.

The old fear that freedom to choose clothes would expose differences of income and the girls to permanent traumas of decision-making seems to ignore the modern teenager and his environment. For one thing, clothes are generally much cheaper than they used to be. In addition, most teenagers tend to be much more scruffy than before, and think nothing of spending the whole day in jeans, shirt and pullover (the standard uniform), especially at coeducational schools where they don't have to strive for an instant, dramatic, impact on the opposite sex. Perhaps they take more trouble at dances, but I doubt it.

4 · Coeducation

Coeducation is probably the innovation for which the progressive schools are most famous, although Abbotsholme never adopted it, and Gordonstoun remains an unrepentant boy's school. Although it is now common in day-schools – and was in Scotland, long before the progressive movement existed – it remains exceptional in boarding schools, where the public-school single-sex tradition still rules.

The historical reasons for coeducation are varied. A leading aim was to break down the homosexual atmosphere of the single-sex boarding schools. Another was to lift the suppression, secrecy and ignorance surrounding sex. Coeducation was also associated with the battle for women's emancipation. Girls and boys should be made as similar as possible: hence the well-known jibe that coeducation makes masculine women and feminine men. Finally the progressives thought that a community which excluded one sex was bound to offer an unreal and artificial preparation for life in adult society.

The sceptics believed that coeducation was bound to lead to promiscuity. Nothing could have been further from the desire of most coeducators. They saw coeducation as something that would restrain the sexual instinct by inhibiting romantic associations. As the headmaster of Bedales told me:

Boys are able to see girls and girls to see boys as people rather than as creatures of the opposite sex. One doesn't want to take the romance out of life, but when boys at public-schools meet girls at dances, tennis-parties, etc., they are meeting them under over-romanticized conditions, which makes matters much worse. I say that it is only when you can have the other situations – laying the breakfast table together, studying alongside each other in class, that you really get a balance.

The coeducational ideal was that of comrades rather than sexual partners. There was a strong appeal to the idealism and moralism of youth. Teachers tried to focus their pupils' atten-

tions on Higher Things – community spirit, good causes, etc. –
in order to remove lower temptations. (At Gordonstoun, the
Outward Bound ideal of service, with its corollary of being in
training, still plays this role.) They were aided by the children's family backgrounds – high-minded, often Quaker and
nonconformist. The result was that anti-sexual traditions were
established at a number of pre-war schools which proved very
potent: sex, I was told by an old pupil, was considered very
'un-Bedalian'.

With the aid of these devices the progressives were able to
cling to the comforting view that sex was really something
that started after school, except possibly in some shy, utterly
delightful and naïve fashion. Sexual precocity was seen – and
still is – as a sign of psychological disturbance. Thus the present principals of Dartington Hall write: 'when a boy-and-
girl relationship begins to cause anxiety, it is almost certain
that the underlying factor in the situation will be the emotional instability in one or both due to a breakdown in the
family situation. . . .'* This would have been fair comment
thirty years ago, but today they are deceiving themselves – or
the parents.

Of course, the progressives were not so naïve as to imagine
that the appeal to idealism would alone suffice. In the earlier
period, idealism was reinforced by strenuous activity. Public-
school masters had long known that idleness is a powerful
source of temptation. As one headmaster put it: 'My prophylactic against certain unclean microbes was to send the boys
to bed dead tired.' Progressive-school manual and estate work
(as, in a more traditional setting, Gordonstoun's Outward
Bound activities) had a function similar to public-school
games. Indeed, one of Reddie's chief criticisms of games was
that they did *not* send the boys to bed dead tired: most pupils
were bored by them.

The Bedales mixed-aged dormitory system is also seen as a
defence, with older pupils being encouraged to take responsibility for advising and helping younger ones. The constant
circulation of pupils round the school – they rarely stay in the

*The Independent Progressive School, ed. H. A. T. Child, p. 53.

same social unit for more than one term – is designed to break up cliques and prevent the concentration of 'bad' influences. Even more important, coeducational schools rely upon 'the strength and intimacy of the relationship with adults'. Social convention is not nearly as antagonistic to staff–pupil friendships as it is at most public schools, with the result that the teachers get to know their pupils very well and divert dangerous thoughts into safer channels. At Bedales this informality is symbolized in a nightly ceremony when the staff line up to shake the hands of the pupils as they file out of hall after evening assembly. Badley always used to claim that he could tell at a glance by looking into the pupil's eyes whether anything was 'wrong'.

At any rate, that was the theory: what is the contemporary practice? Do boys and girls sleep with each other? The answer, of course, is that they do: indeed it would be surprising today if they didn't. The proportion is probably fairly small, though there is no reason to believe that it is lower than the national average for the age-group. Opportunities are plentiful, especially at Dartington Hall, where the boys and girls have separate study-bedrooms in mixed blocks. The following story, told me by a sixteen-year-old Dartingtonian, illustrates the gulf between theory and reality:

You know, we all have to be in our rooms by 12 o'clock. Well, there I was having it off with this girl, when I was discovered missing from my room, and a big hue and cry was raised. . . . The Childs were summoned [they live a few miles away from the school]. A friend warned me and I slipped out into the grounds, and came back at 4 o'clock, as cool as you like. Mrs Child asked me where I'd been, so I said I'd been having these fits of depression and needed the night air. They fixed up an appointment with a head-shrinker in London. . . .

At Bedales about two years ago, there was a big 'purge' following the discovery of empty whisky bottles and used contraceptives in the loft above the central hall. No doubt abortions are discreetly arranged from time to time. This ambiance must be expected to grow in the future, and pose an increasing problem for coeducational boarding schools.

The sad fact is that the current teenage revolution has left the progressive schools way behind. The main factors have been increased teenage spending power, and the whole world of teenage entertainment and fashion that has gone with it; the growth of libertarian and permissive values, leading to the effective loss of control of adults over the adolescent generation; finally, perhaps, a feeling of futility in face of the Bomb. 'What would you do if you heard the Bomb was coming?' one boy was asked. 'Sleep with Brenda,' he replied.

The whole phenomenon may be seen more broadly as an extreme reaction against the repressive Puritanism of previous ages. In a strange way, most progressives were part of the Puritan generation. Of course, they attacked feelings of guilt and original sin and so opened the way for the complete repudiation of the Puritan ethic. But, at the same time, they hoped to replace it by a kind of cultural evangelism which similarly excluded the lower self. They assumed that youth was naturally high-minded, pure and aesthetic. Stern repression was therefore unnecessary. It had only to be lifted for these qualities to flower in all their splendour. Many of them now feel that they have let loose a monster. Their legacy has been the culture of pot and pop. Today they reassure parents that a full and varied programme in a country setting will keep the swinging world at bay for a few years more. But the fact is that, in most schools, the programme is no longer attractive enough to compete with Carnaby Street and the discotheque. The pop idol has, for many of today's progressive teenagers, replaced the sandalled, bearded prophet of a brave new civilization.

The progressives are trapped. They search round desperately for explanations. The Childs write:

Our commercial world has discovered how to make more money than ever out of this fundamental drive and does not care how it makes it. Young people are subjected to a ceaseless barrage of sex propaganda in the Press, in films, in the theatre, in advertisements, in the sexy novel, much of it exalting sexual satisfactions as the most important of human gratifications. Add to this the almost universal availability of cheap contraceptives and it is small wonder that the forces battling against restraint are on the retreat.*

*ibid., p. 52.

No doubt Mrs Mary Whitehouse, of Clean Up T.V. fame, would heartily agree!

Even Neill confesses himself baffled by the 'new shallow sophistication' of the young. (An article in the *Weekend Telegraph* called Dartingtonians 'swinging to the point of world-weariness'.) He writes in his latest book:

The young have come to see through the pretences and morals of their elders. They realize they have been lied to and cheated. . . . It was not youth that made the H bomb: it was age. But youth knows that it is powerless . . . [it] rebels but in a futile way. Its Beatle hair, its leather jackets, its blue jeans, its motor-bikes are all symbols of rebellion but symbols that remain symbols. In essentials youth is still docile, obedient, inferior; it challenges the things that do not matter. . . .*

Summerhill, of course, is the school most popularly associated with sexual freedom, but in fact it is a great deal more 'moral' than either Bedales or Dartington Hall. Life at Summerhill is very public and the direct democracy made possible by small numbers develops a strong community feeling. In addition, most of the children are very young: at the time of writing there are only half a dozen over fifteen. Summerhill's image chiefly derives from the very libertarian instincts of Neill's books. He asks: why did God give youth a sex instinct if He did not intend it to be used? But Neill is too cautious to put publicly into practice what he preaches, though on occasions he has been prepared to turn a blind eye to a love affair. At Kilquhanity, small numbers, youth and a strong family atmosphere impose similar restraints. It is also a much more active school than some of the others.

The whole question of coeducation is now being debated in the boarding-school world. Atlantic College wants to go co-educational: even some public schools are making tentative experiments in this direction. Is it a good or a bad thing?

The exponents of coeducational boarding face a very real dilemma. For coeducation to be real, it must consist of more than a separation punctuated by carefully supervised 'mixed' occasions. But a genuine mingling in the conditions of privacy

*Talking of Summerhill, p. 131.

and freedom now likely to prevail must lead to boys and girls sleeping together in the school. The great premise of the early coeducators that this would not in fact happen is now illusory. And as most schoolmasters are far from being prepared to accept this eventuality, coeducation means importing into any school a whole new group of unsettling conflicts. In fact, the progressive school now exhibits, in a coeducational setting, many of the features of the traditional single-sex public school: the illicit and furtive sex, the discovery, the expulsion – all of which makes nonsense of the progressive claim to have established new bonds of confidence and honesty between children and staff. The utter traditionality of this ritual, so different from what the progressives envisaged, is scarcely concealed by the Childs' flat description: 'we say that in this field, as in many others, restraint is the price of freedom and ... if any individual is unable to exercise it Dartington cannot be the right place for him or her.'*

There are other arguments against coeducation. A shrewd criticism was expressed by Reddie of Abbotsholme, who saw it as an 'excellent example of applying to children the conditions that may suit adults' – an unkind thrust since this was precisely the progressive charge against conventional education. A second criticism is expressed by a contributor to the *Bedales Chronicle*: 'I thought that boys at Bedales who felt they weren't a success with girls (and vice versa) were too young to have the consequent misgivings forced upon them.'†

Finally, it is very doubtful whether the public schools today really encourage homosexuality, as their earlier critics claimed. The most active boy homosexuals probably turn out to be the most vigorous heterosexuals;‡ while the monastic seclusion which previously produced what Robert Graves called 'pseudo-homosexuality' – a kind of delayed adolescence – is rapidly vanishing.

*H. A. T. Child, op. cit., p. 53.
†Spring, 1964, p. 39.
‡D. J. West, in *Homosexuality*, p. 127, writes '... the frequency of homosexual indulgence at school has probably more to do with the strength of the sex drive than the direction it will take in later life.'

Geoffrey Crump, a Bedales master before the war, argued that coeducation 'does appear to cause a permanent undercurrent of restlessness and excitement, which makes concentration difficult. . . .' This raises a question about the function of a school. Should a school aim as far as possible to approximate to 'real life'? Or should it be a place set aside for certain purposes? This distinction is important. If I attend a language course I do not insist that it be coeducational, because that is irrelevant to its purpose. On the other hand, if I go to a dance I would certainly expect to find girls there. The public school always aimed to be a microcosm of life, providing all the ingredients necessary for healthy development. It was single-sex because it thought the other sex was unnecessary for that age. The progressives thought that it was. The answer surely is that it *is* important for teenage boys and girls to mix; it may not even matter if they sleep together; but it is not necessary that they should do so at school. The boarding school, in short, should abandon some of its totalitarian claims. Weekly boarding could be a conceivable solution. Atlantic College, for example, grants its pupils long week-end exeats, without question. This seems much more sensible than establishing a girl's section on those isolated Welsh cliffs, and importing into the school a basically intractable problem.

5 · Government

Perhaps the most distinctive feature of the public school was its system of boy-government, the prefect system. Originally developed as a pragmatic response to the problem of maintaining order and supervision in large boarding communities with inadequate and incompetent staff, it evolved into a highly conscious technique for training leaders to run the empire. From this point of view public-school education as a whole may be regarded in Platonic terms as a preparation for the task of governing an imperial society.

The earliest progressives did not attack the principles which underlay these arrangements. They too believed in training a 'Directing Class' (to use Reddie's phrase). But they started with the assumption that the existing leaders were no good. Everywhere in government they saw incompetence, selfishness, idleness. No wonder a 'labour question' had arisen when the country was governed by a pampered aristocracy and a self-seeking plutocracy. They traced these misfortunes to faulty methods of education. And it was in the existing structure of the prefectorial system that they discovered a most potent source of the malaise. In their eyes the hedonistic athletocracy which governed the late Victorian public school exhibited all those vices of privilege without responsibility to which they attributed the social unrest of adult society. They aimed to diminish the privilege and increase the sense of responsibility. By so doing they hoped to attain their ideal of a purified Directing Class to run the nation.

But the early progressives were not just Tory democrats, though this strain ran pretty strong in Reddie, and indeed in Hahn. They also believed in 'participation'. This required not merely an emphasis on responsibility, but a diffusion of responsibility. The public school as they saw it was divided into the 'successes' – the gifted scholars and athletes round whom everything revolved – and the 'failures' whose 'talents' were never developed. Everyone, they felt, ought to be given a chance to make his individual contribution to the life of the whole. From the earliest age pupils were to be given definite tasks and responsibilities; to be brought into the running of the school. Thus although on the one hand the progressives set out to improve the quality of the leader class, their other innovations – removing privileges and diffusing responsibility right through the school – tended to break down the distinction between 'leaders' and 'led' and pave the way for a more democratic and egalitarian form of government.

The libertarian progressives carried this trend to its logical conclusion. They argued that only a democratic community could be truly harmonious and cooperative. What was required was not only a diffusion of responsibility, but a diffusion of decision-making as well. This fitted in much better with the optimistic and democratic intellectual current of the post-1918 period. This was the heyday of 'self-government'. Pupils were elected to office by popular vote; laws were framed by school parliaments; discipline was handed over to judicial tribunals. True friendship would replace the relationship of leader and led, which the progressives believed was necessarily based on force or fraud. 'The bigs hit me, so I hit the smalls; that's fair,' said a ten-year-old boy to Bertrand Russell, in parody of what the progressives believed to be the fundamental principle underlying the prefect system.* The alternative vision was charmingly described in the *Summerhill Chronicle*:

> We try hard to raise children by loving them so that when they grow older they too will love not only their families and friends but have a love in them big enough to put a stop to a silly thing called War.

This view of school life was obviously incompatible with corporal punishment. Both the early and later progressives were united in rejecting it. As much ink was spilled on this question as on that of competitive games. The earlier progressives were less militant about their repudiation. They thought corporal punishment was the result of an insuffi-

Autobiography, Vol. 2, p. 154.

ciently interesting educational programme which constantly tempted pupils to mischief. If the programme offered could fully absorb the pupil's energies and affections then the need for beating would disappear. There was a subtler, though related, reason. People like Reddie and Hahn were great character-moulders. Outward conformity was not enough for them: they wanted inward assent. Beating aimed at securing the right *behaviour*: it could not implant the right *motive*. This reason for rejecting beating has influenced all the progressives to a greater or lesser extent, except possibly Neill, who didn't aim to influence anyone. He had a specific reason for getting rid of corporal punishment. Most of his 'bad' pupils had been beaten all their lives in an attempt to improve their behaviour. Constant beating if anything made them behave worse. It was clear that corporal punishment could have no place in his scheme of therapy.

Neill was greatly influenced by Freud, and Freudian theory has further discredited the corporal punishment idea. Basically the Freudian therapist believes that the only way of removing symptoms is to expose causes: if the cause is dealt with, the symptom will disappear. Corporal punishment, by contrast, is closer to 'aversion therapy', which seeks to eliminate the symptom without bothering too much about the cause, which it believes in any case to be inaccessible. The most modern psychology would appear to offer some support to the old public-school idea that for most childish misdemeanours beating is the quickest and simplest way of 'wiping clean the slate'.

One further argument had a great influence on all progressives and this derived from the Quaker rejection of any form of violence, which in politics led to pacifism. Basically, the Quakers believed that it is evil to offer violence against any form of God's life; that violence begets violence, thus progressively brutalizing all relationships and making war inevitable. With their optimistic psychology they believed that the appeal to love, gentleness and reason would secure the results that coercion inevitably failed to secure. This kind of thinking became very popular in the largely pacifist decade following the First World War. The prevention of further wars seemed to require the elimination of violence from the family and school. For the libertarian progressives the rejection of corporal punishment was thus linked to the repudiation of a school authority which rested ultimately on force. Force had been tried and found wanting: a new way was needed.

*

Gordonstoun's aims, as we have seen, do not suffer from understatement. Who but Hahn would have dared call his head boy 'The Guardian' – and got away with it? Hahn saw the word and the function in their Platonic sense – a person of superior virtue who is also a protector. This is how he liked to think of the whole prefectorial cadre, renamed 'Helpers'. Lower down responsibility is diffused among no less than 19 Captains, 8 Heads of Services, and 8 other officials. The attempt to provide as many boys as possible with something to do, as well as a characteristic pomposity, is reflected in some of the titles: Captain of Lost Property, Captain of the Linen Room, Captain of Bicycles, and an even stranger-sounding Captain of Guests. I suppose that, in a school tucked away in a remote corner of northern Scotland, no one notices the incongruity of these appellations.

We have seen how the progressive schools tried to get away from the idea that promotion should depend upon sporting prowess. The chance ability to hit a ball to the boundary was (rightly) considered by Hahn far too insubstantial evidence of the requisite powers of leadership and dedication. Nor was intellectual ability to be the decisive factor as in the Arnoldian conception. No: the criterion of promotion was to be virtue. The schoolboy leaders, in the words of Gordonstoun's Warden, 'should indeed be swift and bold, if in addition they were gentle and lovers of the truth'.

Thus, from the moment of his entry into the school, the Gordonstoun boy is confronted by tests or hurdles which he has to surmount in order to aspire to higher things. In fact, Gordonstoun life may be described as one long obstacle race. These tests are designed to fortify the character for more exalted challenges. After a term or so of 'trial', the boy is granted the 'privilege' of wearing the school uniform, scanty though that is. At this point he encounters his first great hurdle in the form of the 'Training Plan'. He is required to keep a daily record of the performance or non-performance of certain tasks, for which he is entirely responsible. This is called a 'training in self-honesty'. Thus each day he has to brush his teeth, have cold and hot showers, go on his morning run, do press-ups and skip sixty times. Then there are the 'Great Temptations' to be resisted, especially one called E.B.M. (Eating Between Meals). Other temptations may from time to time be added to the list by the housemaster, the more private ones marked with a cypher. Through the deliberate creation of guilt the boy is steeled in habits of self-discipline necessary for the next stage in the ascent.

Hahn's greatest achievement, in the eyes of his admirers, is to have breathed fresh life into old and worn-out institutions. The public schools have for many years awarded 'colours' for proficiency in various sports. These take the form of special blazers, stripes, ribbons, tassels, etc. Hahn, in Brereton's words, 'took the overprized colours ... and used them in a new way. The most worthy representatives of the school should wear them, but these would not necessarily be the fastest runners or the best goal-scorers ...'

The first mark of recognition is a white stripe across the pullover, signifying worthiness to be considered for selection as a Colour Bearer Candidate. With a white and purple stripe a boy becomes a Colour Bearer Candidate proper; and from this body is chosen the Colour Bearer Council, from which in turn the headmaster chooses his Guardian and Helpers. The Colour Bearer Council itself is self-electing, in imitation of the Eton Pop Society (another example of breathing new life into old and worn-out institutions). But there its resemblance to that somewhat frivolous organization ends, since the Gordonstoun version is charged with preserving the moral tone of the school. Its activities are shrouded in the mystery deemed appropriate to a body of such lofty calling:

The sudden announcement that there were no Colour Bearer Secrets therefore took a lot of people by surprise. It blew away many old phogies [sic], ghosts and cobwebs. With the invitation to ask questions about the institution by which our school is run, people found out that the mysterious Salem Document (previously alleged by those who did not know any better, to perform some mystical and semi-sacred part in the mysterious initiation ceremony of Colour Bearers) was nothing more than an extremely long and pompous document signifying very little indeed. Because such myths have now been dispelled ... it is possible to write and publish articles such as this one, which last term would have been considered sacriligious and almost blasphemous.*

As we have noted, Hahn is a great character-moulder. He has endeavoured to put into practice Reddie's dictum that *every* aspect of schoolboy life should reflect the official values and purposes of the school. At most public schools there are two distinct levels on which life is lived. There is the official level, representing 'What the School Stands For' – classwork, chapel, games, societies, etc; and there is the unofficial, or 'subcultural' level, the inner life of the schoolboy society, with all its slang, petty hierarchies, distinctions and conventions (including that of a perpetual war of wits with the authorities). This subterranean schoolboy life is admittedly not very pleasant or edifying; but it opposes a very strong barrier to the totalitarian aims of the moulding schoolmaster. It is the domain of the bully and the cheat. But it also harbours the rebel, anyone who will not conform. It was this private sphere which was anathema to most progressives, none more so than Kurt Hahn. They saw only its bad sides: its cruelty, its primitivism, its amorality. They attributed its existence to the fact that the official values made insufficient appeal to the pupils. If only the instincts and appetites which nurtured the semi-delinquent subculture could be channelled into worthy purposes; if only those turbulent and unruly spirits could be turned towards Higher Thoughts, Great Deeds, and Beautiful Objects! This was the dream of nearly all progressives from Reddie onwards. Hahn carried it out with typical German thoroughness. What he did was essentially what Arnold had

*The Nurve, the unofficial Gordonstoun magazine, February 1966.

attempted to do in the 1830s, namely to take over a system of hierarchy and esteem developed by the pupils and reflecting their own values, and inject into it his own exalted purpose of moral leadership.

Whether he has succeeded is more doubtful. While he was there he breathed his own life into his paper institutions, like Arnold, inspiring the whole community with his own insistent purposes. Once he left, what had been real became largely mechanical. The Gordonstoun boys I spoke to were rather defensive about the Training Plan and the whole Colour-Bearer system. Perhaps they felt them to be embarrassing. Nevertheless, it is a tribute to the school's moulding environment that they arouse very little irreverence or criticism.

Will Hahn go down in history as a second Arnold? It certainly seems possible. His undoubted success with the staidest of the English squirearchy illustrates an unexpected phenomenon: the recurrent English need to have their inchoate and muddled strivings articulated with an audacity, clarity and grandeur that can only be provided by a foreigner or at least by someone very un-English in temperament. Viewed in this light, Gordonstoun can be seen as the public-school system carried to its logical conclusion. It marks the final transformation of the anarchic boy-republic encountered by Arnold into a disciplined regiment inspired by a great ideal. Whether the times are ripe for a second Arnoldian revolution, whether Hahn will go down in history as an interesting oddity or as the forerunner of a new impulse in education, only time will tell.

With Atlantic College, we are back once more to solid, English common-sense. Whereas Gordonstoun sets out to capture both body and soul of the pupil, Atlantic College is content that he should participate fully in a very demanding programme, without worrying unduly about what he thinks or attempting to impose a moral censorship. As the age of entry is sixteen plus it is assumed that boys who come are in some sense sympathetic to the school's aims. The older age-group and the international character of the school have forced the abandonment of many characteristic public-school practices – prefect system, compulsory chapel and so on – while there has been no attempt to impose Training Plans or Colour Bearer Councils. There is an elective system for all the main posts, and all internal matters not affecting the staff are discussed between the headmaster and the Student Council. This system of 'guided democracy' seems naturally appropriate to the needs of Atlantic College's age-group and of an international student body. It was not imposed *a priori* in deference to the fixed conceptions of a founder, and so functions much less self-consciously than at many other progressive schools where ideological commitments have been made which sometimes seem ill-attuned to the needs or desires of the pupils themselves.

Thus at Atlantic College there is some measure of self-government without the slogan ever having been used. The libertarian progressive schools in theory have elevated it into a central principle: but in practice they have failed to make much real progress in that direction for reasons which should have been obvious from the start. The headmaster inevitably reserves the major powers to himself. Admissions, staff appointments, academic policy and health matters all lie within his province. No school which entrusted these concerns to its children would have much chance of survival. In addition the headmaster has to handle social and legal relations between the school and the larger community. He might thus forbid activities simply because they offend public opinion or would give rise to legal action. Independence might give greater latitude for experiment, but no school can be too far ahead of public opinion, and the most radical school can only be as radical as its parents allow it to be. All these considerations naturally limit the role of self-government.

Indeed, nowadays one often gets the impression that it is the idea rather than the reality which keeps self-government going. It is so much part of the progressive credo that to scrap it seems an unthinkable betrayal. It also has its public-relations uses. The self-government meeting at Summerhill, for example, is a big 'draw' for visitors, whose five-shilling contributions furnish a sizeable chunk of the school's income. A contributor to the *Bedales Chronicle* remarked of an interminable meeting: 'But it has served its purpose. Now the

Headmaster can say to visitors – "Oh yes, we do have a student government."'

Summerhill and Kilquhanity are very small schools: numbers fluctuate round the fifty mark. Hence direct democracy is possible, even though the younger children may not be fully aware of what is going on. Every week these two schools hold a meeting of the whole community (staff as well as children) which reviews the problems which have arisen since the previous meeting. First it hears the report of the judicial tribunal on offences and their punishments: defendants have the right of appeal to the full meeting. Most of the offences are very trivial – petty annoyances perpetrated by one child on another, or upon a member of staff. These offences are reported by the victims to the tribunal, which only acts upon specific complaints, the theory being that only behaviour which gives rise to complaints is deemed worthy of communal attention. The victim is generally asked what he wishes done, and he generally demands a fine, a public warning, or restitution of damaged or 'borrowed' property. At both schools, there is strong social disapproval of bullying, and anyone who suffers from it is fully backed up in complaining to the tribunal or community meeting. Because the complaint is to the community itself rather than to the staff, there is no suggestion of 'sneaking' or 'telling tales'.

Indeed one of the main arguments for removing disciplinary powers from the staff is that this breaks down the traditional hostility between staff and pupils, thus enabling the teachers to know what goes on and prevent much of the bullying and unpleasantness that in conventional schools goes largely undetected. On the other hand, Bedales, where teachers and pupils are very friendly, had for many years a traditional system of initiation and bullying comparable to that of any public school. New boys were subjected to the 'brush torture' described in the *Bedales Chronicle* as the 'savage massage of the chest with a hard-bristle hairbrush' and also to 'agg-agg', the same treatment applied to the knuckles. More surprising were reports of anti-semitism, for example teasing a boy because he had a Jewish nose or a Jewish way of speaking. The bigger the school, it seems, the less effective are the benefits of staff–pupil intimacy.

At Summerhill a characteristic report of the tribunal committee runs as follows:

Paul versus Earl for throwing matches at him. Earl fined sixpence. Alice versus Julie for chucking raisins around. Julie doesn't get any raisins next week. Emile versus Mort for hitting him at supper. Mort to eat supper last all week. Lou versus Ben for putting shoe polish on his trunk. Dropped with a strong warning.

In this particular case Earl appealed against his sentence, and the following discussion took place:

Earl: I think I was fined too much.
Chairman: State your case.
Earl: I didn't intentionally throw the matches at him, and besides they weren't lit.
Chairman: That's beside the point, Earl. Lit or not, it's a stupid thing to do.
Earl: I didn't see him there anyway.
Paul: He damn well saw me there, and threw them at me.
Earl: I did not.
Chairman: No cross talk now. How much do you think you should be fined?
Earl: Threepence.
Neill: What was he fined for? I can't hear you...
Chairman: He was fined sixpence for flinging matches at Paul, and now he wants it lowered to threepence. All right. All in favour that Earl is fined threepence instead of sixpence. All against. You're still fined sixpence.
Earl: Oh, hell!*

At Kilquhanity, a 'strong warning was given to Sean not to make faces at Hilary' and the scribe noted 'a request not to call Mike names. Names, except Cocoa Bean, are a 6d. fine.' At Kilquhanity there is much less fining than at Summerhill; on the other hand all the offences are published every week in the school's magazine, *Broadsheet,* so this may be considered sufficient deterrent. Delicate susceptibilities are respected.

*These accounts are taken from *Summerhill: A Loving World*, privately printed.

'Jeremy: I would like people not to swear so much. Strong warning to Stephen.'

Many of these problems arise from lack of privacy. That great topic of discussion – bed-times – which seems to have sustained the Summerhill Meeting for almost forty years would simply not arise if children had their own bedrooms as they do at Dartington Hall. It is the lack of occasion for such social conflicts that makes the Dartington Moot a much less central institution than its equivalents at Summerhill and Kilquhanity.

At Summerhill and Kilquhanity, self-government, then, is largely a complaints system, especially suited to the needs of younger children, who cannot look after themselves, and require communal protection for their persons and property. These schools lack entirely sixth-formers who no doubt would find the proceedings trivial and tedious. In addition, really serious breaches of rules or persistent anti-social behaviour cannot be dealt with by the tribunals – the headmaster has to be called in.

The rule-making functions of the school parliaments are much less important. At Kilquhanity, the Council almost never makes or changes rules: the only attempt in the last two years was to relax the smoking rules, heavily defeated. At Summerhill, the weekly meeting discusses bed-times, smoking, behaviour in the town and other such matters and is given considerable latitude for experiment, but even here decisions tend to be subject to 'overriding considerations' introduced by the headmaster. Neill addressed the Summerhill meeting as follows on bed-times:

I know this is something we have talked about, but I feel I have to bring it up again.... You kids are running around this house at all hours, and as I said before, it's becoming a health problem, not a government problem. My concern is the health of the children. If you can't keep the laws you make, then the staff will decide about bedtimes, and then we'll make it a strict school. Is that what you want? I just can't afford to have kids get sick. The school can be closed for that.

Over the years, the sphere of health has gradually encroached on the sphere of government. The most notable instance is smoking. Both Summerhill and Kilquhanity now forbid it under the age of sixteen, and at Dartington Hall it is confined to the children's own rooms. Neill makes no pretence that it is a 'government' decision:

I made a law at the beginning of this term (1962) about smoking under sixteen. I made this law because the government told all schools to discourage smoking among children, and Summerhill can't stand out against the whole of the schools of England.... Now, a lot of people are smoking under sixteen, and quite openly. ... Well, I'm going to tell you all something. You have to choose whether you are going to smoke here or not. If you're going to smoke here, you're not coming back. ... I can't punish you. Only the community can punish, but I can say, all right, if you don't want to live the Summerhill way, you're not coming back. ... So don't feel you can come here, and do as you like. You can't.

It may be argued that self-government, even in this limited sense, achieves nothing that could not be better achieved by benevolent adults. If teachers are fully adult they will be able sufficiently to distinguish between necessary and unecessary rules; and complaints can be dealt with much more informally and expeditiously by the adults themselves. Against this three points may be made. The complaints system, administered by children themselves, does seem to bring to light bullying, teasing and various other forms of annoying behaviour which would tend to go undetected because of the ban on telling tales. However kind and understanding adults are there is a barrier between them and the children: younger children especially identify with their gang and not with the adult. For the same reason, community decisions and punishments seem to cause much less resentment, for the child is being judged by those who have roughly the same outlook and values as himself, rather than by those whose judgement must always be suspect in his eyes. Finally, self-government is a very wholesome check on adult pomposity and abuse of power. At Gordonstoun, for example, one housemaster prides himself on the perfect order and tidiness of his domain: everything has a place and everything is in its place. There was not a speck of dust anywhere. This reflected a peculiar adult view of the world, quite unnatural to adolescents and, incidentally, un-natural to most adults. It is the subjection of children to these small adult manias that is avoided by giving children some freedom to manage their lives: for no child would dream of enforcing such a system either upon himself or his fellows.

At Summerhill and Kilquhanity self-government is kept go-ing by the small size of the schools which makes possible direct democracy, the 'complaints department' which provides the staple of most meetings, and strong headmaster support. At Dartington Hall and King Alfred School, Hampstead, the posi-tion is different. At Dartington the separate study-bedroom arrangement eliminates most of the personal clashes, at least in Foxhole, the senior section of the school (children above thirteen). With 140 pupils, direct democracy has inevitably given way in part to the representative system with elected committees – Agenda, Dining Room, Food and Common Room – to handle communal administration. King Alfred's is a day school, so there is much less for the Council to do. Here again, there is a partly representative system, with elected delegates from each form, together with some of the older children. At both these schools there is a lack of business sufficient to sustain continuous interest. At Dartington Hall a motion 'that the school should refrain from buying South African produce' was passed by sixty-one votes to one; and at King Alfred's the headmistress made a vigorous plea in favour of a well-deserving charity; but this is hardly the stuff out of which thriving self-government is built. At Dartington the committees are staffed with difficulty and meet intermittently; the Moot itself has gone for long periods into retirement: separate living quarters tend to encourage individual, rather than communal, interests.

Nevertheless, at both these schools the School Council does have a definite function, which is to defend traditional liberties and customs against innovating headmasters. At Dartington, as we have seen, a proposal to call free periods study periods in order to improve the attitude to work was heavily defeated. A motion to make gym compulsory was also lost; and though the Moot was forced to accept a proposal (December 1964) to confine smoking to children's rooms, it was able to reject fines for breaking the rule. At K.A.S. the fear of innovation strongly emerges from the following account of a Council meeting:

Next, Andrew Elton asked the Heads if they could inform Council 'in advance' of any proposed changes in the school. This plea seemed reasonable enough for it would give Council the power to discuss the proposals, and hear the reasons for and against. Surprisingly the Heads objected, for they claimed that it would interfere with their duties, but this is clearly not so for Elton only asked for discussion and not that the Council be allowed to alter the Heads' decisions. They said that discussion would create a bad feeling, but surely more bad feeling is created if a change is sprung on the school, rather than if reasons for it can be heard and discussed. Council held this view also, and insisted that the Heads kept them informed. . . .*

At many progressive schools, the arrival of a new headmaster has produced a 'tightening-up' of control. The excessively libertarian and somewhat romantic headmasters of the thirties and forties have been replaced by more contemporary-minded chiefs, intent on getting better academic results, reducing smoking and improving behaviour. When the School Council obstructs their plans, they tend to ascribe its truculence to unthinking conservatism and seek various stratagems to get their own way, which in turn undermines the reality of self-government.

At Bedales, the Advisory Council voted its own dissolution soon after the arrival of the new headmaster, Timothy Slack. His comment was as follows:

I don't know to what extent I influenced this – I didn't broadcast my feelings, but it was known that I thought it to be rather a worthless institution, the preserve of the barrack-room lawyer talking a lot about the constitution. . . . We now have a more informal meeting two or three times a term, when I invite people to come through into this room and we discuss anything they wish to bring up.

No doubt the new head, who had had no previous connexion with the school, found particularly galling references to the Bedales 'way of doing things'. He thought that the right solu-

*Locus Classicus, the un official K.A.S. magazine, 1964.

tion was to give the pupils definite responsibilities – such as finance and club activities – but otherwise to retain control in his hands. 'There is nothing more dishonest,' he said, 'than to give people the feeling that it is their decision, when you know it must be your decision.' It is in fact this pretence that responsibility lies with the Council when in fact the headmaster has no intention of accepting decisions contrary to his wishes that has proved the bane of most attempts to run self-government systems.

Progressive headmasters are very prone to talk about the 'right use of freedom', which, in practice, means running the school according to the headmaster's idea of how it should be run. It is very doubtful whether this type of self-government can work with sophisticated and intelligent children; and although Neill at Summerhill concedes greater latitude than any other headmaster, one reason for the relative success of Summerhill self-government is the youthfulness and naïvety of its citizens.

Again, it is very hard to make the process interesting. This is not simply because there is not enough for the Council to do; it is because administration is generally boring. Where representative institutions exist all the work is done by the few children who have a taste for it; the only occasions when the mass of children participate is when some big issue, directly affecting their liberties, comes up. It is this boredom that has always defeated the liberal goal of a participating democracy. Populations, adult and child, it seems, only participate in times of crisis.

On the other hand, what pupils do seem to appreciate is the right to be consulted and to have their say when important decisions are pending. The true function of the school parliament, in short, is to criticize the government, not to legislate or administer itself.

PART TWO

Reddie
of
Abbotsholme

6 · A Public-School Education

The English progressive school movement was born in the imagination of a shy and idealistic adolescent boarding at Fettes public school in the 1870s. Cecil Reddie came from middle-class Scottish parents – his father, a civil servant, rose to be Deputy Comptroller of Naval Pay. The death of both parents had left him an orphan at the age of thirteen; and his school for the next six years became his whole life.

The English public school probably leaves a deeper imprint on the characters of those who attend it than any other educational institution. Its secret is simple. Adolescence is a time of intense emotions, possibly the most intense that people ever experience. The passions have been kindled, but are not yet under control. The public school both amplifies and concentrates them. It amplifies them by throwing people together in close and intimate relations and by providing them with a rapid succession of emotionally charged events and experiences; it concentrates them by focusing them on one place and on one small community. People may leave their school loving or hating it, or both; they rarely leave indifferent to it.

Not only is there this intense concentration of emotion in an isolated community, but the outlets provided for it within the community are extremely limited. In the late Victorian public school there were basically three: the chapel, the playing field and beautiful youths. Dr Arnold had elevated the chapel from being a place where boys let loose rats, as in Keats's day at Eton, into a most powerful agency of moral and aesthetic inspiration. Associated with the chapel were all those big words beloved of the Victorian schoolmaster: Beauty, Truth, Honour, Loyalty, Purity, Obedience and so on. The culture of the spirit was supplemented by the muscular Christianity of the playing fields. Organized games were initially devised to keep boys occupied in the day and tired at night:

from this pragmatic beginning arose the cult of athletics, which became in effect the religion of the late Victorian public school. The beautiful youth was a sex substitute, in an age when the normal difficulties of boy-girl contact in Victorian society were reinforced by total segregation during the adolescence. At the public school, the romance between boy and girl was transformed into the 'romantic friendship' between elder and younger boy which is a stock theme of so many public-school novels. That the baser instincts also enjoyed considerable scope is proved by the plentiful correspondence devoted to this subject in the pages of the late-Victorian *Journal of Education*. The tension between the Platonic ideal and the all-too-frequent evidence of corruption was a formative one for generations of future schoolmasters and clergymen, among them Cecil Reddie.

The psychologist would no doubt explain Reddie's career in terms of a successful sublimation of his physical passion for young boys into an attempt to serve them, and at the same time preserve them from the temptations to which he was subject. The repressed pederast emerged as the apostle of the Platonic ideal in education. This conclusion gains plausibility from a reading of Reddie's own memoir of his adolescence, written before Freud made self-knowledge necessary and concealment desirable.

Reddie's biographer, B. M. Ward, notes how his 'highly sensitive nature' was 'sorely perplexed with the trials of adolescence'. But Reddie himself gives a somewhat more elaborate account of his difficulties.

We had, indeed, as early as we can recall, a bias towards idealizing not only the absent but the present. And amid our new surroundings this tendency grew apace, and unceasingly we kept constructing in our imagination an olympus of heroes, built out of the most perfect types we found around us, as objects of reverence and worship.

As he grew older and attained prefectorial responsibilities, he began to have doubts about his Olympus. 'We grew,' he noted, 'more critical.' His Gods 'one by one ... had fallen from the pedestals upon which youthful enthusiasm had placed them, leaving, however, undimmed the memory of moments of earlier heart-whole worship, never to be forgotten.'

His disillusionment with his comrades was reinforced by doubts about the syllabus. Instead of the 'beautiful stories of Roman and Hellenic heroes' which the notion of a Classical education had led him to expect, he was offered a diet of 'stammered reading and semi-English translation of Greek and Latin literature in class' and 'unending excursions after dull grammatical rules'. He turned, in reaction, to natural science, but this he found 'too purely intellectual and cold'.

His metaphysical yearnings might have been satisfied by religion, but 'the Divine Figure placed before us ... seemed to have little connexion with England in the nineteenth century, or with the life of Boyhood.'

On all sides, the terrible gap between the ideal and the real 'was producing day by day a feeling of hopeless division and discordance'. 'Our disenchantment,' he goes on, 'threatened to bring cynicism or indifference.' But at this critical moment, salvation came. The young Reddie happened to meet a 'lady relative, somewhat our senior. Her womanly intuition ... dispersed the gathering gloom.' Thereafter he felt more sure of himself and his mission.

Having failed to find among those of his own age 'the perfect ideal we sought', he turned 'to the younger generation, resolved, if it were possible to find favourable material, to strive and create in more plastic boyhood the ideal we had failed to see incarnate in grown youth.'

But 'plastic boyhood' apparently resisted for long his attempt to mould it. He recalled a 'period of inactivity'. He admits that his young companions found his conversation 'tedious'. 'They and we inhabited different worlds, though in the same room.' Once again the solution to his difficulties came 'suddenly and unexpectedly'.

A friendship with a youngster supplied the needed link. Our wish to educate him produced in us a passion for knowledge unfelt before. ... And this incident really decided the future. ... For it was this youngster who, years after, persuaded us to attempt to be an educator.

One can just imagine the scene. The crackling fire in the study, the cups of tea; the tall, dark, intense Senior Prefect, his eyes blazing with the enthusiasm of his mission, talking compulsively about idealism, perfection and purity; and the bright, cheerful youngster, wondering what it was all about, half-longing to escape to the more congenial society of his companions, yet strangely moved by the hypnotic power of those eyes, and by the intensity and passion of the oration. In this manner Reddie, happy at last, spent his last year at Fettes. 'We lose a most useful, if not the most useful, college prefect by his going,' wrote his housemaster on his last report in the summer of 1878. 'I anticipate a successful future for him.'

7 · The Idea Takes Shape

Reddie first turned to education because he believed that he had a mission to protect adolescents from sexual vice. This aim was always in the forefront of his educational career; but it came to be linked to the larger aim of reforming society. The two were never clearly distinguished in his own mind. He wanted to fashion his uppper-class adolescents into a heroic mould: to be beautiful, brave and pure. And what better occupation for heroes than to run the country? Walt Whitman, the American poet, had the same obsession with his 'bands of comrades'. Both were adolescent fantasies masquerading as a policy of social revival.

Reddie's desire to reform society was not exceptional; nor was his belief that this could best be done through the school. The Victorians tended to believe that all problems would ultimately be solved by better education, This faith has survived virtually intact to the present day, despite powerful evidence to the contrary.

But Reddie's public-school experience gave him an additional bias in favour of social reform through education. The public school embodied the idea of the school as a community. Boarding had a great deal to do with this. Being places where the boys actually lived, rather than travelled to for specific purposes, the public schools came to be seen as miniature societies: everything pertaining to the life of childhood was their legitimate concern – intellectual learning, social relations, moral development. It was natural for public schoolmasters to think in terms of educating the 'whole man' and not just the 'mind'; and it was their proud boast that they produced a certain type of man, instantly recognizable, and specially fitted for leadership in industry and empire.

Reddic accepted without question these very far-reaching aims of public-school education; what he began to question were some of the methods. He came to ask: why, if all-round development was the aim, was there such a concentration on games to the exclusion of, say, manual work or aesthetic pursuits? Some reformers, working from within the system, were already beginning to make pertinent criticisms of a similar kind. For example, Edward Thring, headmaster of Uppingham, argued that to gear the whole system to the needs of the scholar and the athlete was grossly unfair to the ordinary boy who was neither. According to Thring 'every boy, however unpromising he might appear, had some latent talent ... could do *something* well.'* It was the school's job to discover what that 'something' was and give it opportunity for expression. This view tied up with something Reddie had experienced at his own school: the fact that, despite the school's grandiose aims, most boys passed through school life largely untouched by official purposes and activities. The Public school lacked the secret of engaging the 'affections' of the 'ordinary' boy for the enterprise of education. Religion was 'too remote'. The Classics were meaningless except for the future pedant; games were enjoyed by the handful of gifted athletes.

As the progressive school movement developed the criticisms started to go even deeper. Badley, one of Reddie's followers, posed the question: how, if the school is to be regarded as a microcosm of society, even of an improved society, can the exclusion of one sex be justified? He introduced coeducation into his school, Bedales. Following the First World War, the school reformers began to ask another set of questions: did not perpetual rifle-drilling turn the public-schoolboy into a dangerous militarist? Did not corporal punishment brutalize him? Was the prefect system the right kind of training for a democratic society? Surely the nation required more individualism and less of that team-spirit which had led it unthinking to the blood-baths of Flanders? Yet the feature of all these questions which links them to the public-school outlook is that they accepted implicitly the view that it *was* the school's task to develop the whole range of desirable individual and

*David Newsome, *Godliness and Good Learning*, p. 221.

social aptitudes, to educate the 'whole man', though a new and improved version of him.

At Edinburgh University, where he studied medicine and chemistry, Reddie read Disraeli, Carlyle and Ruskin; met the poet Edward Carpenter, and through him was introduced to the writings of Walt Whitman; flirted briefly with the views of such socialists as Hyndman and William Morris; in short came into contact with a body of thought which may be broadly described as Romantic.

It was natural that Reddie should be attracted to Romanticism. The emotional side of his nature, as he himself admitted, had been starved at school; he was a man of strong passions and feelings generally kept under an iron control. While he worked conscientiously on a chemistry thesis of monumental dullness, his trapped spirit sought release in the heady visions of the Romantic poets and artists who proclaimed the doctrine of man's power and freedom to transcend the crippling limitations of society and circumstance. 'Man is born free but is everywhere in chains,' Rousseau had proclaimed. Attributing his own spiritual incarceration to an educational system that had cramped, repressed and twisted the deepest yearnings of his adolescence, Reddie conjured up a school that would set the children free; not admittedly in the sense of being free from adult direction, but free to realize the power that was in them, free to become confident, assured, god-like, in their response to the world around them.

The central preoccupation of the Romantics was in fact the release of power in the individual so that he might come to realize his glorious destiny. Blake and Rousseau had both talked ecstatically about the divine potential of the child destroyed by faulty and 'unnatural' social arrangements – whether those of the school, home, church or political structure. But – and here the Romantics differed from the *philosophes* of the Enlightenment – they saw this 'power' to be released not primarily in intellectual terms, but in spiritual and imaginative ones.

Indeed Rousseau's identification of intellectual life with spiritual decay was naturally attractive to a young man grinding out page after page of a mammoth work on the industrial applications of saltpetre. 'Study,' wrote Rousseau, 'corrupts man's morals, is prejudicial to his health, destroys his constitution, and often spoils his understanding.' He replaced reason by feeling – '*Cogito ergo sum* is superseded by *je sens, donc je suis*.'* 'An upright heart,' Rousseau declared, 'is the first organ of truth,' and he went on to advance an aesthetic theory of virtue which was to be very influential among early progressive educators: 'the good is only the Beautiful put into action . . . the degree of Taste we possess depends much upon the refinement of our feelings'. His critique of schoolmasters – 'the lame teaching others to walk' – was vigorously echoed by later reformers who characterized the teacher as a narrow-minded pedant, intent on forcing his arid categories on to the life-seeking spirit of childhood.

To Rousseau can be traced not only the vigorous and liberating elements in Romantic thought, but also what Croce has called its 'perversions' – notably its antiquarianism and nostalgia expressed in the attempt to recover a mythical Golden Age of the past, whether in the form of the cult of the Noble Savage, or a pietistic medievalism, or an over-romanticized view of 'original innocence'.

The escapism contrasts oddly with the dominant strain of optimism inherited from the Enlightenment, and fortified by the new evolutionary theories of Darwin. Increasingly the optimism becomes divorced from society, becomes other-worldly – a return to 'natural' living, a withdrawal from active involvement in social improvements into a kind of romanticized Christianity such as theosophy (which we shall consider later) or the establishment of Utopian communities dedicated to the realization of private visions in rural settings. The progressive movement in education partakes to some extent of all these 'perversions'. The progressives, like the Romantics, were men who felt that they had been vouchsafed a blinding flash of clarity. They felt that they held the key to a most marvellous future. Unfortunately the dead weight of inherited custom and habit proved far more difficult to dislodge than they

*Quoted in Peter Coveney, *The Image of Childhood*, p. 41.

imagined; all kinds of unforeseen problems arose; and insofar as things were changing they appeared to be doing so in the wrong direction. Escapism was the product of disillusionment with social action; its corollary, an increasingly frenzied and unrealistic search for the 'short-cut' to progress and happiness. All these elements were more or less present in the writers whom Reddie studied, and were to give to his own aims and methods that characteristic 'crankiness' which later became such a marked, if rather endearing, feature of the progressive school movement.

Was social regeneration to come from the top or from the bottom? There were two groups who might to some extent be considered free from the prevailing 'corruption' of liberal, industrial, society: the aristocracy and the workers. The workers were oppressed; the aristocrats, resentful. Either source of social disaffection might be tapped and utilized for the programme of national revival. The progressive decision to work through the traditional governing class was crucial for the future development of the English movement. It tied it to increasingly marginal groups. When Reddie expounded his doctrine of a revived Directing Class in 1909, Sir Robert Morant, the Permanent Secretary of the Board of Education, commented that Reddie had confined his address to 'the educational requirements of a dwindling class'. In a sense Reddie's choice was natural: not only was he a product of the public-school world, but mass education in the 1880s was still a very novel conception. Nevertheless, the concept of a revival through a regenerated aristocracy, in sharp opposition to the dominant impulses of the age towards democracy and equality, is an example of that escapist strain in Romantic thought which we have just mentioned. This is even more clear when we come to examine the content of the education advocated for the Directing Classes.

The contrast with America is interesting. There the progressive movement from the first aimed at transforming the *national* system of education. Differences in culture were decisive. In America education for the masses was already a reality; in England still an aspiration. Moreover, in America

it was mass schooling which, faced by the problem of integrating different racial groups through the school system, had
developed along those communal and non-intellectual lines
which provided an obvious setting for progressive ideas. In
England, by contrast, the only school system through which
the progressive reformer could plausibly work was the public-
school one. Thus while John Dewey launched the American
progressive movement in cooperation with the public authorities in Chicago, Reddie borrowed £2,000 from a friend to buy
an Elizabethan manor house with Gothic additions set in the
heart of the Staffordshire countryside.

Certainly he never considered any other alternative. His
whole experience had been with upper-class adolescents; he
knew little about the masses except that they were insubordin-
ate. He was a complete autocrat who never doubted that some
were born to rule and others to obey; he would never have
tolerated any sharing of control of his 'miniature kingdom'
with local authorities. His sense of property was so strong that
when the mortgage on the building was finally paid off he
rolled on the grass with joy. He believed in order, method and
efficiency, which required leaders, not committees; he was convinced that national regeneration must come from the top,
not from the bottom.

Later progressive headmasters like Neill of Summerhill and
Curry of Dartington Hall would have preferred to work with
ordinary children. However, they found no scope for experiment within the state system. Thus they were forced to charge
fees, which in turn meant that they too were educating, however reluctantly, the 'directing classes'. They thus got themselves and other schools which followed them into a false
position: democratic institutions catering for an élite. Reddie's
position did not suffer from this inconsistency. Abbotsholme
and those schools which it largely inspired – Bedales, Gordonstoun and latterly Atlantic College – believed passionately that
it was their task to make the upper classes morally fit to regenerate the national life.

How was this to be done? Disraeli's Young England movement of the 1840s was too obviously a fraud as a regenerating

political force, consisting as it did of debauched aristocratic dandies. Clearly the morals of the aristocracy itself must be reformed before it could plausibly give political expression to the anti-commercial spirit.

This programme of aristocratic regeneration was summed up in Carpenter's phrase – the simplification of life. Ruskin provided the theoretical starting point with his attack on the prevailing tenets of political economy.

Keynes has noted that England in the nineteenth century was 'so organized socially and economically as to secure the maximum accumulation of capital'. In his book *Unto This Last* published in 1862 Ruskin attacked the doctrine of accumulation. Wealth can only be justified if it 'avails towards life'. This gives the first definition of wealth: articles that can actually be used. But clearly their possessor must have the capacity to make good use of them. Thus ownership cannot be separated from virtue. Wealth, Ruskin said 'is the possession of the valuable by the valiant'.

That part of wealth due simply to the mania for accumulation Ruskin called 'illth'. It was illth not wealth that caused social strife.

Ruskin's first point, then, was to establish that wealth in its true sense is independent of quantity. But acceptance of this view required a certain attitude to possessions. After all, the possession of costly art treasures entailed a considerable amount of accumulation: yet the purpose of such accumulation would be consumption rather than investment; use, rather than ownership: hence it would be wealth rather than illth.

Ruskin attacked this justification of accumulation with the argument that great possessions limit human freedom. The chains, which according to Rousseau imprison freedom, are the conventions of an 'unnatural' society. Freedom is to be found in returning to a more 'natural' existence, shorn of the 'furniture of the ordinary world', in Sir Isaiah Berlin's phrase. In his satire *Sartor Resartus*, published in 1838, Carlyle attacks the extravagant dress of the Regency period. 'The beginning of all Wisdom,' he writes, 'is to look fixedly at Clothes with armed eyesight, till they become *transparent*.' For it is only when a man sees himself, and is seen by others, in a state of nakedness, that he begins to glimpse his full potentialities:

> To the eye of vulgar Logic what is man? An omnivorous biped that wears Breeches. To the eye of Pure Reason what is he? A Soul, a Spirit... Round his mysterious ME, there lies, under all those woolrags, a Garment of Flesh (or of Senses) contextured in the Loom of Heaven....

In short, the worship of externals (such as clothes and other possessions) hides a man from his 'higher' self and thus destroys the freedom and happiness that springs from self-realization.

The appreciation of these principles Ruskin hoped would cause people to seek 'not greater wealth, but simpler pleasure; not higher fortune, but deeper felicity'. His aristocrats of the future would live a life of healthy manual toil:

> We once taught them to make Latin verses and called them educated; now we teach them to leap and row, to hit a ball with a bat, and call them educated. Can they plough, can they sow, can they plant at the right time, or build with a steady hand?

True to his precepts he led Oxford undergraduates 'for a time to road-making and like serviceable labours, spade and hammer in hand, amid the astonishment and laughter of the British Philistines'. He maintained that he never painted better than after washing down with his hands, on his knees, the wooden stair of the Swiss hotel in which he was staying. Ruskin believed that manual work was one of the proper ends of life, whereby man fulfilled something fundamental within himself. The false definition of the gentleman as someone who never used his hands arose, in his view, 'from the fact that work – hand work is not yet sufficiently identified with ... Culture' – an attempt by Ruskin to re-establish an earlier usage of the word 'culture' as a whole way of life and not just the pursuit of certain aesthetic and intellectual activities.

In his effort to direct the soul towards true felicity Ruskin placed great emphasis on beauty. Like Rousseau, he believed in the soul rising to the good through the beautiful. The ennobling of the soul was to be achieved through the cultivation of good taste, which he defined as 'the instantaneous preference of the noble thing to the ignoble'. Thus to Ruskin aesthetic education was moral in purpose. The function of beauty in all its forms was to release and fortify the nobler feelings of man.*

Beauty was to be sought not only in communion with Nature and in a purified sexual relationship (fruits of the simplification of life) but also in the improvement of the urban environment – hence the somewhat bizarre Gothic additions to the depressing industrial environment.

Like manual work, aesthetic appreciation was encouraged because it produced 'more personal soul'. But the utilitarian purpose was always prominent. Ruskin associated Philistines with avarice. 'As a nation we have been going on despising literature, despising science, despising art, despising nature, despising compassion, and concentrating our soul on pence.' A true refinement of the spirit would never have permitted the physical ugliness and squalor of the huge industrial slums. With the desire for acquisition weakened through a 'right understanding of the ends of life', social harmony would once more be restored. 'The training which makes men *happiest in themselves,*' Ruskin concluded, 'also makes them *most serviceable to others.*'

*

In 1885 Reddie returned to Fettes as assistant science master and, in the words of Ward, 'at once set to work to put into practice a scheme to provide the younger boys with a properly organized and wholesome instruction in sex; and created a secret society for this purpose called the Gild of the Laurel.' Possibly for this reason Dr Potts, the headmaster, gave him every encouragement to look for a new job, and in 1887 Reddie became a master at Clifton College in Bristol.

A year or so before he had met the poet Edward Carpenter and in 1888, after leaving Clifton, he spent six months with Carpenter at Millthorpe near Sheffield, where the proposal for

*Whitman had much the same philosophy of beauty.

a new school was finally hatched. Carpenter's influence on Reddie was so great* that it is necessary to say a word about him.

Others spoke of the New Life; Edward Carpenter practised it. His father, an amateur philosopher and a Brighton magistrate, 'lived the life of a respectable *rentier*, with its usual aims and ideals', a life which Carpenter was later to describe in his poem, *Towards Democracy*, as 'deadly Respectability sitting at its dinner table, quaffing its wine, and discussing the rise and fall of stocks. . . .'

His adolescence at Brighton College in the late 1850s closely resembles Reddie's. He hungered 'for the love of comrades' and loved to press against his heroes unnoticed in a football scrum 'or even to get accidentally hurt by one of them at hockey. . . .' But his 'fund of romance and intense feeling . . . latent in so many boys and capable even of heroic expression' was never utilized; the 'hunger of the heart for friendship' never satisfied. The curriculum was equally disappointing. School subjects were completely divorced from the emotions. All was 'grammar and syntax'; 'never . . . was any attempt made to make us understand the subject or the plot or the literary interest' of Homer and Virgil and the Greek plays so assiduously crammed for scholarships.

At Cambridge, where he became a tutor in Mathematics, similar misgivings arose over the quality of academic life – 'these chit-chat societies, these little supper parties, these lingerings over wine in combination-room after dinner – where every subject in Heaven and Earth was discussed, with the university man's perfect freedom of thought and utterance, but also with his perfect absence of practical knowledge or of intention to apply his theories to any practical issue'. In any case, Carpenter noted, 'what avail was the brain, when the heart demanded so much . . .?' For Carpenter salvation came through the American poet Walt Whitman. In 1868 he read the *Leaves of Grass* and later the same poet's *Democratic*

---

*J. H. Badley, founder of Bedales, wrote: 'Abbotsholme owed much of its first inception to Edward Carpenter with his practical Socialism and the high value he set on manual work . . .'

Vistas. 'From that time forward,' he recalls, 'a profound change set in within me.'

Whitman represents the American version of the revolt against commercialism. In place of the 'arid' life of the intellect, he offered the rude health and well-being of manual work; a vision of the eternal primitive at one with Nature. 'I will go to the bank by the wood, and become undisguised and naked, I am mad for it to be in contact with me.' Whitman has been called the Poet of Democracy, but he was the poet of a physical aristocracy, a band of comrades, beautiful and brave, who would purify society.

Carpenter soon resigned his fellowship, and, after some years of lecturing in university extension courses, bought a small-holding at Millthorpe, there to cultivate his new ideas of simple living and to work as a market gardener. 'I felt . . . the need of physical work, of open-air life and labour – something primitive to restore my over-worn constitution.' There he wrote numerous books and pamphlets, including one called *The Intermediate Sex*.

His views are a curious amalgam of Whitman, Thoreau,* Ruskin, Carlyle and Hyndman. In *England's Ideal* (1887) he launches a bitter attack on the upper classes and urges them to place their lives 'on the very simplest footing'. The English gentleman creates 'frightful poverty' all round him by his parasitic style of life. He 'wears clothes in which it is impossible for him to do any work of ordinary usefulness'; he suffers from 'constipated manners and frozen speech'; lives in a 'jungle of idiotic duties and thin-lipped respectability that money breeds'; is encumbered by useless property. This way of life is strongly reinforced by his education ' . . . a cheap-jack education, an education in glib phrases, grammar, the art of keeping up appearances, [that] has nothing to do with bringing anyone into relation with the real world around him – the real world of humanity, of honest daily life, of the majesty of

*In his book *Walden* (1880), Thoreau, a New England intellectual, describes how he built a house on a small piece of land where he grew the main articles of his own food and claimed as a consequence that he found undreamt-of spiritual peace and contentment.

Nature, and the wonderful questions and answers of the soul. . . .'

Conventional upper-class life Carpenter was convinced was a *prison*: 'Plain food, the open air, the hardiness of sun and wind, are things practically unobtainable in a complex *menage*.' 'No individual or class,' he concludes, 'can travel far from the native life of the race without becoming shrivelled, corrupt, diseased. . . .'

*

Ruskin, Whitman and Carpenter were poets and artists; they clothed the programme of national revival in a kind of Romantic haze. Reddie was both a Romantic and a positivist; he sought to establish it on a scientific basis. From Edinburgh he had gone to Göttingen University to read for a doctorate in Chemistry. He was immediately impressed by the quality of German life. 'Wherever one turned,' he wrote, 'there was method, clearness, organization. . . . Every day in Germany one felt the mind expanding and the fog melting away.' It must be remembered that Germany at the time was widely regarded as the model for the future development of the industrial state. Bismarck was supposed to have 'solved' the social question by his mixture of strong government and social reform programmes. German culture was contrasted with English philistinism; the agrarian paternalistic Junkers seemed to many to provide a model for a revived English aristocracy; the 'organic' theory of society, expressed in idealist philosophy and the rhetoric of the *Volk*, seemed superior to liberal notions which appeared to lead straight to class-war. Yet despite these traditional features of German life, its superior organization of science and production made it a very 'modern' nation, threatening to break England's commercial and imperial dominance. Those hard-headed imperialists like Lord Milner, fearful of imperial decline, looked precisely to German 'method, clearness, organization' above all to German 'discipline' to restore England's national greatness. Individualism might have won an empire but it was now threatening to lose it. Amateurism, ignorance, muddle, selfishness, must all be banished if England was to retain its great position.

None of this was as remote from the preoccupations of Ruskin and Carpenter as might be imagined; or rather it shows what may follow from the attempt to translate what is essentially a poetic statement or feeling into a social philosophy. Certainly Reddie found no difficulty in reconciling the two. He was both a Romantic inspired by a lofty vision, and a planner, convinced that, in the progress towards Utopia, nothing must be left to chance. It is an unpleasant combination, but not an unusual one. 'We found these two sides of our nature,' he wrote, 'coming together . . . into a very happy harmony.'

There is something very Germanic in Reddie's attempt to secure a union between theory and practice. The English have never lacked ideals; but on the whole they have been content to run their ordinary lives according to 'common sense'; which in practice has meant compromise between conflicting requirements and opinions. Hence they have never been particularly worried by the logical inconsistencies in their behaviour. It was this element of 'muddle' in the English character that was gradually to convert Reddie into a violent Anglophobe and a fanatic Germanophile. Reddie was not really opposed to the English public-school tradition: he wanted to force the public school to live up to its aims. It believed in training character, yet 'crammed' pupils for examinations; it preached the virtues of cooperation and team spirit, yet its whole ethos was competitive. In short, it had capitulated to the commercial spirit. Reddie's educational system was designed to secure a revival of the English upper classes according to certain principles; every detail of the school environment must be planned to achieve that aim: there could be no 'inconsistencies'. Everything must be harmonized and integrated. The same attitude is to be found in Kurt Hahn of Gordonstoun. It is the apotheosis of the 'moulding' view of education.

It is not, therefore, in the least surprising that Reddie turned to Germany for a pedagogical plan; equally it is not in the least surprising that he found one.

In 1893, four years after founding Abbotsholme, he visited

the University of Jena, where Professor Rein was expounding Herbartian pedagogy. Herbart's aim had been to mould completely the child's personality, in so far as that was independent of hereditary influences. He developed a theory of learning admirably suited to his purpose. Basically, he was a sensationalist: he postulated a simple soul or mind subject to 'impressions' – sense impressions, and intellectual and emotional impressions formed the character, not the bad ones. Partly sions. The educator's task was to ensure that only the good impressions formed the character, not the bad ones. Partly this was to be done by so controlling the environment that only the good impressions got in. But Herbart realized that it was impossible to control all that passes into the child's mind. He therefore devised a scheme of instruction designed to strengthen and fortify the good impressions. Education consisted in the assimilation of a new impression to the mass of impressions already in the mind. This assimilation could only take place if the mind was 'ready' for it; if, in fact, the new impression in some sense followed on from the previous impression. Thus it was essential that these impressions be presented in the right order and properly related to each other – in particular, the emotional and the intellectual ones. By this means the stock of good impressions would be systematically enlarged, augmented and fortified, so that eventually the child himself selected only the good impressions and thus took over responsibility for his own development. 'Those only wield the full power of education,' Herbart wrote, 'who know how to cultivate in the youthful soul a large circle of thought closely connected in all its parts, possessing the power of overcoming what is unfavourable in the environment and of dissolving and absorbing into itself all that is favourable.'

Unlike Blake and Coleridge, and to a certain extent Rousseau, Reddie did not believe that goodness sprang from the 'intuitive soul':

> I may not hope from outward forms to win
> The passion and the life, whose fountains are within.

For Reddie the soul itself is the source of nothing: it develops only in so far as it is nourished by association with what is 'favourable' in the environment. In Wordsworth's case this is Nature. Reddie too believes in the educative influence of Nature, but he adds many other things to his 'circle of good impressions'. His criticism of traditional education is not so much that it destroys something 'essential' within the child, as that it fails to bring to flower certain potentialities. Thus it failed to nourish the feelings and affections which are of equal importance to the intellect in understanding the world. It also failed to offer protection against the 'impure passions'. Once again, Reddie does not see these passions as 'innate', in the sense of the original-sin theorists. Reflecting upon his own experience at Fettes, he was convinced that these passions developed because traditional education was too passive: it made no attempt to exploit its pupils' other, more vital, potentialities, leaving an emotional vacuum into which the Devil was all too prone to step. Professor Rein's pedagogy offered great hopes of plugging this particular educational gap. No longer would Reddie's Olympus of heroes topple 'one by one ... from the pedestals upon which youthful enthusiasm had placed them. . . .' Pure in thought and deed they would glide imperceptibly from beautiful adolescence into healthy manhood, protected by 'circles of thought' excluding all that was vile and poisonous. Reddie returned from Jena feeling that 'we had behind our aims the arguments of an entire philosophy'.

Acceptance of this philosophy helps to explain the totalitarian elements in Reddie's system – as it does those in Kurt Hahn's. Blake's 'original innocence' is compatible with noninterference, because 'goodness' is seen as something innate. In Reddie's scheme it has to be planned or 'nourished'. The debate about the permissible amount of adult 'interference' in education came later to dominate the progressive school movement. Its intellectual roots can be traced to this associative-intuitive split in Romantic thought.

Reddie's talks with Carpenter at Millthorpe produced a definite plan for a new school designed to give effect to all the proposals for the 'regeneration of life' then in the air. Other collaborators were drawn in: R. F. Muirhead, a Scotsman, who was then an Army tutor in London and a mathematician, agreed to help, as did William Cassels, also a Scotsman and a farmer, who contributed £2,000. Lowes Dickinson, just down from Cambridge and strongly influenced by Greek theories of life, was also involved, though less directly. A house and estate in Derbyshire by the River Dove were leased from 1 August 1889; and the school opened with sixteen boys in October.

The arrangement was that Reddie should be headmaster; Cassels would run the estate; and Muirhead would teach mathematics and act as treasurer. But this arrangement did not long survive serious conflicts of principle and method. The two Scotsmen wanted a democratic triumvirate: Reddie wanted complete authority. Cassels saw the school as essentially an agricultural community whose object was training for work on the land; Reddie regarded it as an educational laboratory. Muirhead and Cassels therefore presented Reddie with an ultimatum: he should hold the headmastership at a week's notice and if he did anything the others objected to he was to be deposed and his place taken by one of them. Reddie refused, and Muirhead and Cassels thereupon resigned. Reddie was left in sole charge, determined in future to be absolute ruler of his 'miniature kingdom'.

8 · An Education for the Directing Classes

> The Tertiary School I am endeavouring to organize is not intended to suit the whim of a few faddists, but the normal wants of the Directing Classes of a Reorganized English Nation.

Thus wrote Reddie in his evidence to the Bryce Commission on Secondary Education in 1894. He had no interest in the education of the mass of the people, except that they should be trained to obey the ruling class; a purpose which he believed would be admirably served by compulsory military training to cure 'lack of honourable subordination, and lack of unselfish patriotism'. The trouble with the existing directing classes was that their selfishness had unfitted them for leadership, giving rise to social discord. It was also precipitating the disintegration of the Empire. Reddie was a staunch imperialist: he believed in the civilizing mission of the English race; and in 1898 promised a book 'giving a criticism of the present educational outlook in relation to the Future of the Anglo-Keltic World Dominion'. He believed that that world dominion was in grave jeopardy owing to the excessive individualism and selfishness of English life: it lacked an organizing principle which would subordinate every activity to a grand design – something he admired particularly about Germany. 'No one,' he wrote in 1898, 'seems to ask how can this Nation's property be best managed ... in the interests of the immortal English People which has been offered the Empire of the World.' A visit to Oxford did nothing to cheer him up:

> While the Union plays at Parliament, and Parliament plays the fool, the Empire slips from our grasp. If Oxford did her duty, artizans would not want 'labour members', or substitute for 'cultured selfishness', the still worse selfishness of the ignorant.

Social cooperation would be secured not by democratic consultation but by organizing national life on the principles of aristocratic unselfishness and service. The new school would mirror the future life of the 'Reorganized English Nation'. 'The Abbotsholme estate,' as Reddie noted in 1894, 'constitutes an *ideal miniature kingdom* ... it contains ... all the main factors which produce a civilized community' (except, he might have noted, the 'factor' of women: but as we shall see, he did not regard this as essential for adolescents).

The principle of hierarchy was therefore not abandoned but reinforced. Reddie was the captain; his masters, the (somewhat mutinous) officers; his prefects, the non-commissioned officers; his boys, the crew. But this hierarchy – based on that of the public school – was just the framework. Ruskin had denied that 'an advantageous code of social action may be determined irrespectively of the influence of social affection'. Gentleness and justice must mark the relationship between classes. Reddie's method of creating his 'organic' community was to work upon the interests and feelings of his pupils. It was only if those were 'on the side' of the new enterprise that it could succeed. 'If there is one thing more than any other which we have aimed at cultivating at Abbotsholme it is this – that we have made such a strong endeavour to develop, illuminate and guide the *affections* of the boys.'

Today, educational sociologists distinguish between 'instrumental' and 'expressive' forms of education: the first aimed at imparting knowledge and skills; the second at establishing 'affectively charged relationships of normative involvement' (to quote a particularly ghastly expression from a recent text). Reddie, as Kurt Hahn did after him, based his educational design on the 'idealism' of adolescents, especially their strong capacity to love and attach themselves to people. The school would be bound together by bonds of love – between master and boy and boy and boy. This love he saw as Platonic rather than sexual; on the one hand it expressed the natural admiration of the younger boy for his elders; on the other hand, it expressed the natural feeling of responsibility and tenderness of the elder boy for the younger one.

He saw this reciprocal love relationship as a kind of analogue to social relationships between the classes in an improved society. The school song, based on Whitman's poem *The Love of Comrades*, gave it exalted expression:

> Come! We will make the Continents inseparable;
> We will make the most splendid race the sun
>   ever shone upon;
> We will make divine magnetic bands:
> With the life-long love of Comrades.

The example of the three hundred at Thermopylae was cited as a historical illustration: the lack of more recent examples highlighted the difficulty of translating it into practice under modern conditions. Love might make Abbotsholme, but it could plainly not make the world go round: a truth that all the progressive reformers were destined to discover in one context or another, as they sought to make the world a better place.

Feeling was not only an instrument of training: it also offered a way of understanding the world.

There is only one subject-matter for education, and that is Life in all its manifestations. Instead of this single unity, we offer children – Algebra, from which nothing follows; Geometry, from which nothing follows; a couple of Languages, never mastered; and lastly, most dreary of all, Literature, represented by plays of Shakespeare, with philological notes and short analyses of plot and character. ... Can such a list be said to represent Life? ... The best that can be said of it is, that it is a rapid table of contents which a deity might run over in his mind while he was thinking of creating a world, and had not yet determined how to put it together.*

Reddie would have heartily agreed with all this. The trouble is: it is easy enough to teach Algebra, but how does one teach Life? or even 'live' it? Life is clearly not a single thing like an apple. It is nothing less than the sum total of everything that goes on in the world.

If the purpose of education is to increase a person's understanding of, or capacity to enjoy, life, then the problem is where and how to begin. It may be true that life in some ultimate sense is a 'single unity', but for educational purposes, at any rate, Humpty Dumpty has to be broken up into little

*A. N. Whitehead, *Aims of Education*, p. 10.

pieces. Whitehead's basic criticism, shared by all progressive educators, was twofold: first, it was the less important of the little pieces that formed the 'subject-matter' of traditional education; secondly, Humpty Dumpty was never put together again: there was no unifying thread which linked the subjects of study to each other and to the ultimate 'wholeness' of life.

Standing in the way of an attempt to restore the 'unity' of the educational process was the so-called Doctrine of Faculties. This was the view that the world was to be 'understood' by means of different capacities or faculties residing in the soul – faculties such as cognition, the senses, imagination, memory and so on. (Different thinkers drew up different lists.) The object of education was so to cultivate the faculties as to develop 'understanding'. Each particular faculty was thought to correspond to a branch of knowledge and to be developed or 'trained' by its study. Thus in D'Alembert's* scheme the world was to be understood through Memory, Reason and Imagination. Corresponding to Memory was History; to Reason, Philosophy; and to the Imagination, Poetry. His detailed system of human knowledge looked something like the plan opposite.

Two main 'progressive' criticisms could be levelled against this 'detailed system'. First, the vertical lines which separated the activities of Memory, Reason and the Imagination were quite unreal; they prevented that 'wholeness' of perception which the Romantics sought. Secondly, 'understanding' was sought in largely mental terms. It is true that D'Alembert's scheme left room for the imagination, but it was never properly assimilated to his general theory of understanding and was, in any case, given a very subordinate role. The thinkers of the Enlightenment believed that the world was to be understood principally through scientific 'laws' uncovered by empirical inquiry. As knowledge progressed laws would become increasingly generalized and simple until in the end 'the universe ... would only be one fact and one great truth for who-

*Jean D'Alembert (1717–83), a leading *philosophe* whose 'Preliminary Discourse' to Diderot's *Encyclopaedia* (1751), from which this chart is taken, was the manifesto of the French Enlightenment.

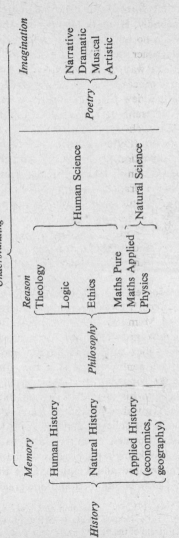

ever knew how to embrace it from a single point of view'.*

This at first sight seems identical with Whitehead's view of the world as a 'single unity'. However, whereas the *philosophes* were hopeful that eventually the world would be understood by some universal law that summed up all the other laws, Whitehead was thinking much more of flashes of intuition or mystic insight that suddenly revealed connexions hitherto obscure. This philosophic quarrel has been a basic dividing line in modern education: between those who believe that education is primarily concerned with book-learning and those who do not.

The roots of the reaction against book-learning are varied and by no means disreputable. For Reddie and other reforming schoolmasters of that generation classroom learning was associated with cramming for Latin and Greek scholarships; in short with a narrow and stultifying pedantry that had no relation either with the real world or with the life of the child. Making the syllabus more practical or 'concrete' (as Reddie called it) was an attempt to satisfy both needs. Modern conditions required 'practical' men, not theorizing amateurs unencumbered with any relevant knowledge; equally, to be effective 'learning' must spring from some need or interest of the child, and as the child tended to be interested in 'things' and situations in the world around him, those interests should form the starting point in education. In addition there was the attempt, started by Thring at Uppingham, to make education more meaningful to the 'non-academic' boy; this resulted in a wide variety of 'activities' being included in the curriculum – a practice which the New School Movement elevated into a theory with the title of 'Learning by Doing'. But there was more to the progressive school's anti-intellectual bias than that.

There was, for instance, the reaction against competitive examinations. As these are thought to be a somewhat recent growth it is surprising to find that already in the 1880s educational reformers saw them as the main enemy. Indeed, most public-schoolmasters of that period would probably have been

Preliminary Discourse, p. 29.

surprised to find their institutions described, as they were by Reddie, as 'steam-driven factories for turning out by the dozen hastily crammed candidates for examinations'. In his evidence to the Bryce Commission in 1894 Reddie wrote: 'Amid the confused whirl of examinations, teaching is impossible; and amid the struggles to cram, teachers have forgotten education, whose real work is the development of power and the building up of character.' One reason for the revolt against the examination system was that it was 'selfish' rather than 'cooperative'; in short, the *laissez-faire* system applied to education. In so far as the school was supposed to be a microcosm of a revived national life, Reddie naturally set his face against what was supposed to be the chief vice of the old order. The second objection was that examinations tested in fact the least important aspects of education, 'book work, words apart from things, analytic studies, and memory work'. If success in getting people through examinations was to be the criterion for judging a good school, then it was plain that academic aims would be given priority over the more important ones – 'character building'.

Finally there was the Romantic legacy. As we have seen, the *philosophes* did not doubt that the world had 'meaning'; but they assumed that the 'universal laws' could be discovered by means of rational, scientific, inquiry. But to the progressives – who followed the Romantics in this respect – scientific inquiry leads only to a knowledge of separate things; it can only solve 'second-order' problems. To the Romantics the rationalists were 'the poor in spirit, pursuing soulless and largely mechanical activities, and completely unaware of the deeper problems of life and philosophy.'* They associated the rationalist approach with book-learning, the amassing of facts and information, the suppression of the deep, vital, urges of man; and contrasted it with the liberated world of the passions and emotions, the insights of the mystics and creative artists, the symbolic unity of man with nature. Reddie expressed the essence of the Romantic doctrine in a sermon in the Abbotsholme chapel in 1904:

*Karl Popper, *The Open Society and Its Enemies*, Vol. II, p. 216.

. . . we cannot understand adequately external nature – the trees, the hills, the clouds, or the atoms and molecules in our Chemical or Physical Laboratories, or the animals and plants in our Aquaria and Gardens – unless we not only look at them as things at a distance from us, but endeavour to feel ourselves into them, and incarnate ourselves in imagination in their tissues and substance. We must look at them, in short. . . not merely analytically. . . . but we must feel in them the connecting links which constitute the very life itself.

Any educator with a romantic turn of mind would stress the primacy of direct experience over the vicarious experience of books. Many would go further: book learning actually 'disrupts' the communication system between man and the universe, making it impossible for him to live 'fully', react 'authentically' and 'spontaneously' to people and things, cutting him off from the deeper layers of understanding. Hence it produces unhappiness, dissatisfactions and a perpetual feeling of frustration.

Both Reddie and someone in many ways so dissimilar to him as Neill of Summerhill were 'irrationalists' in this sense. They disliked book-learning and at best regarded it as a supplement to other kinds of learning. They would have agreed with Coleridge that 'deep thinking' can only be nourished by 'deep feeling'. The cultivation of the feelings thus came to replace the cultivation of the mental 'faculties' in their scheme of things.

Since irrationalism assigns primacy to the emotions it is clearly compatible with both the best and the worst impulses of man; rationalism, it can be argued, by suppressing both, makes the world a much safer place to live in. For the progressive urge to base education on the 'heart' of the child is perfectly compatible with, say, a Nazi system of education.

Seven years after its foundation Abbotsholme was visited by Dr Lietz, who returned to Germany to found his *Landschule* movement based on Abbotsholme practice. In 1897 he published a book entitled *Emlohstobba* (Abbotsholme in reverse), which eulogizes Reddie's school. While at the school he describes an 'extraordinary dream':

He sees a mighty funeral pile, and upon it blazing a vast accumulation of books. ... In his dream [he] sees millions of children dancing delirious with joy, around this mighty bonfire. A crowd of persons, most wearing spectacles and all an angry frown, essay to quell these deafening shouts. Are they the teachers of bygone centuries, or of this? ... He hears a wail of anguish as they bemoan this deed of Vandalism, this obscurantist fiery holocaust, amid which *their* world of culture, art, and science, crumbles in final dissolution.

But, on a sudden, there is silence. For, like a Phoenix, rising aloft out of the quivering flames, appears a majestic youthful Form, his body sheathed in glistening armour, and on his dazzling helm a golden crown. Announced by clash of arms and trumpet-blast Heralds spring swiftly forth, and amid deafening acclamations proclaim the accession of a new Monarch – destined to give to a dying world an *Education which shall teach men to Live*.

To be fair to Reddie, he held the 'balance' between the intellectual and emotional aspects of education better than that. Just as he relied upon a combination of 'instrumental' and 'expressive' methods to attain the 'normative ends' of the school, so he approached the teaching of subjects in a 'double way' – analytically and imaginatively. In addition he continually stressed the interrelations of the individual subjects.

He justified his 'dual' approach by what he called 'the law of polarity'. Just as the physical world is governed by repulsion and attraction, so is the human world governed by self-will and love. Thus there were two different ways of looking at the world which Reddie labelled masculine and feminine. The masculine approach was self-willed and intellectual, the feminine approach loving and emotional. The best education should combine both.

Thus, looking at them [things] from the masculine point of view, as made up of distinct particles, and feeling ourselves into them in the feminine manner, as having an influence upon each other, we are enabled to bind together our thoughts and feelings, so as to get an absolute unity of our conception as to this mysterious Universe and our relation to it.

Religion was no more than 'the study of the whole of things, without and within'.

*

One of Abbotsholme's first teachers, F. B. H. Ellis, has recalled the principles upon which Reddie organized the curriculum:

It was explained that the aim of the Abbotsholme education was to
develop all the faculties and qualities of the boys by an enlarged and
revised curriculum, by interlocking subject with subject so that each
should explain and enforce the other, and by adapting all to the environment. . . . More time was devoted to English, French and German;
Greek disappeared, and Latin was confined to the elder boys, with
little time allotted. Science of various kinds bulked bigger, and hygiene,
elementary economics and some book-keeping were added. Music,
drawing and handwork were no longer regarded as extra accomplish-
ments to be pursued in spare time, but became compulsory. . . . Games
. . . were to some extent replaced by gardening, navvying, physical drill
and other outdoor occupations. There was a complete planning of the
boy's whole life at school, and the leisure which was left to the boy . . .
was comparatively small.

Not only was the boy's life planned to the last detail, but that
of the masters as well. Reddie insisted on absolute obedience
and subservience to his ideas. 'As regards the *Teaching Body*,'
he noted, 'the aim has been to make the Staff an Organic
Unity'. The result was that staff turnover was very high. True
to the ideas of Dr Rein of Jena, he insisted on the careful preparation of each lesson as a distinct whole, arranged in definite phases so as to render it more easy of assimilation. He
loved nothing better than to discuss the application of general
pedagogic principles to the teaching of vulgar fractions. Nor
was hygiene neglected while mathematics was taught. Special
desks were obtained from Stuttgart whose object was to prevent any malformation of the spine through sliding forward.

Equal attention was devoted to planning the new school
buildings:

To us personally the English houses, railway stations, etc, seemed
most inadequate. All were the outcome of the English fog and in-
sularity, want of ideas and lack of social co-operation. All bore the
stamp of selfish individualism, and all preached mental and social
chaos. . . . In a School designed to develop Harmonious Growth this

would, we knew, be fatal. For a school like this it was essential to have a Kosmos. The buildings, we felt, moreover, ought to symbolize the whole Theory of the School, as the human body summarizes and fore-tells the history of the soul. Accordingly, we commenced betimes to excogitate our plans.

The new wing, opened in 1900, embodied the results of this 'excogitation'. Double walls made it cold in the summer and warm in the winter; window fittings were constructed of gun metal to prevent rust; the new chapel was filled with bas-reliefs of philosophers, warriors and noble youths, to turn the thoughts of the boys towards the Ideal.

Everywhere the attempt was relentlessly pursued to find 'connexions' between subjects, and to approach the same sub-ject from different angles. 'Very fine Geography lesson about the battles which had been fought in Belgium,' noted the thir-teen-year-old G. Lissant Cox in his diary for January 1893. Reddie, as many others, saw geography as the 'link between the Natural and Human Sciences'.

In pursuit of his aim of making the curriculum directly rele-vant to modern life, history led on directly from the death of Henry VII to 'all kinds of general questions, such as the Eng-lish, their character, their outlook, and what the Germans could teach them....' Chemistry, and physics too, was ap-proached from the human angle, the 'law of polarity' fur-nishing that larger framework that Reddie regarded as so essential. Nature study was taught from 'the opposite sides' – the cosmic polarity again – of objective and subjective know-ledge. 'Elementary facts of physics on the one side, the laws of personal life and of social health on the other. Elementary physics leading to dynamics and chemistry; hygiene and the boys' relation to the school and to each other, developing into economics....'

Reddie defined the aim of 'brain work' as 'to train the boy to deal with *things* as well as with *words*; to pass upward from the *concrete* to the *abstract*'. The first principle of instruction therefore was the use of the 'concrete case' or 'object lesson'. Abbotsholme itself was an 'object lesson' of how society should be organized in a 'cooperative' way; but within this 'miniature kingdom' there was no shortage of 'concrete cases' illustrative of general principles. In fact the whole school was so organized that every activity and object in it should furnish lessons about something. Unexpected events were eagerly utilized to provide object lessons. 'No boy who was in the upper part of the school in those days can have forgotten the Immortal Gumby, a local artisan who had proved himself a fraud in some work undertaken for the school and thereafter became a concrete case.' Estate work and other manual activities were encouraged not only to inculcate a respect for 'manual work' which would ultimately lessen class-antagonism, not only to teach skills suitable for the 'colonist', not only to bring boys into contact with beauty, but also to furnish 'object lessons' for classroom teaching:

The outdoor work and play . . . all are intended to bring the boy into contact with *things*. . . . But the impressions got in this way straight from Nature and from material existence have to be organized and made a mental possession. This is done in the class-room. The whole section of the work called Naturalistics . . . is co-ordinated indoors with drawing, mathematics, and the study of the sciences in their elements . . . so that the impressions and experiences outside furnish the subject matter one day for the class teaching; and the principles developed in the class-room are applied and followed out next day when the boys return to their outside occupations. . . .

Thus studies would progress both *upwards* from the concrete to the abstract and *inwards* from the material to the spiritual. (Reddie more or less equated these two processes.) 'The external parts of animals,' he declared 'will be studied before their internal organs. . . .' As may be imagined, he was a great believer in the Platonic Doctrine of Forms. This was the view that material forms (or qualities) were very poor reproductions of perfect spiritual forms that had no existence in the material world. A man was 'just', a body 'beautiful', or ink 'blue' in so far as each corresponded, however imperfectly, to some 'ideal' form of Justice, Beauty and Blueness. The object of education was to create as far as possible 'ideal types' for the pupils to model themselves on in order that their inner lives might be progressively 'refined'. These 'ideal types' might be historical figures, artistic, literary and musical creations or even (though Reddie was always disappointed in this hope) the masters at the school.

The most 'ideal' of them all, of course, was Jesus Christ. Religion, in short, was the subject that most clearly revealed the 'ideal'; it was in some sense the culmination and summation of all the other subjects.* It completed the 'circle of thought" At the end of each term Reddie anxiously plotted, on the report forms, each boy's progress towards the ideal, with the aid of the new science of 'Statistiks'.

If the aim of the chapel service was to express and sum up everything that was noblest in life in such a way as to impress the pupils, a serious difficulty at once presented itself. Various passages in the divine texts seem to run counter to the 'manly' aspirations of boyhood. In the Beatitudes, for example, Christ promised that the meek 'shall inherit the earth' and blessed the 'poor in spirit'. As we have seen Reddie had no time for the 'poor in spirit'. His solution was simple: he inserted into the Beatitudes more appropriate sentiments: 'Blessed are the heroes who persevere with manly fortitude: for they shall subdue the earth.' The Ten Commandments, too, were infused with the very un-Mosiac sentiment: 'Reverence, therefore, every manifestation of love, according to its degree; and seek to ennoble it, both in thyself and others, by becoming thyself a lover and radiating forth the divine afflatus to inspire others with that heavenly gift; for love shall purge away every sin.' In the same spirit Reddie purged the Bible of any characters who might be considered unworthy 'models' for 'the young mind' and regretted that he could not get rid of Abraham entirely. 'Before very long,' he declared, 'the world will certainly be forced, in the interest of improved education, to revise the Bible, if it is to remain the textbook of religious instruction.'

---

*Thus, for example, the three lessons on Good Friday were the death of Socrates as related by Plato, the death of Oliver Cromwell as related by Carlyle and the story of the Crucifixion. Chapel service included readings from Shakespeare, Cromwell, Milton, Blake, Carlyle and Ruskin.

'This is too serious a task for a hard-worked schoolmaster,' he added modestly. But if the traditional content of religious instruction was somewhat decreased by the omission of certain passages and rituals, it was immensely expanded by the attempt to gather the whole universe under the religious umbrella. Readings from Buddha, Mohammed and Confucius emphasized the universality of man's aspirations; while great symbolic festivals such as hay-making were designed to express the connexion between God and Nature.

The chapel at Abbotsholme at any rate dropped one traditional function: Reddie's pupils were spared the horror of a Philippic from the pulpit inveighing sternly and obscurely against 'unclean practices'. Reddie was indeed determined that boys should be kept clean (both inside and out) but, as in every other sphere of education, he believed in tackling the problem from a number of different, if complementary, angles, so as to build up a whole 'tone' that was conducive to the highest moral standards.

Just as he regarded the staff as an 'organic unity' so he regarded the school as an 'organic unity' between staff and boys. On first becoming a teacher he was appalled at the 'lack of frankness' existing between masters and boys; that 'the mere fact of being a teacher by profession raised an immense wall, unknown before, between us and our pupils'. It was this barrier that prevented the staff from understanding 'Boy Nature, its doubts and difficulties'; and it was this barrier that Reddie was determined to break down. Masters were encouraged to live very much the same life as the boys, to share the same routines and disciplines, in fact, to regard themselves as older and wiser boys. Essentially Reddie continued to see himself as a Senior Prefect – 'on the side' of the pupils, or at least of their higher selves, against those who strove to destroy and pervert the splendour and purity of 'Boy Nature'. Throughout his life he tried to re-create that 'friendship with a youngster' which he had formed at Fettes in his last year. Cooperation in this sphere, as in so many others, was to replace competition. 'Exaggerated competition,' he wrote, 'is the source of Lust.' 'At Abbotsholme,' noted a Dutch visitor, 'the antagonism which usually exists in a school between boys and masters has been avoided by the same means which will end the struggle between capital and labour, i.e., by cooperation and participation. ... The result is an expanded life for all.' How true this was it is hard to judge: few masters appeared to stay long enough to achieve much in the breaking-down of barriers; and while they stayed they generally exhibited a marked coolness towards Reddie's educational objectives. Nevertheless, the attempt to break down staff-pupil antagonism in the interest of a purer 'tone' became an important principle of the new education.

Other expedients were borrowed from the Gild of the Laurel days. In an early memorandum on Abbotsholme, he listed as one òf his aims: 'To organize silently and secretly a body of selected natures to undertake the helpings of the sick, and the watching over the weak.' The spirit too was invoked to redress the temptations of the flesh. Carpenter in his autobiography had traced bad habits to the starving of the boy's need for affection. Reddie proposed to conquer lust with love. In one of his lectures he declared:

If we want to cure what is usually called 'immorality', it is before all things necessary to train the boys to love. ... Is it not natural for boys to love each other? Is it not a fact that the very best types in every school naturally tend to this? Then along comes a black-coated ignoramus, with memories of past perversions; unable, amid the squalor of our commercial age to understand the enthusiasm even of the age of Shakespeare, still less of earlier epochs.

With this view it is hardly surprising that Reddie did not consider coeducation the solution to 'perversion'. 'This coeducation notion,' he wrote in 1899, 'is entirely of feminine origin' and what was worse 'comes from the United States'. 'No need,' he added, 'exists for such heroic salvation if boys of normal nature are allowed to live a sane and rational life such as they have here.'

As part of the drive for sexual purity Reddie instituted systematic instruction in hygiene. This was not simply instruction of the 'facts of life' variety, though this was one valuable consequence. The body, to Reddie, was much more than just a physical object. It was the tabernacle of the soul. Hygiene was thus concerned with the care of the body, both inside and out. It is hardly an exaggeration to say that the prime activity of Abbotsholme was the cultivation of the body in the belief that this would at the same time purify the soul. 'To render the body strong, clean and lovely,' Reddie wrote in the first school prospectus, 'is a religious duty.'

Lessons in hygiene were thus given pride of place in the curriculum, and the anatomical drawings were supplemented by busts of Greek youths and warriors to ensure that the proper object of bodily care was borne constantly in mind. The lessons were 'logically' arranged to proceed from the 'outside' to the 'inside'. 'We study skin before bones. ... We study the teeth before the stomach.' Nor were other connexions neglected:

Each boy at Abbotsholme is taught how to manage the house he lives in – namely, his own body – and this study we call Hygiene. He also learns how the community – the school – is to be kept wholesome, and this study we call Economics. Thus the economics of the boy's body is interrelated in our curriculum with the hygiene of the school community.

The economics of the school community, it will be recalled, was designed to illustrate the economics of the larger society, so that the study of skin and teeth led quite logically, in Reddie's view, to the study of the laws of supply and demand.

However, Reddie always believed that practice should take precedence over theory; and so the main hygienic lessons were embodied in innumerable sheets of rules, printed on the Abbotsholme press, which regulated, down to the minutest detail, every bodily function of the waking and sleeping life. Each list was headed by a question; there would then be a discussion of the points at issue; and finally a series of injunctions embodying the conclusions of the discussion.

Our new boy goes to take off his boots and finds, staring him in the face, beautifully printed and framed Rules for the Boot-room. When he reaches his bed-room he finds Dormitory Rules. He enters his set-room and finds similar printed sheets. ... If he needs clothes, he finds a monograph on clothes just at the needful place. ... Once perfectly conceived and perfectly expressed, so that error is impossible, such rules will last for ever, ready to speak from the wall whenever needed. . . .

When a boy rose at 6.15 a.m. (6.55 in the winter) from a sleep which Reddie had taken immense pains to ensure was undisturbed by evil dreams, he went on a brief run, followed by a cold bath. After this invigorating start, he put on his Abbotsholme suit and his Abbotsholme shoes. Reddie, like Carpenter, was a great advocate of the simplification of clothing. 'Eleven layers of cloth separating man from God,' Carpenter had remarked in horror at the elaborate Victorian dress, and speculated that

The reason why in our modern times the curious intellect is so abnormally developed, the brain and the tongue waggle so, and fingers are so nervous and meddlesome, [is] because these organs alone have a chance. The rest are shut out from God's light and air: the poor human heart grown feeble and weary in its isolation and imprisonment, the sexual parts degenerated and ashamed of themselves, the liver diseased, and the lungs straitened down to mere sighs and conventional disconsolate sounds beneath their cerements.

Reddie was determined to avoid these disasters. In a long sheet of rules headed *What is the Educative Value of Life in Dormitory?* he argued strongly that boys should see each other naked as much as possible and concluded that 'three-quarters, if not all, of the evil thoughts and evil actions of youngsters, in connexion with this matter, arise from ridiculous and unnatural attempts to prevent, by hook or crook, boys getting a sight of the naked body.' Complete nudity was forbidden by the climate as well as by convention, but Reddie decreed that 'Abbotsholme boys should wear as little clothing as is compatible with health, comfort, and decency.'

The sartorial customs of the Victorians were carefully examined from the hygienic point of view and found wanting. Starched shirts produced congestion of the lungs; starched collars, sore throats; pointed shoes, corns and bunions; belts, ruptures; cotton and linen were inflammable; dyed garments, 'unnatural'. All these were therefore abolished. Abbotsholme boys dressed entirely in wool (Carpenter recommended woad).

The jackets were fitted with outside pockets to simplify their design; trousers were tucked into long socks just below the knees; and were sustained by specially designed 'hip straps' fitted with 'safety buckles'. Shoes were square to enable the toes to waggle (sandals were worn in the summer). Berets replaced the usual caps or boaters.

So much for the purely physical aspects. But clothes also served a metaphysical purpose.

One of the leading ideas of Abbotsholme [Reddie wrote] is that the Human Body, hammered into shape from without by the forces of Nature impinging upon the plastic Protoplasm, and changing its form from within as it expresses the various thoughts and feelings of the inner life, becomes, step by step, as it reaches higher conditions, a representation of the Ideal Form, a symbol of the Divine Beauty. If we regard the Body in this light, we cannot desire to have its beautiful form injured in any way by subjecting it to imprisonment in the artificial livery of civilization.

Thus the 'materials and shapes' of the Abbotsholme clothes were specially chosen to 'aid the proper growth of the body, and to show off its structure and beauty of form' and at the same time, by presenting to the observation of the boy his own companions' shapely forms, to assist his imagination to mould his own body into an ever closer approximation of the ideal form.

After chapel and breakfast came Dormitory Parade, in which the boys were expected to clean their teeth and make their own beds, both in accordance with specific instructions laid down in the rules. (True to his championship of the claims of wool over those of linen. Reddie abolished sheets and had his boys sleep between blankets.) The boys then, somewhat strangely, went off to violin practice, but this was followed by the big moment of the day. 'During the first Period, 8.30 – 9.15, the boys visit, in batches under captains, the earth cabinets in the garden.'

Reddie was convinced that indoor lavatories were a potent source of evil; and under his regime Abbotsholme reverted to more natural and 'wholesome' practices. In addition, so convinced was he of the need for regular movements that the boys were forbidden to visit the earth cabinets except at the appointed hour. The instructions for the use of the cabinets were particularly precise.

The Cabinets are to be used in the following manner – The Occupant will face towards the light ... not towards the door, and will stand, or stoop, with his heels on the rests provided for the purpose. After use, dry earth should be thrown down to absorb all liquid and cover completely all solid matter.

The cabinets were to be cleaned out weekly. 'Human beings,' Reddie proclaimed, 'should be as clean, at least, as Cats.' This requirement apparently applied in lesser degree to the workmen on the estate. They, too, were provided with an earth cabinet 'near the Potting Shed' but it was considered sufficient to have this cleaned 'by the Groom' 'once a month'. As the boys emptied their excrement from the earth closets they were encouraged to reflect that 'the lowliest functions of our nature can subserve great ends, for all rejected by the body is employed to nourish the garden crops; and what is too often a source of disease, becomes here a source of wealth.'

Luncheon was taken at the improbable time of quarter to eleven. Reddie was convinced that diet influences, not only health, but intellectual and moral stature. Meat stimulated the passions.

If boys at school are fed upon highly inflammatory food they are apt to lose control of themselves and to have fits of irritability, leading very often to moral vice. Whereas, those fed upon a cooler diet of cereals and vegetables run far less risk of these storms of super-abundant vitality.

(Reddie also thought that the weather affected moral conduct, but was, unfortunately, not in a position to control it.) The diet at Abbotsholme appears to have been excellent. The school itself grew thirty-eight different vegetables (Reddie was always precise in matters like this); the bread was wholemeal and home-ground; fresh eggs, butter and fruit were available in abundance and meat was of the very best quality. (He was, he notes somewhat ambiguously, foiled in his attempts to produce his own butter by the 'class prejudice' of the school's servants.) To cap it all, there was Abbotsholme Pudding, a special recipe which Reddie himself claimed to have devised, but was in reality a kind of muesli (oatmeal and fruit). The boys sat down to a Gregorian sung grace, and ate their Abbotsholme Pudding under Leonardo da Vinci's *Last Supper* to remind them 'in what spirit such meals should be taken'. On their way into the dining room, they would have passed an immense picture entitled *L'Ange des Splendeurs,* depicting, in the words of one of the pupils, 'an angel (who has come down from heaven) trying to save a youth from the serpents of vice and evil which surround him, and beckoning him upwards to better things'. 'Dr Reddie,' recalls an old boy, 'was an incurable symbolist and liked a canvas to be cluttered with objects that had a higher meaning.' Symbolism, in fact, oozed from every pore of Abbotsholme in Reddie's day. Every object and event was clothed, however scantily, with a Higher Purpose. Every picture was expected to lead the boy on to Higher Things. Art at Abbotsholme was definitely not for art's sake, but a sentry keeping vigilant guard over the pupils' morals.

In the afternoon there was estate work, which combined in a practical way the culture of one body (hygiene) with the culture of many bodies (economics). Tea was at six o'clock, followed once more by violin practice. There was then a Social Hour devoted to 'quiet, healthy, and rational amusements'. (Reddie discontinued this institution for a number of years after he came in one evening and heard 'Marquis ma. sing "Two little girls in blue" – [he] said as we had degenerated to singing comic songs there would be no more social evenings'). Reddie was certainly no believer in free time, which he regarded as 'one of the chief sources of the corrupt imagination and conversation found in schools'.

Dormitory life was meticulously planned. After much 'excogitation' Reddie hit upon the figure of seven as the optimum population of the dormitory.* It was a 'mixed aged' dor-

*'For the conversation to be general, without the need of splitting the room up into sections, 7 is not too many. If there are more than 7, it is impossible for all Boys to join fairly in the conversation, or to get to know the other Boys well enough to overcome the shyness inevitable at first. If the number is smaller, the Captain has really not much opportunity of

mitory so as to give an outlet 'for the natural feeling of affection
and admiration felt by Youngsters for Older Boys, and the
natural feeling of affection and desire to protect felt by the
best types of Senior Boys towards the Juniors'. Each dormitory had a Captain (an elder boy) who was responsible for its
discipline and 'tone'. At the end of every term, he had to give
a report on each of his charges, commenting on his cooperativeness, moral standards, cleanliness and so on. It was his
task also to give the boys in his dormitory those 'minuter dir-
ections about washing, etc.' which the compendious sheets of
rules might have missed.

'On reaching dormitory, all must undress at once; but, before getting into bed, wash the face, and chest, and feet in
cold water; and clean the teeth with the proper powder; and
so go to bed clean inside and out.' These ablutions were carried out in special washbasins designed to keep the water in
constant circulation. Having made sure that the 'pure air of
heaven' was blowing through the room through the seven
open windows, the boy would then attempt to fall asleep in the
correct posture.

*

How did the boys react to all this? There is heartening evidence of their natural resilience. They smoked and ate forbidden 'tuck' clandestinely; they built houses in trees and
pulled up the ladder so that Reddie could not get at them. Of
course, the headmaster's grand design was seriously jeopar-
dized at the outset by the failure of the staff to play their
allotted role as 'heroic' guides and counsellors: the succession
of eccentric foreign masters afforded endless opportunity of

learning the business of Government; and, of course, the smaller the Dormitory, the more risk that a bad tone might conceivably become adopted by
all. It is most unlikely that with ordinary care a Dormitory of 7 would all
be infected together, and as long as a single Boy keeps clear of evil, there is a
check on the growth of evil, and a tolerable certainty that it will be discovered and put down. The number 7 is, then, a compromise. It aims at
avoiding the danger, on the one hand of too few, and, on the other hand, of
too many.' From *What is the Educative Value of Life in Dormitory?* which
was posted in each dormitory.

evading both the rules and the claims of the 'affective relationship'. Occasionally there were more fundamental revolts. Reddie attached enormous significance to the harvest festival; for three days in the year everything was centred on collecting and stacking hay, in what was meant to be a kind of mystic symbiosis with nature. As an old boy recalls:

Whatever the idea [of Abbotsholme] this haymaking was its annual festival and C.R. its high priest. This all went on every summer, and one summer was like another until the terrible happening I have rashly dared to chronicle. I think it must have been in '98 or '99. A whisper swept through the school. Our festival had been outraged. Haymaking was suddenly stopped and the school flung back into the classrooms. Norman Wilkinson* had said to C.R., 'After all, it's your hay.'

Had C.R. come upon Norman asleep under a tree, or reading a play? Whatever the precise circumstances . . . it is clear that Norman had been detected in a grievous lapse from haymaking probity, and great indeed was the wrath of C.R.

But the boy gave blow for blow and his words became more and more wild. He said that school haymaking was really a commercial proposition and that its purpose was to save the wages of professional haymakers. Very wrong indeed, but we were thrilled to the marrow.

On the whole, though, there is little evidence about the influence of the Abbotsholme ideal on the physical, mental and spiritual development of the boys, or on their subsequent careers. It seems a fair guess that the exalted idealism of the place appealed most to those boys least able to live up to it – in other words, to those who suffered most from bodily and spiritual imperfections. Such a boy was Lytton Strachey, who was a pupil for a couple of terms in 1893–4, before ill-health caused his withdrawal. Freakish in appearance, physically weak and uncoordinated, he developed a love-hate attitude towards the Abbotsholmian, and indeed the whole public-school, ideal of beautiful forms which necessitated the ironic disguise of his portrait of Dr Arnold, based to some extent upon the original of Dr Reddie. For, as in the case of Reddie himself, idealism is often the counterpart of introversion: the

*Later a theatrical producer.

construction in the mind of a world of heroes, of lofty aspirations, of exalted relationships, arising from a consciousness of one's own actual inadequacy, or inability to communicate freely with other people. The leaders of Dr Reddie's physical aristocracy probably glided through life largely untouched by the lofty sentiments of the school. But this is necessarily speculative. What we are left with are occasional fragments of the 'philosophic' speculations of the boys themselves: and the following, reprinted from the *Abbotsholmian* of 1894, must have gladdened Dr Reddie with the confirmation that one, at least, of his pupils was making satisfactory progress towards the ideal:

Xerxes was a youth who, a few years ago, was suddenly inspired with the advantages of having a strong and healthy body to live in. Since then he had devoted his time and thought to the realization of his ideal, and success might already be said to be his.

One evening, after having had his games and bath, he was strolling towards his friend's home, in a mood of healthful langour, content with everything and everyone. In a few minutes he was with his friend. 'Ah, Histius,' cried Xerxes, 'you are not well.' 'That is true,' said Histius. 'I have well nigh broken down. Lately I have been too much occupied in finishing a book which I am writing to think of going out for a recruiting [*sic*] walk. The result is as you see. What a pleasure it must be to be so strong and healthy as you are. Life must be to you one great joy.

And yet, after all, perhaps I am playing a greater part in the world than you. The ideas which I conceive and embody in my writings will, when read by the people, be more or less the motive forces of their actions in the future. Thus my range of action spreads over a large area. At times when I feel my physical inabilities strongly, I console myself with the thought that my body is not of so much moment as it appears to be. Were it so, death would destroy the most noble work of a lifetime. But I look at it that death, which vanquishes the body, does not destroy the unearthy and aspiring soul. So the preference of cultivating Ideals to that of my physical structure, appears to me to be the only real thing of use to the world and to myself.

'What say you to this, Xerxes?'

'I cannot quite follow your philosophy,' said Xerxes. 'Yet, methinks, that men who have well-cultured physiques do play a part in the world. The admiration felt in seeing a beautiful healthy form fulfils a useful part in education, for it tends to re-mould the beauty in the admirer; and then the harmonious result causes life's lessons to be clearly perceived and purposes achieved. Should unhealthy conditions prevail in the body, the disorder will prevent or cloud the knowledge to be gained through the perceptions of sense. And surely this limitation would be a loss. Again, the possession of a well-developed physique endows one with the power of pursuing life's studies with energy.'

'You are right,' replied Histius. 'I was looking at the matter in rather a narrow light. After all, the best plan is to have a cultured mind in a healthy and beautiful body.'

9 · A Bizarre Autocrat

Abbotsholme was dominated by Cecil Reddie from the moment of its foundation in October 1889 to the moment of his retirement in March 1927. His headmastership opened with sixteen boys and a quarrel with his collaborators and supporters; it closed with two and the suggestion that he must never come near the school again. Over the years, disappointment and frustration had increased his eccentricities. Headmasters, like Oxford dons, are very prone to peculiarity, as social pressures towards conformity are much reduced, allowing small manias and obsessions to grow luxuriant. Marriage, no doubt, would have been a powerful corrective; but Reddie's affections were engaged elsewhere. Masters too were sacked if they questioned his views.

Increasingly he came to believe that the rot in the English character had spread much further than he had imagined; and that the New School Movement could make no further progress until other causes had been dealt with. The vagueness and muddle of the English character he attributed to the haphazard manner in which the English language had grown up; and he denounced English spelling with a vehemence which could certainly have been reserved for greater tragedies. He installed in the chapel as a war memorial a bas-relief of a naked youth (taken from Blake's *The Radiant Lover*) and on the plaque beneath it the names of the war dead were remembered in 'non-caps' (non-capital letters) – smith, unwin. His own speech was punctuated by strange words with which he hoped to replace conventional ones 'devalued' by incorrect usage. He championed a new 'Perpetual Calendar' designed to eliminate the 'illogicality' of the existing one; he wanted to rotate musical notation by an angle of 90 degrees so that the notes on the sheet ran parallel to the piano keyboard; he interested himself in the occult.

He had hypnotic eyes and was a great, even 'memorable'

talker, though a look of 'extreme pain' would come across his face if anyone tried to change the subject of conversation. He lived in a world of 'non-caps', quill pens, blue chalk and Gregorian chants. He terrified and fascinated the boys by turns. In the early days, there was an atmosphere of excitement, uncertainty and adventure. The masters were strange, Germanic and short-lived; Reddie was always apt to do the unexpected – such as leading his pupils on a midnight expedition against an obstreperous neighbour who claimed a 'right of way' over the Abbotsholme estate. 'The pupils,' recalled an old boy, 'loved their Headmaster because he too was a dreamer'; and their support and affection for him in retirement at Welwyn Garden City after 1927 softened what might otherwise have been an intolerable exile.

He was too bizarre, autocratic and fanatical ever to establish the school on a stable footing; and it would undoubtedly have closed down in 1927 had not the old boys come to the rescue. Admittedly its troubles were not entirely his own fault. The Boer War and the First World War both hindered its growth at a critical point in its fortunes; Reddie's own health deteriorated in the first years of this century and he collapsed completely in 1906, spending two years in America recuperating. But the main troubles stemmed from his own personality. The most serious obstacle to Abbotsholme growth was his inability to hold his staff. By July 1900 when the new buildings were opened the school numbers had crept up to sixty-one; but next term occurred the 'great Row'. One master left in the middle of the term; another collapsed; the resignations of two more followed. Some of the parents becoming alarmed, thirteen boys were withdrawn and the numbers fell to thirty-three. While Reddie was in America the staff tried to prevent his return by circulating rumours about his morals; and though these were quashed, numbers were once more affected. During the war, Reddie's pronounced pro-German feelings did not help recruitment and at one point numbers fell to thirteen.* (It was rumoured locally that he flashed lights from

*A large proportion of the masters and boys were German and they were, of course, immediately withdrawn or interned.

the school building to guide passing Zeppelins.) An old boy has provided a vivid picture of Reddie in his period of decline:

> Always a complex combination of devil and saint, the devil now took command. His temper was ungovernable. He shouted, stormed, and raged. He seldom came into class without a cane. Teaching, what there was of it, was thrown completely to the winds, and instead we suffered tirades against the English, against women, and against public schools. Only Germany was extolled, although at that very time German bullets were tearing Old Abbotsholmians to death. His classes became reigns of terror, and rested like a dead weight upon the happiness of the boys. Even bathing was spoilt, with C.R. always present shouting at us to do this and that, and in particular compelling us to dive seven or eight feet into the water without any proper instruction.

In the 1920s more staff rows and an increasing fatalism, bitterness and crankiness on the part of the headmaster produced a slow and inexorable decline, so that in 1927 Dunlop and Hilderbrand were the only boys left in the school. How much the school's ill-fortune was due to Reddie himself can be judged by its recovery under the new headmaster, Colin Sharp. The decline was immediately reversed. In three years the school had passed Reddie's peak figure of sixty-one boys; by the outbreak of war its numbers were over one hundred.

A high proportion of the staff were always foreign. Their stay seldom exceeded one term and their knowledge of English left much to be desired. They had heard about Abbotsholme and its aims; they came to see for themselves; and soon left to start similar schools in their own country. Thus Abbotsholme, like Summerhill later on, had a paradoxical position: it became internationally famous, without ever being firmly established in its own country. Reddie, with his perverse Anglophobia, generally endorsed foreign imitations of Abbotsholme, while condemning English attempts to extend his principles. The most famous early visitor was Dr Herman Lietz, who stayed for a couple of terms in 1896–7, and, as we have seen, wrote a eulogistic account (*Emlohstobba*) and returned to Germany to found the Land School Movement: it was through Herman Lietz that Kurt Hahn, founder of Gordonstoun, first made contact with the Abbotsholme ideal.

Of course, the German schools drew upon their own literature for inspiration, especially Goethe's *Wilhelm Meister*. If anything, they were even more symbolic than Abbotsholme. In 1897 the French sociologist Edmond Demolins published his book *À quoi tient la supériorité des Anglo-Saxons?* which attributed the decay of France to cramming for examinations and the stultifying influence of the family, and cited Abbotsholme (which he had not visited) as an example of that 'all-round education' that had created the British Empire. Demolins never understood that Abbotsholme was not typical of the English public-school system and ignored the fact that the British Empire was won long before public schools had been heard of. Nevertheless his book ran through six editions in six months; and thus encouraged he started the École des Roches outside Paris. In 1910, Dr Friedrich Grunder, a Swiss, who had taught for a short time at Abbotsholme, published *Les Mouvements des écoles nouvelles* and founded a 'New School' in Switzerland. Reddie was terribly worried lest he should not receive the recognition he felt to be his due, or lest his work should be misrepresented. In a letter to Grunder in 1910 he writes:

Ferrière,* for instance, in writing a panegyric on my very intimate friend, Dr Lietz, wishing to exalt his subject, says that, until Dr Lietz came to Abbotsholme, nothing of any vital value existed there. This must have been most unpleasant for Dr Lietz, who would, of course, be the first to disclaim any such thing. And Professor Rein, on his first visit here in 1896 ... would not have advised Lietz to come here at all, had he felt Abbotsholme was without vitality....

The most famous of Abbotsholme's English 'colonies' and one which caused Dr Reddie great pain was Bedales, founded by J. H. Badley in 1893. Badley was born in 1865 of a middle-class family which he described as 'Liberal in politics, Puritan in morals, Evangelical in religion'. At Rugby he enjoyed boxing but was dissatisfied with the narrow Classical curriculum,

---

*Adolph Ferrière, a Swiss, who in 1899 founded the International Bureau of New Schools and was active in the international coordination and development of the New School Movement.

though he excelled in it. He enjoyed, too, the feeling of responsibility when he was made head of his house. He gained a first in Classics at Cambridge in 1887 and then, like Edward Carpenter before him, he started reading Whitman. This led on to Carpenter himself, Morris and Ruskin. The latter's *Unto This Last* 'first woke in me an awareness that beyond the sheltered garden of art in which I had been content to wander lay a world with problems and struggles that must be faced.'

While walking in the Rhineland in the spring of 1889, steeping himself in the lyrics of Heinrich Heine, he received a letter from Lowes Dickinson which mentioned a plan to form a new school 'that would retain what was good in the Public School system, but with a practical rather than an academic training, in the setting of a country life and its interests'. Badley joined Reddie in 1890 and remained two years. He found much to admire in the new school, but like so many others found Reddie impossibly autocratic. He was 'the most striking example known to me of the teacher whose personality so completely dominates and moulds his pupils that, for the time at any rate, they are apt to lose their own individuality in their readiness to adopt his ideas, feelings and habits.' A further complication was that in 1892 Badley got married and Reddie hated married staff. So he determined to found his own school and in January 1893 Bedales opened in Sussex with three boys. In 1900 it transferred to Petersfield in Hampshire, where it has been ever since.

Badley, like Reddie, wished to retain what was best in the public-school system; but unlike Reddie he believed that cooperation must be attained by democratic, not autocratic, methods. From the first, therefore, there was an atmosphere of freedom and permissiveness at Bedales unknown at Abbotsholme, and a much greater encouragement of individuality. Another important divergence was Badley's conversion to coeducation, mainly through the influence of his wife. This caused Reddie particular mortification. As we have seen, he believed that it was natural and indeed noble for adolescent

boys to love each other; and saw that the introduction of
girls would inevitably destroy the beautiful relationships of
his Platonic cosmos. Strangely enough, he did not object nearly
as much to the introduction of coeducation in the German
Land Schools.

Otherwise, Bedales developed very much on Abbotsholme
lines. There was the same emphasis on estate work to replace
compulsory games; cold baths were *de rigueur*; the school
was filled with Higher Life symbolism; the mixed-aged dormitory was retained though the Abbotsholme rules were dis-
carded. In diet, clothing, hygiene and religion Badley followed
very much in Reddie's footsteps. The difference was that he
had the ability to put across these ideas without that German
logic and fanaticism that alienated the middle-class English
parent. Bedales, though in some ways – such as coeducation –
more revolutionary than Abotsholme, was definitely less
'cranky' and was thus more successful. It was also more
genuinely experimental. Reddie's educational plan was completed by his visit to Jena in the early 1890s and thereafter
was never changed. Badley was much more alive to new
developments. He grasped the relevance of advances in psychology for educational thinking; he incorporated Montessorian
principles into the junior and infant departments (Reddie had
no interest in younger children); he experimented with new
teaching methods such as the Dalton System. Bedales was thus
enabled to advance in what would now be regarded as a genuinely 'progressive' direction. Abbotsholme, on the other hand,
trapped in the progressivism of the 1890s, became increasingly
conventional as Reddie's successors sloughed off the eccentricities of the first head without adding anything to the
original mixture.

PART THREE

Neill
of
Summerhill

10 · A Calvinist Upbringing

Alexander Sutherland Neill was born in the town of Forfar, Angus, on 17 October 1883, the third of eight brothers and sisters. (His mother actually gave birth to thirteen children, but five died young.) His grandfather on his father's side had been a coalminer with the family name of MacNeill: his father, who rose somewhat in the world by becoming a schoolmaster, dropped the Mac. His mother, Mary Sutherland Sinclair, was also a teacher: her mother – Granny Sinclair – had been the sole survivor of twenty children (the rest died of T.B.) and lived with the Neills. She used to give young Alexander peppermints, and was very religious.

Neill's father, George, was the dominie of the Kingsmuir School, Forfar, with a salary of £120 a year. As a schoolmaster he seems to have been a kindly, if somewhat pedantic, pedagogue. As a father he was stern and remote, determined that his offspring should make good through education. Neill recalls: 'He used to hold up a boy as a model for us, a frail little chap with glasses, who never played a game in his life, but . . . wept if he wasn't at the top of the class. . . . He is now a railway porter I believe.' His mother he loved dearly, 'too dearly' he says. Although a kindly person, she was something of a snob, determined that the neighbours should recognize her children to be a cut above those of the ploughmen and farm-labourers. While her husband wanted the children to be smart, she saw to it that they looked smart. Willie, the oldest son, was the bright boy who took all the prizes and went on to St Andrews University. He was the parents' favourite and could do no wrong in their eyes. He later became a minister. Neill himself was closest to Clunes, his sister, though he hero-worshipped his elder brother.

Lower-middle-class respectability was perhaps the keynote of Neill's family life. His mother made sure that the children had stiff starched collars even on weekdays, and wore herself out washing clothes and keeping the house scrupulously clean. English was spoken in the home, while with his schoolmates Neill spoke dialect. Of them, he has written, 'Most ... were children of farm workers, poor, ill-fed many of them, often ragged, tough, mischievous ... they left school at fourteen to work on the land.' Games with them would be broken off to pore over school textbooks. 'Time for the dogs to gang hame,' they would shout derisively as Neill and Clunie responded to the stern parental summons. Neill grew up envious of those children whose parents had no ambitions for them. 'You'll end up in the gutter,' his father would roar at him, but in vain.

For Neill had what would now be called a 'learning block'. 'I was obedience personified,' he recalled, 'although in the long run my obedience was never satisfactory. Obedience made me stare at Allen's Grammar, and then something inside me negatived everything by refusing to allow me to learn it.' He was, however, passionately interested in things: 'My pockets were always filled with bits of string, chunks of old iron and brass, nails, screws.' In addition, he was something of an inventor, and applied his talents to improving the penny-farthing bicycle.

I had read about levers, and concluded that if the pedal cranks were about three feet long the power of driving would be enormous. I at once saw the difficulty of getting two long cranks to revolve without touching the ground, and I elaborated some Heath Robinson sort of mechanism that would make them fold up telescopically as they reached the bottom of their stroke. After an engineer had laughed heartily at the idea and explained its impossibility I gave up.

The surface of his life was placidly rustic. Every morning and evening he fetched milk from the farm. The roads were empty except for a few bicycles, and he and his friends used to hang round the pubs on market days, hoping that some farmer would give one of them a penny for holding his horse, which was the sum of their pocket-money. There were few interruptions to the routine: the annual school picnic was one of them; the big market-day was another, when the children would throng the funfair and the credulous rustics would exchange their hard-earned money for worthless trinkets and merchandise persuasively offered by glib, itinerant salesmen. To outward appearances, the youthful Neill, tall, gangling, with big feet and ears that stuck out (his nickname was Saucers), was very much like his companions, more prone to daydreaming perhaps, but not in any way remarkable.

But surface appearances are deceptive, especially those of a small, dreamy, Scottish town. George Douglas, in his novel *The House with the Green Shutters* – Neill's own favourite – has portrayed in suitably nightmarish prose the claustrophobic concentration of guilt, hate and madness in a small community whose energies have been bottled up by a repressive Calvinist ethic and by the lack of any real work outlets. (Ibsen's plays convey much the same feeling.) Neill has often been accused of caricaturing Christianity as a religion of Hell-Fire, yet there is little doubt that the God of the Scottish kirk was a harsh taskmaster, a God of cold winds and black frost, of long, howling nights, and mighty winds battering against bleak hills, rather than a God of sunlight and warmth and joy. Moreover, he was a God whose judgement always threatened. Death was commonplace: and every few weeks an elaborate funeral ceremony would mark the passing of relations and friends. Death to Neill was 'the great judgement . . . a kind of grand School Inspection and I for one knew that I would fail, for my copybook was all blots'.

Of his early childhood he has written of:

The kirk bells and the dreadful Sabbath when you could only take a walk in stiff collars and cuffs, never being allowed to play on the Lord's Day. The total dark cloud that hid sex. . . .

The kirk itself was merely the outward symbol of the kill-joy spirit; the interminable sermons, merely incidents in the profound melancholy of Calvinism. Later Neill wrote:

We were not specifically taught religion: it was in the air, an atmosphere of negation to life. . . . Without being told we knew precisely the milestones on the broad road that leads to destruction: sex, stealing, lying, swearing, profaning God's day (this comprehended nearly everything that was enjoyable).

The association between sex and sin was early established in his mind:

> When I was six my sister and I discovered each other's genitals, and naturally played with each other. Discovered by my mother, we were severely thrashed, and I was locked in a dark room for hours, and then made to kneel down and ask forgiveness from God. It took me decades to get over that early shock.

This incident Neill obviously considered as crucial to the whole of his later sexual development. The association of sex with sin convinced him that romantic love was the only kind that was 'pure': 'I fled from raw sex into the realm of idealistic sex.' He also developed what he described as a 'sister-fixation' which evidently made it very difficult for him for a long time to fall in love with a real person. He compared the girls he met to Clunes, and not surprisingly found them inferior. Finally he traces to his mother's snobbery the search for a girl of superior social class. Overshadowing everything was a total ignorance of the physiology of sex. With this background it is not perhaps surprising that all his early love affairs were doomed to frustration and disappointment, and that he did not get married till he was over forty. Equally, it is not surprising that growing self-awareness brought a deep and lasting revulsion against a system of upbringing that denied him for so long the chance of happiness. However, he makes it clear that this was his personal fate: 'I seemed to take on the whole burden of the family's sins.' His brothers and sisters passed through their trying Scottish adolescence relatively unscathed. Why should Neill alone have been so particularly affected? External repression cannot be the sole factor in subsequent unhappiness. The individual obviously brings something personal to the experience which determines the way it affects him.

It was no doubt partly because his mind was occupied with these questions, that Neill, despite considerable ability, failed to achieve anything at school, and was the only one of his brothers and sisters not to proceed to secondary education. He had, at the age of fourteen he recalls, only one talent – 'I could write copper-plate.' His father made him apply for clerking jobs and his handwriting got him one in Edinburgh in a gas meter factory.

I can still smell the damned place. So at 14 I went a hundred miles away to lonely lodgings and, I think, 6/– a week pay. I had months of homesickness and misery. I kept imploring my parents to take me home, promising that I would study hard for the Boy Clerks' Competitive exam. My father thought that the Civil Service was a fine institution. They took me home and of course I couldn't study. They then sent me to be a draper's assistant in Forfar, hours 8 to 8 and 10 on Saturdays. My chief job was to deliver parcels. My big toe joints got inflamed and then stiff... and I had to give up the job. My parents held a meeting about my future. Said my mother: 'George, why don't we make him a teacher?' 'It's about the only thing he is fit for,' growled my father.

So he enrolled, at fifteen, as a pupil teacher in his father's school. Methods of teaching had changed little over the previous fifty years. There was one teacher (the headmaster) who taught everything. 'While he took Standard IV for Reading, Class V would be doing sums. Class III would be looking vaguely at a map waiting for him to come over to teach some Geography.' With the start of Bell's monitorial system in the 1820s it had become customary for the teacher to employ elder boys to help out, without salary, thus satisfying the Victorian demand for education on the cheap. The teacher himself was paid by results in getting his pupils through the standard tests laid down by the School Board, again satisfying the Victorian demand that money should show some return for its use. Instruction consisted in cramming the Three Rs and assorted subjects into the pupil's mind and ensuring they were firmly lodged there with the aid of the 'tawse' or punishment strap.

Neill was undoubtedly a late developer. After four years as a pupil teacher he sat an entrance examination for a Teacher Training College, coming 103rd out of 104 candidates. He was now an ex-pupil teacher and got a job at Kingskettle, East Fife, at a salary of £60 a year. He has given us some glimpses of his life at this time. His headmaster, Calder, was a stern disciplinarian who had boils on his neck. He 'tawsed the pupils most savagely and expected me to do the same.' Comments Neill: 'I had to be on the side of authority when my own desire to play had not been lived out.' He was not, according to his own account, an admirable person. 'Status,' he writes, 'was the only thing that mattered to me then.' He joined the Volunteers; he worked for the Tory party against Asquith in the election of 1906; he sat in conventional ecstasy through a performance of Henry Irving. He acquired some reputation as a drawing-room wit. Girls he continued to view through a romantic, upper-class haze:

I did not idealize common girls: I aimed higher. The girl I loved was always quite unattainable, always in a rank of society that was far above mine. ... There was nothing consciously sexual about it all: I never even in imagination thought of kissing them. I was satisfied to have seen them pass in the street, and if the adored one happened to glance in my direction my joy was complete.

He fell desperately in love with a fifteen-year-old girl pupil, Margaret, but could never bring himself to give any sign: her memory haunted him for years, and added further to his difficulty of establishing contact with 'real' women.

With these social aspirations, the prospect of a life spent in the lowest grade of the teaching profession (maximum salary £100 a year) began to look decidedly unappealing; and he decided to go to university. The Reverend Aeneas Gunn Gordon taught him Greek, and his interest was stirred by mathematics. Two years of further study were combined with a job at Newport; and finally, in 1908, with the entrance examination successfully passed, Neill, aged twenty-five, enrolled at Edinburgh University. From this belated intellectual flowering, Neill drew firm conclusions. Forced learning was a waste of time: the pupil would give outward obedience, but his interests would be elsewhere. These interests would only take an intellectual turn when a definite purpose had formed in his mind, the achievement of which required learning: interest, in short, was a function of a specific aim. No doubt the aim would come sooner if the pupil were freed from guilt about his body.

At university he switched from Chemistry and Physics to English, studied under Professor Saintsbury, and got a second-class Honours degree. He edited the university magazine, contributed to the Glasgow Herald and wore coloured shirts. He won £40 in a literary competition, and saved it up carefully; consciously reacting against the spendthrift university ways of his brother Willie, whose repeated requests for cash had worried his parents and made life miserable for the rest of the children. (To this day Neill admits to a 'queer meanness' in money matters.) Like many others who have devoted their lives to criticizing the academic establishment, he was always very proud of his M.A., which, in a rather curious way, he saw as establishing his intellectual *bona fides*.*

University life left a mixed impression. The English course he later described as 'a sham ... we read books about books ... what Coleridge or Hazlitt had said about Shakespeare.' Professor Saintsbury 'knew the beauty of literature, but could not get it across the footlights.' Neill was considerably older than most of his fellow students and was conscious of the disparity between their intellectual and emotional development, a contrast heightened by the Scottish educational system with its fine intellectual traditions and stern Presbyterian morality. Freed for the first time from the strict domination of home and kirk, students revelled in their liberty; and the rowdiness of student life in Scotland far exceeded anything south of the border. One of Neill's favourite passages in *The House with the Green Shutters* describes the students ragging a weak lecturer:

It was a bear garden. The most moral individual has his days of perversity when a malign fate compels him to show the worst he has in him. A Scottish University class – which is many most moral individuals – has a similar eruptive tendency when it gets into the hands of a weak professor. ... This was a morning of the kind. The lecturer, who was an able man but a weakling, had begun by apologizing for the condition of his voice, on the ground that he had a bad cold. Instantly every man

*Neill has objected to this, commenting: 'I never use it, even on the school prospectus.' On the other hand, it gets an honourable mention in every book he has written.

in the class was blowing his nose. One fellow, of a most portentous snout, who could trumpet like an elephant sent his handkerchief across the room. When called to account for his conduct, 'Really, sir,' he said, 'er-er-oom – bad cold.' Uprose a universal sneeze. Then the 'roughing' began, to the tune of 'John Brown's body lies a-mouldering in the grave' – which no man seemed to sing, but every man could hear. They were playing the tune with their feet. . . . At last the lecturer plunged wildly at the door and flung it open. 'Go!' he shrieked, and pointed in superb dismissal.

A hundred and fifty barbarians sat where they were, and laughed at him; and he must needs come back to the platform, with a baffled and vindictive glower.

'A learned neurotic,' Neill tartly observed, 'is not any different from an unlearned neurotic.' University students 'have been taught to know but have not been allowed to feel'.

At university Neill discovered a flair for writing and he decided to become an author. He got a job as assistant editor in the Edinburgh publishing house of Jacks, and spent a year sub-editing a one-volume encyclopedia of theirs and then helping to write Jacks Self-Educator. Many of these rather dismal tomes which enjoyed a great vogue in the early days of adult education can still be had in second-hand bookshops. Neill himself contributed chapters on literature and mathematics, and wrote a piece on sketching with his own drawings to illustrate it (omitted). Though most of his literary opinions were 'second-hand', one passage on style he recalled with pleasure:

'Lucy in vain sought the dreamy realms of Morpheus, but the dismal wailing of feline wanderers kept recalling her to the stern realities of a grim world.' This is merely a flowery way of writing: 'Lucy could not sleep because of a cats' concert on the tiles.'

He later looked back on his contributions with a self-deprecatory pride which is characteristic.

A job in Fleet Street followed, as Art Editor of a new venture, the *Piccadilly Magazine*. The outbreak of war in 1914 killed it stone dead, and Neill returned to Scotland, applying for the headmastership of Gretna Green school. He got it and became 'for the first time . . . conscious of education'. A year later (he was by now thirty-three) the publication of *A*

Dominie's Log brought him to the attention of the public as an engaging and humorous schoolmaster, with distinctly unorthodox views. It was the first chapter in the spiritual Odyssey that was to take him from Gretna Green to Summerhill.

11 · New Horizons

Every schoolmaster was required to keep a 'log-book' of the day-to-day happenings of the school attendance, illnesses, marks, etc. 'No reflections or opinions of a general character are to be entered in the log-book,' the Scottish Code sternly decreed. Neill resolved to keep a private log in which 'I shall write down my thoughts on education'. His first book thus consists largely of incidents from his everyday life as a schoolmaster, written up daily or weekly, which serve as a peg or text for his general observations on children, education, literature, national characteristics and anything that came into his head.

He later described his first book as 'groping'. Certainly, it is not in any sense a coherent critique of the existing education set-up; rather it consists of a sprinkling of doubts about what was expected of him as a schoolmaster.

> I began to challenge the system [he later wrote] ... when I began to wonder what bearing decimal fractions, the Long Parliament, the exports of Peru had on the lives of children who were destined to go out as farmworkers and blacksmith.

This was, and is, a familiar complaint. The purpose of mass elementary education, in the words of the standard text-book on the subject, was 'to train the poor to an honest and industrious poverty which knew its place and was duly appreciative of any favours received'.* Adam Smith had argued that education enabled people to 'see through' the pretensions of agitators and 'interested complaints of faction or sedition', thus binding the people more firmly to the established order. With the spread of democracy the need to 'educate our masters' to a true appreciation of the 'national' interest – that is, the interest of the ruling and possessing class – became even more press-

*H. C. Barnard, *A Short History of English Education* 1760–1944, p. 62.

ing. Disaffection was seen largely as the product of ignorance:
the best guarantee of social stability lay in the 'civilization' of
the proletariat through the Three Rs and other improving disciplines. A further motive which came to the fore in the increasingly competitive industrial struggle of the late nineteenth
century was the creation of an efficient labour-force. The study
of boring subjects was supposed to develop 'habits of industry' which would serve in good stead for the boring work of
the factory. Vocational considerations came to play an
increasing part. 'Practical subjects' were gradually added to
the curriculum, while the Three Rs would serve as a useful preparation for the minor clerical jobs created by industrial
expansion. Education for Neill's children was thus seen primarily as a process of 'breaking in' and 'disciplining' savage
children and potentially savage adults, 'fitting them for the
work of life' not specifically, or vocationally, but by giving
them the right 'attitudes' and a certain minimal general
understanding. This civilizing, or, to use a more neutral word,
socializing, function had long been performed by the church,
which justified it theologically with the doctrine of original
sin. With the increasing importance of the electorate, and their
increased utility as wage-slaves, it was thought necessary, by
deliberate policy, to add education, hitherto confined to the
minority, to the battery of socializing agencies.

One extremely important further function of working-class
education must be noted, for it effectively stilled the protest of
those who might otherwise have resented this 'moulding' of
the working class to fit them into a reactionary social order;
and that was its function of enabling the bright working-class
boy to 'get on'. If education were regarded primarily as an
opportunity to get on, then any curriculum or system, however sterile, could be justified as 'relevant' to the child's future,
simply by virtue of its job allocation functions.

Neill himself toyed with the meritocratic idea as the answer
to his dilemma.

Our educational system is futile because it does not go far enough.
The State should see to it that each child has the best of chances.
Margaret [a bright girl] should be sent to a Secondary School and to a

University free of charge. Her food and clothes and books and train fares should be free of right.

But the meritocratic solution did not satisfy Neill for long, precisely because it could be so easily assimilated into the notion of 'fitting the child for the work of life'. But suppose the 'work' for which society was fitting the child was stultifying and uncreative? That it was so, Neill had no doubt – 'wage slavery' he saw as the norm. His views echo Blake's: 'Because I was happy upon the heath . . . they clothed me in the clothes of death.' In his first book he quoted Nietzsche: 'If we have a degenerate mean environment, the fittest will be the man who is best adapted to degeneracy and meanness; he will survive.' Should then the task of education be to fit the child for 'a degenerate mean environment'? The task of education, Neill reasoned, was to teach people how to live: the Code wanted him to teach people how to earn a living. There was no necessary antithesis between the two, provided that society gave the individual outlets for creative and satisfying work. But if it did not, then a choice must be made: either to teach children 'how to live', or to adjust them to society's demands, even at the sacrifice of their life potential.

This formulation had revolutionary implications. For given that education's function was mainly to fit the individual to society, it followed that no major educational changes could come about before society itself was transformed. The choice was to be either a lonely pioneer with little influence, or to join a radical social movement dedicated to social change in the desired direction.

But this is to anticipate. In *A Dominie's Log*, Neill simply evaded the dilemma by arguing, in effect, that people should be fitted for the work of life on the job itself, leaving education free for other things, such as developing imagination and self-awareness. In this vein he emerges as the champion of the Ruskin-Reddie view of education: as something ennobling the mind and personality. He wanted to give his children the 'best' in literature and music. Education should deal with 'great thoughts, with the aesthetic things'. 'Sketching, Music, and Poetry,' he wrote, 'are surely intended to make the bairn realize the fuller life that must have beauty always with it.' Sex was a 'wondrous beautiful thing'. The simple rural joys were contrasted with the 'ache of industrialism'. Yet Neill was at best a reluctant candidate for the Higher Life, for the sublimation of his own childish instincts was very far from complete. 'I began these log-notes,' he wrote, 'in order to discover my philosophy of education, and I find that I am discovering myself.'

What he discovered was the child within himself – not Reddie's idealistic adolescent – but a naughty child, full of fun, mischief and irreverence; and with that delightful discovery, the wish to 'mould' the child, to direct his instincts towards Higher Things, vanished. Teaching became for him an emotional exploration of the self – a kind of psycho-analysis. The releasing of the original child in himself, buried under layers of repressions and inhibitions, required him to become a playmate of his children, to take their view, to approve of their behaviour, for by doing so, he was affirming rather than denying himself. In fighting the battle for his bairns' freedom of action, Neill was fighting the battle for his own emotional freedom. By starting with their interests and longings he could attempt to rediscover and relive his own. As the stern dominie vanished, the suppressed schoolboy emerged into daylight.

He gradually dropped the 'tawse'. 'Dignity,' he wrote 'is something I abominate' – precisely because it emphasized his separation from his pupils. 'I try hard to share the bairns' joys': he flew their kites, read their comics and encouraged their shy romances. He found an invaluable aid in his own sense of humour or 'fun', setting such questions as 'Write a humorous dialogue between a brick and the mongrel dog it came into contact with'. The bad boy, he mused, is entirely the result of wrong mishandling. Criticizing the sentencing on two youthful delinquents for stealing he wrote: 'I should have invited the boys to tea, and sent them home with *Comic Cuts*, two oranges, and a considerable bit of chewing gum.'

Thus Neill described his days at Gretna Green. Reluctantly one has to conclude that most of the enlightened school-mastering took place in his own mind. The challenge had barely begun.

In his next book, *A Dominie Dismissed,* his phantasizing is carried one stage further, and becomes more personal. Neill's inner intellectual struggle is dramatized as a conflict between himself and MacDonald, 'a decent fellow with a kindly nature: sometimes I feel that I am quite fond of him'. Then there is Margaret Thomson, whom Neill marries after an affair at once romantic and educational: for Neill is a very didactic wooer, constantly parading his theories of life. This seems to have been the Margaret to whom Neill could not bring himself to speak in real life. Finally, Neill suffers the penalty for his unorthodox views and practices by being ignominiously dismissed. The scene is movingly described:

'Bairns,' I began again, 'I am going away now' ... I blew my nose again ... 'I don't suppose any of you understand why I am going away, but I'll try to tell you. I have been dismissed by your fathers and mothers. I haven't been a good teacher, they say; I have allowed you too much freedom. I have taken you out sketching and fishing and playing; I have let you read what you liked, let you do what you like. ... You and I made the gardens and rockeries; we dug the pond and we caught the trout and minnows and planted the water plants. We built the pigeon-loft and the rabbit-hutch. We fed our pets together. We –' I don't know what happened after that. I took out my handkerchief, but not to blow my nose.

The real Neill did leave Gretna Green about this time, but for much less 'progressive' reasons: he volunteered for the war and was drafted in 1916. Either the Scottish educational authorities were extraordinarily enlightened (which seems unlikely) or his break with traditional school practice did not go nearly as far as implied in his *Dominie* books. With Neill there was no sudden conversion. He is not an impulsive or rash person, prone to ill-sustained enthusiasms. Rather, he is, in many ways, a cautious Scot; and one's dominant impression of these years is that of a slow, tenacious, struggle to break free from his Presbyterian, 'anti-life', moorings.

*

The big turning-point in his life came when he met the American, Homer Lane. Stationed at Trowbridge, Wilts, as a cadet in the artillery, he found himself near Lane's school for delinquent children, The Little Commonwealth. He had previously heard of Lane's work and now visited the school itself, sitting up half the night while Lane expounded his philosophy of education. 'That week-end,' Neill later recalled, 'was perhaps the most important milestone in my life.'

Lane had a genius for dealing with difficult children and also a remarkable knack for making friends (and enemies) in influential circles. After a varied career in America – as a Sloyd instructor* and as superintendent of a rehabilitation centre for delinquents in Detroit (The Ford Republic) – he came over to England and founded The Little Commonwealth in Hampshire, under Home Office auspices.

In his biography David Wills writes, 'This simple, perplexing, humble, vain, wise, foolish, tarnished, innocent, happy and tragic man was half-a-century before his time.' Lane's basic belief was that 'a bad boy is an example of good qualities wrongly directed.' He becomes delinquent when deprived of love and sympathy, and when his impulses have been thwarted by a repressive and condemnatory upbringing. The 'cure' therefore lies in giving love and approval, in Lane's words, being 'on the side' of the boys; and in showing faith and trust in their 'good' qualities by allowing them to manage and govern their own lives – 'self-regulation'.

Both The Ford Republic and The Little Commonwealth had elaborate constitutions, in which the boys participated as officers and citizens of a miniature state. Lane describes dramatic 'cures' based on these principles, as when he participated in an orgy of plate-smashing in order to show an anti-social boy, Jason, that he was 'on his side'; but generally he seems to have relied on the healing properties of a loving and permissive environment. Later on he dressed up these conclusions in Freudian language, but in fact they owed nothing to

*Sloyd, a Finnish word meaning 'skill', was an educational movement that sought to make work with the hands, rather than desk work, the basis of elementary education.

Freud: they were reached intuitively and sprang from Lane's capacity to 'empathize' with his delinquent children.

Lane's views proved readily acceptable to Neill. He had felt himself to be 'on the side' of the child against the adult; had felt obscurely that approval and kindness were the ways to bring out 'any good' there was in children; had felt in his personal life the disastrous effects of a stern, moralistic up-bringing. Lane's doctrine of instincts and repressions provided him with an intellectual justification of his earlier 'gropings'; moreover Lane's 'therapy' seemed to hold out promise of relieving his own anxieties.

He arranged to return to The Little Commonwealth to help Lane after the end of the war; but by that time the experiment had collapsed. Lane was accused of sexual misconduct with one of the delinquent girls; and though an inquiry exonerated him, the Home Office demanded his withdrawal as the price for the continued recognition of the school. Rather than con-tinue The Little Commonwealth without him, the committee of sponsors closed it down; and Lane set up in London as a private psycho-therapist, attracting a clientèle of patients (he called them 'pupils') which included an Indian Viceroy, a bishop and many other notables. Meanwhile Neill, just com-missioned, was invalided out of the army with a nervous break-down.* He moved to London to continue his psycho-analysis under Lane; and at the same time got a teaching job at King Alfred School, Hampstead.

King Alfred School had been started in 1897. Unlike Bedales, it was not a direct offshoot of Abbotsholme, though there was a link through Professor J. J. Findlay, an admirer and friend of Reddie, who became a sponsor; and the first headmaster, C. E. Rice, had taught science for four years at Bedales. The school was coeducational from the start, though the motive probably had more to do with the current battle for women's emancipation than with the emotional desirability of educating boys and girls together: one of the founders, the sculptor Hamo Thorneycroft, named his daughter Elfrida after

---

*It followed upon pneumonia; and Neill explains it as an unconscious desire to escape being posted to the front: consciously he was eager to go.

King Alfred's daughter, whom that far-sighted monarch 'caused to be informed in the Liberal arts', thus ranking her claim to education to be equal to that he desired for his sons. Indeed there was a militantly rationalistic and ethical tone about the new foundation, deriving no doubt from its Hampstead clientèle. There was to be no religious teaching or observance, and the philosophical inspiration was humanist with touches of the theosophical. For the rest the school followed, as far as its being a day-school allowed, the pattern of New Education laid down by Reddie and Badley. A carefully correlated plan of studies 'aimed at interlocking the various branches of instruction instead of treating them as separate subjects'; where possible education was carried on 'out of doors, in garden, field or hedgerow'. Nature study and manual work were given pride of place and rambles and picnics were organized in the Chiltern Hills; prizes, marks and examinations were abolished; and there was no corporal punishment. Energetic propaganda was waged on behalf of the new ideas; meetings arranged, literature distributed, eminent speakers invited and conferences organized. Already by 1900 an 'embarrassing' succession of visitors trooped to Hampstead to see the new 'rational' school in action.

> You need not be proper, though,
> Which is a cheerful thought,
> Except when visitors (our foe)
> Are to the buildings brought.
> They stand and gaze with open mouth;
> In fact they're like lost sheep.
> They come in flocks from north and south,
> Disturbing lessons deep.

This complaint of a K.A.S. child about this time has found an echo in generations of progressive schoolchildren.

It was into this rather self-satisfied community that Neill burst with heresies picked up from Homer Lane: he demanded self-government for the pupils, which was energetically resisted by the head and staff.* It seems though that Neill did get per-

*Another follower of Lane, J. H. Simpson, experimented with classroom self-government at Rugby.

mission to start self-government in his own class; equally clearly it was a failure. The situation was the more piquant in that Homer Lane's youngest son Allen, then aged eleven, was chairman of Neill's class and, as his sister records, was 'in hot water most of the time'. In his book *A Dominie in Doubt*, published after the King Alfred experience, Neill has his 'whacking' schoolmaster, MacDonald, start an experiment in self-government in his village school. The attempt fails, because 'he wants his children to run the school themselves, but to run it according to his ideas of government.'

It was about this time that Neill visited Bedales for the first and only time. 'What do you think of the school?' asked Badley as Neill was leaving. 'A poor place,' Neill replied, 'I didn't hear a single damn all day.'

Bedales, in fact, was following firmly in Reddie's Higher Life footsteps. The buildings had been specially designed by Lupton, a disciple of William Morris, to symbolize its anti-industrial values: Badley promoted Morris dancing, 'jollity', and above all a 'healthy attitude towards sex'. Rabindranath Tagore, the Bengalese poet and theosophist, visited it in 1919, and left as a memento, a poem to world brotherhood:

> Speak to me of him, my friend and say that
> he has whispered to you in the hushed centre
> of fight and in the depth of peace where
> life puts on its armour.
> 　Shrink not to call his name in the crowd
> for we need to turn our eyes to the heart
> of things, to see the vision of truth and
> love binding the world anew out of its
> wreckage.
> 　Speak to me, my friend, of him, and make
> it simple for me to feel that he is.

The catastrophe of the First World War had, in fact, rendered Reddie's scheme for national revival rather old-fashioned. A much more grandiose reconstruction was called for. 'It is a race,' wrote H. G. Wells 'between education and destruction.'

12 · The New Education

Periods of exceptional educational interest always follow great wars. The 1914-18 War, being the greatest of all wars, produced the greatest educational ferment of modern times. It had administered a profound shock to those who had been brought up on the comfortable Victorian assumption of unending progress. The reconstruction of institutions attempted at the Peace Conference was not enough: nothing less than the reconstruction of humanity itself was required to prevent further catastrophes. The *New Era,* organ of the New Education Fellowship, established in 1920 to bring together the various national movements of education reform, defined the task of education as 'fostering the spirit of democratic brotherhood'. 'Freedom, and Tolerance, and Understanding,' declared its editor, Mrs Beatrice Ensor, 'have burst the doors so carefully locked upon them in the secret chambers of the souls of men, and are at present spreading abroad under the restlessness and destruction of these times.'

In seeking to free permanently the spirit of Freedom, Tolerance and Understanding hitherto 'locked up' in 'the secret chambers of the souls of men', the progressives drew inspiration from Theosophy and the New Psychology.

The Theosophical Society had been founded in 1875 by Madame Blavatsky, a Russian lady of obscure origins, loose morals and an impressive record of (faked) occult experiences. From these somewhat unpromising beginnings as a regenerative force the Society had prospered under the leadership of Mrs Annie Besant, who took over when Madame Blavatsky died in 1891.

Born in 1847, the young Annie Wood early experienced intense religious visions. She yearned to be the 'bride of Christ' but instead became the wife of the Reverend Frank Besant, a curate of narrow and pedantic piety, who was scarcely an adequate substitute. In revulsion, she left him, and for years struggled with 'doubts' which were only resolved when she met Charles Bradlaugh, noted freethinker and atheist, in the Hall of Science. Under his influence she plunged whole-heartedly into radical politics, championing such causes as birth-control and taking a leading part in the match-girls strike of 1887.

But her romantic nature could not long rest satisfied with licking stamps for Sidney Webb, least romantic of men, or even expounding from the platform the Fabian remedies for the social discontents of the times. She yearned for something more 'spiritual' and in this mood came across Madame Blavatsky's gigantic *Secret Doctrine: The Synthesis of Science, Religion and Philosophy,* in 1888. Her conversion was apparently instant. In the words of her biographer, Theodore Besterman:

After she joined the Theosophical Society and became a disciple of Madame Blavatsky, Mrs Besant lost all patience with the tedious effort for social regeneration. Her eyes were no longer on the earth; they were again fixed on a distant star, a grail, a hope, an inspiration. One by one, she abandoned the National Secular Society, the Fabian Society, the London School Board, the match-girls' and other trade unions.

It was in this mood that she experienced at Fontainebleau soon after her conversion 'the radiant astral Figure of the Master, visible to my physical eyes.'

'The difficulties in arriving at a true estimate of the Theosophical Society,' writes Mr Besterman, 'are as nothing to the difficulty of obtaining an accurate notion of Theosophy itself.' The most accessible part of the doctrine consisted in an adaptation of the Hindu belief in reincarnation. Life was a continuous process which had started long before the world came into being and which continued on much higher levels in other parts of the universe. There was 'a direct continuity from form in its most primitive manifestations up to and beyond the invisible forms of divinity'. The possibility of divinity was within the grasp of every living creature: a good life would be rewarded by incarnation in a higher form and so on up to the astral sphere and beyond. Occasionally, spirits who had earned their astral reward would be returned to earth as leaders and prophets to help others on the evolutionary path: such were Mrs Besant herself and other leaders of the Theosophical Society. These prophets would be put in touch with the Masters, a sub-section of the Deity residing somewhere in the Himalayas. It was these Masters who sat in judgement on humanity, deciding who would rise and who would fall in the scale of life.

It was not so much that this rigmarole fascinated progressive educators as that leading Theosophists themselves took up internationalist and educational causes with gusto. A leading aim of the Theosophical Society was 'to form a nucleus of the Universal Brotherhood of Humanity, without distinction of race, creed, sex, caste or colour' – an aim that derived from its doctrine that divinity was a potential possessed by all men. It was natural that Theosophists should feel a natural affinity to India: Mrs Besant herself settled there to be nearer the Masters, and immersed herself in the movement for Indian independence, as well as writing prolifically in praise of traditional Indian culture. Theosophy's generous, if vague, internationalism, was well attuned to the hopes and feelings of the post-war world.

Another aim of Theosophy – 'to investigate the ... powers latent in man' – led naturally to education. Mrs Besant's chief assistant, Charles Leadbeater, interested himself specially in this aspect, though his views as to how these 'powers' should be developed were somewhat singular.* It was he too who discovered the new World-Teacher, whose last incarnation had been as Christ, occupying the body of a small Indian boy, Krishnamurti, who was to grow up to denounce Mr Leadbeater and all his works. At any rate, leading Theosophists, like Mrs Beatrice Ensor, plunged enthusiastically into the new educational movements, and provided them with a language suitably uplifting and optimistic.

With Freud we come to someone much more substantial. It is difficult to sum up shortly Freud's impact on the New

---

*Leadbeater's chief educational theory seems to have been a vigorous encouragement of masturbation. (See Besterman, *Mrs. Annie Besant*, p.223.)

Education. Most influential were his basic psychological categories – the libido and the unconscious – rather than his therapeutic methods or his philosophical speculations. But even
these categories were accepted in diluted form. For example,
it was Jung's, rather than Freud's, interpretations of the libido
and the unconscious that won general approval, mainly because they could be more easily assimilated to the other beliefs
of the progressive educators. Jung in particular can be regarded as a bridge between the new psychology and the new
Theology as represented by the Theosophists, humanists, and
the various other non-sectarian advocates of a new religion of
international brotherhood. The Jungian libido, far from being
the agglomeration of instincts and appetites described by
Freud, was more akin to the Theosophist Soul ever struggling
towards higher things; his 'cosmic' or 'collective' unconscious,
the original source of the individual libido, could easily be
transposed into theological language as God or the First Cause.
Jung in short appealed to those educators who wanted to retain
a place for the religious impulse in the new education and who
disliked what they considered to be Freud's morbid preoccupation with sex.

Mrs Ensor herself is a characteristic apostle of the New
Psychology in this form. In 1915 she had conceived the idea of
'forming within the Theosophical Society a group of progressive teachers who would take as the basis of their work faith
in the spiritual powers latent in every child, powers which if
released could create a new world where all might find true
happiness.'* 'Man's supreme achievement,' she editorialized,
somewhat obscurely, in the *New Era,* 'is to bring to blossom
the flower of life itself.'

The central theory of the New Education, then, expressed in
Jungian language, went something like this. Every child was
possessed of a libido or life-force thrusting towards achievement and perfectibility. However, this thrust was deflected
from its true aim by pressures exerted by the unconscious. The
unconscious was the home of that portion of the libido whose
creative expression had been frustrated and repressed by

*Boyd, op. cit., p. 67.

faulty parental and educational methods. Thwarted in its creative and productive impulses, it expressed itself in neurosis, which might take the form of hatred, cruelty and sadism, and the manifestation of which was destruction and war. 'Making the unconscious conscious' – the catchword of the New Education – consisted in removing the repressive forces of the old education, and instead channelling or guiding the libido, gently and with love, understanding and patience, into its authentic modes of expression, thus enabling man for the first time in his history to realize his full potentialities. 'For the satisfactory achievement of our life task,' wrote a contributor to the *New Era,* 'we need to have all our libido in current circulation as it were, and not tied up in unprofitable investments.' Matthew Arnold had expressed much the same sentiment sixty years before:

> Yet the will is free:
> Strong is the Soul, and wise, and beautiful:
> The seeds of godlike power are in us still:
> Gods are we, Bards, Saints, Heroes, if we will.

J. A. M. Alcock, in a lecture to the Education Group of the Oxford Labour Club in 1921, provided a concrete example of the way in which the natural flow of the 'libido' can be blocked by faulty educational techniques:

If you shut a small boy in a room for a given period of time and tell him he must learn arithmetic, and if, during that time his libido is actually in the garden outside, then you are setting up a disassociation in that boy. That means that you are causing him so much psychic irritation that he will weave an authority complex round you. And that may determine a repression and non-development of his mathematical powers, which are an integral part of his intellectual function. ... If, on the other hand, you give him his fling in the garden, and then suggest mathematics, he will probably come to it with his full libido. It will be seen that what I am suggesting is ... a combination of business and pleasure.

This typified the English 'common-sense' approach. Mrs Ensor would no doubt have regarded this as unduly prosaic. 'The problem,' she declared, in a strange mixture of Theosophical and Jungian language, is to maintain a rhythmic harmony between the various channels of expression, so that there is an uninterrupted flow of life through them, thus allowing the individual to tap increasingly the Source, the Collective Unconscious, the Cosmic Life Force. Just as in the Physical body any kind of blockage or disease will inhibit the flow of vitality, so mental and emotional tangles will prevent the harmonious flowing of the life from the All into the individual.

She returned from the second international conference of the New Education Fellowship in Montreux (1922) greatly heartened. The distinguishing mark of the New Education, she observed, is 'the supremacy of spirit over matter, the idea of an *inner* self, which the child can learn, with the help of stimuli which we provide, to express *outwardly,* rather than of an empty vehicle into which we have to instil knowledge....' What was this Inner Self? Dr Adolph Ferrière, by now the editor of the French section of the *New Era*, had defined it 'as the angel within us, trying to overcome our instincts'. Inspired by an address from Dr Jung, Mrs Ensor concluded

Let us develop, as a fellowship, the Collective Unconscious of our group, so that any member, however remote in space from other members, can at any moment become linked to the collective unconscious of the Fellowship . . . and thus gain the inspiration to go on however lonely the road. . . .

The Locarno Conference of the New Education Fellowship in 1927 discussed the 'True Meaning of Freedom in Education'.

People met and talked in groups on street corners or in hotel lobbies; exhibits of special work hung on the walls; the Bakule Czech Choir showed what genius can do in bringing out childhood; there was an evening of national dances; the Germans and others sang their folk songs; ... the great Indian botanist, Bose, claimed a unity of life through his discoveries that trees and plants have nervous organizations quite like ours. Yes, all this makes for international sympathy and goodwill. . . .

Dr Elizabeth Rotten of Germany defined True Freedom as 'the raising to the highest pinnacle of active personality'. Professor Bovet talked about different types of freedom – artistic freedom, curricular freedom, freedom in self government, and thought that real freedom consisted in the extension of these particular freedoms to life itself. Mrs Ensor defined freedom, with characteristic vagueness, as the Law of Relativity 'applied to the Soul'. 'The really *free* man,' she summed up, 'is he who understands his own inner being and through whom the life forces flow, unchecked by inhibitions and repressions: it is he, too, who has perfect physical, mental and emotional control.'

It may well be asked: how did all this differ from the aims of Dr Reddie, whose own school by this time was reduced to barely half a dozen pupils? He too realized that the way to develop 'power' in his pupils was to engage their affections and curiosity on behalf of the educational process and then guide them into the right channels. He would surely have endorsed Mrs Ensor's belief in the 'supremacy of spirit over matter', that 'beauty is a powerful agent of suggestion ... perhaps the supreme evocation of the spirit', and her demand that classroom be filled with beautiful objects. If his methods were not altogether gentle, that sprang more from his authoritarian personality than from a conscious pedagogic principle. The Abbotsholme experiment, in its Bedales form, was able to assimilate Theosophy and the New Psychology without any break in continuity.

One distinguishing mark of the 'new wave' was a much greater interest in the earlier years of childhood. Reddie had been concerned solely with adolescents: the New Education wanted to lay its hands on children from the earliest age, so that money would not later be wasted 'rectifying the damage which had already been done'. Otherwise the changes were mainly changes in emphasis – a greater respect for the child's individuality; and improvements in technique: for in the 1920s the educational market was flooded with new techniques, each, like a patent medicine, proudly bearing the name of its inventor, and each gobbled up by the gullible practitioners of the new education.

Sir John Adams defined the new educational tendency as 'paidocentricism' or 'child-centred' education. Its *rationale* was a belief in the self-educating qualities of the child. 'The

fundamental basis of the New Education,' wrote the inde-
fatigable Mrs Ensor, 'is the realization that all powers and
capacities lie within the child, and that, therefore, all education
must be auto-education. The function of the educator lies
simply in the provision of external stimuli needed to start the
process of auto-education along the avenues by which consciousness contacts environment.'

The most influential advocate of this view was the American John Dewey. He believed that a child learnt through experience. The task of the educator was simply to provide
educational experiences. Dewey never made clear what the
difference was between an educational and a non-educational
experience, but basically the new educators accepted that an
educational experience was something that awakened and
developed the latent 'powers' in a child. Essentially, the pur-
veyors of the new educational techniques offered 'educational
experiences' in one form or another.

One of the first in the field was Dr Maria Montessori. Working with slum children in Rome, aged three or thereabouts, in
the first decade of this century, she was amazed to discover
that 'the normal characteristics of childhood' had hitherto
been concealed under a mask of 'deviations'. Her children
showed 'quite spontaneously' amazing mental concentration,
a love of order and repetition, a preference for work over
play, and a desire for silence. 'It was as if a higher form of
personality had been liberated,' her biographer remarked. The
Dottoressa immediately realized the immense educational
significance of her discoveries. For if these 'spontaneous' effu-
sions of the young child's spirit could be harnessed to learning, then not only could education begin much earlier than
had hitherto been realized, but it could also be conducted in
complete freedom, the child's own 'inner urge' providing the
incentive for achievement. To this end she devised 'didactic
apparatus', such as cylinders, rods, blocks, bells and so on,
whose object was to develop the child's motor and sensory
powers; apparatus 'which corresponds so directly and profoundly to the child's needs that he is attracted to work with it
spontaneously for long periods of time'. 'Montessori free-

dom,' declared Father Drinkwater somewhat ominously, 'is unlimited freedom to do right.' Signora Maccheroni arrived in England to spread the Montessori gospel in 1920, meeting strong opposition from the Froebelians, who had already established something of a 'progressive' monopoly in infant education with their 'kindergartens', dating back to the 1870s.

Maria Montessori had worked exclusively with very young children, but there was no shortage of new techniques to foster the intellectual growth of older children, all based to some degree on the pupils' interests or insights into the problem of learning which had largely escaped the traditional educator. Thus the Dalton Plan, developed by Miss Helen Parkhurst, replaced class instruction by the individual work consignment, spread over a fortnight or a month, which left the child free to organize the distribution of his time between the various subjects as he wished. The Winnetka Technique, devised by the American, Carleton Washburne, was an early anticipation of the Teaching Machine. The pupil's curriculum was divided up into units of achievement or steps which each had to be carefully mastered before proceeding to the next; and he was provided with self-correcting and self-instructing materials which largely dispensed with the need for classroom teaching. Finally the Project Method, based on the ideas of Dewey, attempted to utilize the child's interest in acting, construction, story-telling and so on, for the purpose of recreating cooperatively historical stages in the development of civilization.

Other techniques were designed not so much to foster intellectual understanding (however defined) but to free the imagination and originality of the child through creative and artistic activity. There was Norman MacNunn's education through drama, Professor Cizek's education through art, Bakule's education through music, Dalcroze's education through eurhythmics (a training in bodily grace and harmony through dance), and many others. No self-respecting progressive school in the 1920s could hold its head high unless it was in a position to offer prospective parents a full range of such techniques to stimulate their children's development, both intellectual and creative.

What were the progressives after? The word 'technique' provides part of the answer. The progressives were appalled by the inefficiency of traditional methods even in relation to their stated aims. The old educators wanted the child to learn, yet produced resentment against learning. They tried to instil Christian morality, yet all too often produced only dirty minds and twisted personalities. Whole areas of human potential were barely touched at all: the 'ordinary' boy was virtually ignored. The reason for these failures was not merely ignorance but a belief in original-sin theories of human nature, and hence a failure to appreciate the extent to which the child was potentially an active agent of his own education. The progressives proposed to replace coercive and 'rote-learning' techniques with those that stimulated and made use of dormant interests and potentialities. Stated in this way the progressive revolution becomes largely a revolution in technique and understanding, providing more effective methods for achieving whatever it was that the educator wanted to achieve. It was in this form, perhaps, that progressive ideas had their greatest impact on traditional education. The English progressive schools were to some extent in this period experimental laboratories, testing out new techniques of education which could then be transplanted, in a suitably modified form, to the state system.

But it would be wrong to regard the English progressive schools primarily as centres of applied educational psychology, places for testing out new techniques. Although this aspect of their work was most useful to state education, it was not central to their own interests. Reddie and Badley had both set out to reform the public-school system, and many of their preoccupations and innovations are only significant against a background of public-school boarding education. Coeducation, for instance, was only 'progressive' because it was boarding: in Scotland it had been the day-school practice for years. It stemmed from the belief that it was 'unnatural' to segregate boys and girls in adolescence. Similarly, the onslaught against games, the transformation of the chapel and prefect system, the dethroning of classroom work – all these

made most sense in a total environment, where the school controlled the whole life of the child. In its reorganization of
boarding life, the progressive school movement was a very
upper-class affair, with a limited relevance to the problem of
mass education.

But experimenting with new techniques and reorganizing
boarding education did not exhaust the aims of the movement.
The progressives, as we have seen, aimed at creating a new
type of human being. Many people came into the movement
after 1918 with the definite aim of eliminating the causes of
war through education. Geoffrey Crump, a public-schoolmaster
who went to Bedales in 1919, wrote

. . . the four years' slaughter of those boys whom we had helped to send
to their death convinced me of two things: first, that the main idea that
lay behind what we tried to teach them was irrational, and secondly,
that it was futile. The causes of the War were the direct result of the
ideas that had been instilled into the youth of every European country
for generations. . . . All the conventions that I had accepted and passed
on without question – religious, moral, patriotic, social, I could no
longer accept, or pass on, without question. . . . It was therefore to the
'New Schools' that I turned. . . .

War was not only produced by the teaching of biased history
and the militaristic training of the O.T.C., but also, more
fundamentally, by methods of upbringing which cramped the
personality, producing strains and dissatisfactions, out of
which grew cruelty, envy and hatred. Thus the New Schools
deliberately tried to create an 'international' personality, and
this, in terms of aims, marked their biggest breach with the
public-school tradition.

Finally, the New Schools were incurably romantic. Rousseau, Ruskin, Carpenter and Whitman flowed strongly
through their veins. They emphasized creativity and fulfilment
at the expense of intellectual discipline, an emphasis heightened by the very 'romantic' interpretation they gave to the
New Psychology. To them, as to Blake and Rousseau, the child
was the source of all good, the world, of all evil. They wanted
to liberate the child from society's fetters, so that he might

realize his God-like potential; such liberation would at the same time secure the world from war, which thrived on dissatisfaction and frustration. This romanticism of the individual was inextricably bound up with anti-industrial and anti-technocratic values. Industrialization was seen as imposing an 'unnatural' life on modern man, crippling his capacity for self-fulfilment by tying his development to the needs of an industrial machine that denied creative work and destroyed creative leisure. The progressive school movement in England can perhaps best be understood as an application of Romanticism to education, as an attempt to apply in the school a Romantic view of man and the universe. Certainly it was this side that appealed most strongly to the progressive school-master.

The inconsistencies in the progressive credo boggle the imagination, but here it is only necessary to highlight one: the discrepancy between the belief in 'self-expression' and the definite desire to produce a certain social type. The progressives seem to have believed that 'non-interference' would result in an 'international' personality. But there was really no warrant for such an assumption. In making it they fell into the very common trap of believing to be true what they wanted to be true.

By 1922 the *New Era* was able to list twenty-three New Schools in England and the number steadily grew, though some of the foundations proved ephemeral. Frensham Heights was opened by Mrs Ensor in 1926 as a 'demonstration school' for the New Education Fellowship. The boys and girls were placed in 'houses' called Perseverance, Courtesy and Co-operation. Dartington Hall was also started in 1926 as 'a single branch of a widely planned scheme of rural development in a thousand acre estate, which includes research work in farming, poultry-keeping, forestry, fruit-growing, textiles and nursery gardening.'* Under its headmaster, William Curry, it developed along very 'free' lines. St Christopher's Letchworth, a Theosophical school founded in 1918, advertised 'Free Development and Character Building upon Individual Lines: Unsectarian religious teaching, inculcating tolerance and sympathy in reli-

*L. B. Pekin, *Progressive Schools* (1934), p. 37.

gious matters; open-air work, arts and crafts study; weaving; Dalcroze eurhythmics, etc.' Wychwood Girls School, in an attempt to get the best of both worlds, offered an education 'self-governing and progressive, but with old-fashioned ideals of courtesy and refinement'. In 1927 Bertrand Russell and his third wife, Dora, started Beacon's Hill, near Bedales, whose object was to produce children 'inspired by love and guided by knowledge'.

The characteristic pattern of the post-war progressive school can be clearly discerned. On the intellectual side it offered Montessori departments, Dalton Plans, Project Methods and so on, all designed to make learning more 'interesting' and thus remove the need for rewards and punishments in the classroom. The imagination of the pupils was fostered by all manner of 'creative' activities – arts and crafts, eurhythmics, drama, poetry and music. The environment was rendered beautiful with reproductions of the Masters, and Bach was played at morning assembly. The discipline was permissive. Corporal punishment was abolished and 'understanding' the rule. Children called the staff by their Christian names and constituted themselves as Parliaments, Advisory Councils and Committees to run that portion of their own lives which the staff allowed them. 'Natural' living was encouraged by rural settings, vegetarianism, coeducation, shorts and sandals, and nude bathing. International cooperation was produced by non-sectarian history and non-sectarian religion. The children tended to be forthright in language and careless of appearance. 'Well, goodbye, you bloody old bore,' a little girl at a well-known school was reported to have said to an earnest and well-meaning visiting spinster. 'Problem' children, of whom the 'freer' new schools always had a fair proportion, swore at visitors, blew smoke in their faces, and picked their pockets, to which the visitors reacted with either masochistic admiration, or exaggerated horror. Rumours were rife of godless orgies. When a pastor visited Beacon's Hill, a naked teenage girl was supposed to have answered the door. 'My God,' gasped the astonished cleric. 'There is no God,' she replied, slamming the door in his face.

In fact, despite their fads and eccentricities, most schools were high-minded and rather serious places. Coeducation was supposed to lessen rather than increase sexual desire: Bedales, for example, prided itself on having substituted comradeship for sex, and pointed to the happy, brother and sister, relationship between the boys and girls.

Sidney Unwin, who had been a pupil at Abbotsholme and became a housemaster at Bedales, had no time for free discipline methods:

He set for himself [recalls an Old Bedalian] a terrifyingly high standard of conduct and he expected everyone else to live up to it – woe betide any boy who fell short of it! By example as well as by precept he taught us to be clean, tidy, punctual, hardy, civil and considerate. He had an uncanny way of always being in the path of any who strayed frcm the straight way: his unerring eye missed nothing. . . . The nightly inspection in the dormitories of hands, ears and feet . . . was a rigorous test of careful washing in icy water. On one occasion I remember his producing a lens to determine whether an offending smudge on some boy's toe was dirt or a natural skin discoloration.

This was a side of progressive education that popular comment often ignored; but it was characteristic of a tradition that stretched from Reddie to Kurt Hahn; and was, indeed, the natural expression of that moralism through which the progressives hoped to reform man and, by doing so, change society.

*

Where did Neill stand in relation to the mainstream of progressive development? After leaving King Alfred School, he became co-editor of the *New Era* in July 1920. His editorials struck a new note – 'At our crank schools we find too many ideals' – which provided a welcome contrast to Mrs Ensor's earnest and high-minded prose. It soon became evident that a major quarrel was brewing.

From the outset Neill found Mrs Ensor's emphasis on the Soul distasteful. 'The essential aim of all education,' declared the constitution of the New Education Fellowship, 'is to prepare the child to seek and realize in his own life the supremacy of the spirit.' To Neill this meant repressing the body, giving the child ideals. Certainly those earnest and high-minded spinsters who thronged the world of progressive education had little time for the body. Their characteristic assumption seemed to be that children have a higher and lower nature, the former to be developed by the Montessori apparatus and by the Dalton Plan; the latter to be repressed by vegetarianism and more or less subtly by moral exhortation. Neill was against moral exhortation in any form. 'The bishops and the sandalled crank schoolmaster,' he wrote, 'both agree that the child must be led to the Light. It does not matter whether the Light is the Light of the Cross or the Light of Post-Impressionism; the purpose is the same – to uplift.' For Neill 'being on the side of the child' did not mean being on the side of the God-like adult to be, but on the side of the actual child. He was not interested in promoting good causes through education. 'To teach pacifism is almost as dangerous to children as to teach militarism . . . they want to mould the character.'

In 1921 he attended the inaugural conference of the New Education Fellowship at Calais, where he gave a talk on Freud, and from there went on to stay with friends in Hellerau, near Dresden. In the suburb was a large building designed in 1912 as a Dalcroze school. It was divided into two: Christine Bauer, the wife of the school's architect, ran a small class in eurhythmics, while the rest of the building was given over to a school for local children, run on 'advanced' lines. Neill and Christine Bauer decided to start an international section in conjunction with the other two schools, Neill teaching the German pupils English, while his children used the others' facilities. He had £400 to invest in the project – a large sum in a country crippled by inflation. Friction soon developed between the German and the embryonic international section:

> We differed in fundamentals. The Neue Schule was run by idealists, most of them belonging to the Jugend movement in Germany. They disapproved of tobacco, alcohol, fox-trots, cinemas; they wore Wandervogel clothes. We on the other hand had other ideals; we were ordinary folk who drank beer and smoked and danced fox-trots. Our intention was to live our own lives while we allowed children to live their own lives. We intended that children would form their own ideals.

The Wandervogel or 'Wandering Birds' ('I love to go a-wandering') was a movement founded in 1904 by students and scholars in opposition to the growth of industrialization. 'They camped by night in the forests, read poems and legends around their fires, gathered and sang their own folk-songs, learned the country dances, made friendly contact with the peasants.'* 'Whether it rains or shines,' wrote the enthusiastic Mrs Ensor, 'whether one travels afoot, by train or boat, everywhere in Germany one meets school classes, knap-sacks on their backs, singing as they wander over bridges, up through the forests, across market squares, along rivers and canals. . . .' 'They drink not, neither do they smoke,' was Neill's terser comment. To him they were idealists who hated the flesh; suppressers of their own unconscious desires who 'sing babyish songs and dance childish dances as solemnly as if they were savages worshipping an unknown god'.

It was [Neill recalled] a stirring adventure. We had pupils from every country in Europe except Spain. We took over the German division and then the rows began. The German teachers were all for character moulding. Teachers would not smoke or drink or go to the cinema because they had to be examples for their pupils to follow. I shared a hostel with the German leader. I had the top storey. Of an evening we would all be dancing to a gramophone upstairs, while downstairs the German was reading Goethe or Nietzsche to his flock. One by one they crept upstairs to dance and naturally he was indignant.

The German New School Movement had indeed developed very much along Reddie's Higher Life lines, with a strong additional dose of idealist philosophy. Paul Geheeb had broken with Lietz in 1906 to found a coeducational school, Wickersdorf, in Thuringia. (He left in 1909 to start the Odenwald Schule near Frankfurt.) 'Wickersdorf,' wrote Pekin, 'stood for a definite way of life and a definite artistic culture, based chiefly on the music of Bach, Beethoven and Anton Bruckner, and on the philosophy and literary *Geist* of Goethe and Carl Spitteler.' The German New Schools, in short, represented the extreme development of Mrs Ensor's spiritualist

*Boyd, op. cit., p. 31.

philosophy, and provided the sharpest possible contrast with Neill's views.

Revolution broke out in Dresden in 1923 and Neill removed the international section of the school, which numbered thirteen boys and girls, to Sonntanberg, an old monastery converted into a youth hostel, situated on top of a mountain in the Austrian Tyrol. The children spent a glorious six months skiing, but the Austrian peasants Neill wrote 'were the most hateful people I had met'. The idyll came to an end when an Austrian bank failure robbed him of his savings. He returned to England and started up again in Lyme Regis, where 'we miss the snow, the sun, the interplay of nationality, the music, the art, of central Europe.' His three years abroad had given him a taste for music and an international outlook. His experience of the Wandervogel had confirmed his suspicions of all Higher Life education. Psycho-analysis in Vienna from Wilhelm Stekel, an erstwhile Freudian, had made him further conscious of himself and his mission.

His break with the *New Era* had come early in 1923. The occasion was an editorial by Mrs Ensor, championing, with her usual enthusiasm, a new 'method' designed by the Frenchman, Monsieur Coué. Coué's panacea was auto-suggestion: by the adoption of certain techniques an individual could 'will himself' to follow or avoid certain courses of action. His theory puts one irresistibly in mind of that ingenious invention designed to save Victorian youths from impure thoughts – the pocket card. One such youth wrote ecstatically to its inventor, Dr Dio Lewis:

I do not know in what terms to express my joy that all this is past. I found it difficult at first to control my imagination but I soon fixed the thought of danger so that, when a lascivious fancy appeared, it startled me and immediately I took from my pocket the Card you so warmly advised, on which I had written ten words, each suggestive of some subject in which I was interested. Looking over this card, I had no difficulty in changing my thoughts. This policy, with vigorous exercise and plain food, has given me complete victory.*

*Quoted in Leslie Brewer, *The Good News*, p. 23.

Neill declared auto-suggestion to be the 'negation of the new dynamic psychology', for it took no account of causes. In reality, every suggestion was conditioned by the unconscious. Through auto-suggestion the 'conscious mind is either trying to cheat the unconscious, or the unconscious is acquiescing in the suggestion, and using it for its own purposes'. The whole point of psycho-analysis was to rid the patient of his elaborate system of self-suggestion and rationalization and 'tell him the truth about himself'. Coué, Neill added characteristically, must be wrong, because he was so popular. More generally, he attacked the *New Era*'s championing of suggestion in any form:

I spend much of my time here, in Germany, fighting the school reformers on this very point. They will form the child's character; they will so live their lives as to be examples to their children. They read Goethe to a tableful of hungry children whose interest is entirely given to food. They surround the child with all the noble influences. It is all suggestion, and it is not one whit better than the suggestion of the old Puritans who told the child he was born in original sin. I assert that every suggestionist believes in original sin; he tries to make the child better . . . as if God didn't know his job.

Beatrice Ensor defended the 'orthodox' *New Era* line. Every child had 'impulses towards perfection'. The educator's task was to develop these impulses. He could not escape from suggestion. 'Mr Neill, himself, is a constant suggestion to the children around him.' Personality is a suggestion 'and therefore the teacher is *bound* to influence his pupils.' The whole point was whether the influence is to be unconscious through personality or whether the teacher coerces his pupils into adopting a special point of view. 'If there is no coercion individuality is strong enough in the free child to assert itself. . . .'

This debate might seem to be of little more than academic interest today, but in reality Neill had put his finger on a point to which the new educators were extraordinarily blind: the totalitarian potentialities of the new methods. The old education was wrong because it was ineffective: there was all the difference in the world, according to Mrs Ensor, between 'sug-

gestion presented in such a form *that it is rejected*' (italics
mine) and 'suggestion, presented through environment, atmosphere, an attractive personality or apparatus designed to fit
the needs of the developing psyche, which is more easily accepted by the subconscious and becomes auto-suggestion, in-
volving expansion of consciousness'.

The exciting and dangerous enthusiasm provoked by this
new insight into the unconscious is well expressed in the following piece contributed by a teacher to the *New Era,* with its
hopeful anticipations of Brave New World and Big Brother.

Our 'calling' will become a scientific profession, with recognized
experts and specialists within our own ranks. Psychological 'suggestion'
will be deliberately employed in training the imagination and character.
The writer employs it regularly with splendid results. . . . A psychological history sheet of every scholar will accompany him throughout
his whole school career . . . intelligent employers will demand such
sheets. He will leave school, not according to chronological age, but
according to fitness to leave. He will have more individual freedom and
choice (under guidance) than at present. . . .

After reading this passage it may be possible to feel more
charitable to the old whacking schoolmaster, precisely because
his methods *were* crude and ineffective.

In his criticisms of the Higher Life schools and in his debates with Mrs Ensor we see Neill adopting an out-and-out
libertarian position. The instincts of the child are good, he
declares, echoing Homer Lane. They must not be moulded,
however subtly and understandingly. But this only represents
one side of his thinking: he is neither intellectually nor emotionally ready for such a sweeping affirmation. Intellectually
he was deeply influenced by the pessimistic turn in Freud's
thought after the First World War. Freud found it increasingly difficult to assimilate the war's destructiveness and irrationality into his previous account of the personality. Hitherto
he had ascribed neurosis to a conflict between instinctual desires and social suppression. After 1920 he postulated an innate urge to self-destruction which he called the death instinct.
It was this death instinct that caused man to murder his own
flesh, and, as a compensation to murder the flesh of others

(morally and, in war, physically), in the service of Higher Things.

Emotionally, Neill was not yet prepared to face the implications of a complete affirmation of the child's instincts – implications for sex education, or for the relationship between the school and society. The purpose of sex education, he declared, was sublimation; masturbation was the result of an insufficiently interesting environment.

'The teachings of moralists,' he declared in his book *A Dominie in Doubt*, 'are not enough to account for the fear and hate of sex, for instance.' A child, even if reared 'miraculously ... by electricity on a desert island ... would later enter human society with a masochistic, death-seeking psychology.' In other words, the child was born to fear, shame and guilt. What then could education do?

Neill himself did not suggest any answer. But the difficulty solved itself as more and more of his time came to be spent with 'problem' (maladjusted, neurotic and delinquent) children. Although later Neill insisted that he was forced to work with such children, there seems little doubt that part of him at any rate welcomed the opportunity. He was fascinated by psychology and in 1926 declared that he was no longer an educator but a child psychologist – a description of himself that is retained in the latest edition of *Who's Who*. Moreover, work with difficult children was a kind of escape from unresolved intellectual and emotional dilemmas. It was a way of avoiding a full commitment to an out-and-out libertarian position, since such children were almost by definition 'special cases'. For them complete 'release' could be justified on therapeutic grounds, on the model of Homer Lane. 'A man,' Neill declared, 'speaks from his complexes. I am probably interested in criminality because I am unconsciously a criminal.' It would be more accurate to say that he was interested in 'problem' children because of his *consciousness* of his own problems.

The books that he wrote in the 1920s are all 'problem'-orientated. They dealt with special cases. The educator and the parent could ignore most of the radical implications for 'normal' children. In fact the educators tended to ignore the books altogether. Educational psychology had become immersed in the problems of intelligence testing; while academic psychology was busy experimenting with rats and other animals. Freudians accused Neill of misapplying the Master's ideas and methods; while Jungians disliked his emphasis on the genitals (even of problem children). On the other hand, laymen and young teachers read him with great enjoyment; and his books had a wide sale in Scandinavia and Japan (always on the look-out for new ideas). His greatest direct influence has been in the treatment of maladjusted children. David Wills, Otto Shaw, Lucy Francis and others have run special schools largely inspired by his ideas. On the other hand, he has inspired few 'progressive' schools; the main movement regards him as stimulating, but mad. The exceptions are Kilquhanity House, Scotland, started in 1940 by a disciple, John Aitkenhead, and Burgess Hill, London, which acquired, for a few years before its collapse, a headmaster with definite Neillite tendencies – and a notorious reputation.

In 1927 he moved his school – Summerhill – from Lyme Regis to Leiston, Suffolk, its present site. For £3,500 he acquired 'an ugly but not depressing red-brick nineteenth-century house tucked away behind Leiston station'. It stood in the middle of several acres of derelict ground, gradually cleared over the years to make room for a playing-field, tennis court, railway carriages and other odd buildings. He brought with him to Leiston two dozen problem children – and also a wife.

She was Ada Lillian Neustatter, a divorcee some years older than him. He had first met her in 1918 at King Alfred School, where her son was a pupil. At that time she was married to Otto Neustatter, a German civil servant (the Dr Otto of *A Dominie Abroad*), and it was as his guest that Neill stayed in Dresden. She was an Australian who shared Neill's enthusiasm for educational reform, though not apparently for self-government; and it is clear, from Neill's moving memoir written after her death in 1944, that she provided the 'practical' side of the partnership. To Summerhillians she was known as Mrs

Lins. The marriage, though 'ideal', was childless; it was his second marriage, to Ena Wood, the present Mrs Neill, that finally made him a father at the age of sixty.*

*He describes the upbringing of his daughter, Zoe, in his book, *The Free Child* (1953).

13 · Problem Children

From 1923 onwards Neill's experience, as he records, was mainly with 'difficult' children. He had to deal with incendiaries, thieves, liars, bedwetters and other kinds of neurotics and delinquents. He came to the conclusion that childhood neurosis was entirely due to the attempt to implant morality. 'I believe that it is moral instruction that makes the child bad. I find that when I smash the moral instruction a bad boy has received he automatically becomes a good boy.' Moral instruction in its positive sense – moral exhortation – consisted in giving the child ideals – he must be good, work hard, keep clean, etc., etc. These ideals generally ran contrary to some childish interest or habit. Consequently, exhortation was reinforced by prohibition, designed to make a child fearful or guilty of these interests or habits by the use of such expressions as 'tut-tut', or such words as 'dirty' and 'naughty', backed up with threats of punishment – in this life or the next – or by emotional bribery ('Mummy will not love you if you do this'). Its characteristic and most harmful application was in the sphere of sex, though it could be employed to inhibit any behaviour of which the adult disapproved. The result of moral instruction was to create a conflict between instinct and ideal (or in Neill's words 'between inherited right and acquired wrong'); more particularly, to focus a child's interest on a forbidden activity, thus accentuating the psychic conflict between his heightened interest and the guilt engendered by its indulgence. The tension produced by this conflict might express itself in specific neurotic or anti-social behaviour, or simply as a general state of nervousness, anxiety, unhappiness.

Elsewhere Neill speaks of childhood neurosis as the consequence of a lack of love or affection. Some of his case-histories – such as the boy who smashed furniture because he thought his sister was getting too much of his mother's love – would

seem to be examples of lack of affection rather than of moral instruction. However, since he defines love in such a way as to
exclude moral instruction, the question of which is the prime
cause of neurosis becomes irrelevant. For Neill love essentially
signifies 'approval': one cannot love a child unless one ap-
proves of his instincts, which means that one refrains from
giving him a 'conscience' about them by moral instruction.
Moral instruction he sees as the adult's self-hate or self-dis-
approval projected on to the child. The moralizing adult does,
in a sense, love the child, but that love has got so mixed up
with his own problems that its expression is twisted and thwarted. When dealing with children whose lives have been starved
of approval, it was essential to be wholly 'on their side'; to
avoid any temptation to interfere with their pursuits or direct
them to more 'desirable' ends; the assumption being that such
attempts would certainly lead to an identification with previous 'disapproving' or 'moralizing' adults, thus removing
the possibility of a cure.

This was strikingly brought home to him in Hellerau, when
he failed to cure a teenage girl's 'authority complex'. As she
left the school after six months' vandalism, he said to her,
'Well, I didn't help you much, did I?' 'Do you know why?'
she said with a dry smile. 'The first day I came to your school,
I was making a box and you said I was using too many nails.
From that moment onwards, I knew that you were just like
every schoolmaster in the world – a boss. From that moment,
you could not possibly help me.' 'You are right,' said Neill.
'Good-bye.'

Neill's 'cure' as expounded in the *Problem* books was to
give full encouragement to the particular neurotic symptom
through which the child currently sought release; to give him
full opportunities for 'creative' sublimations; to undertake,
where necessary, direct analysis in order to uncover the roots
of the neurosis (he called them 'private lessons'); and more
generally, to provide a loving, approving and permissive atmosphere, which would enable the child to 'unwind', relax, be
himself.

'The whole idea of my school,' wrote Neill in *The Problem*

Child, 'is release; is the living out of an interest.' Where the neurotic symptom was expressed in anti-social behaviour this meant encouraging it, however destructive it might be, just as Homer Lane had encouraged his delinquents to smash crockery and furniture. 'If I were painting a door,' Neill wrote, 'and Robert came along and threw mud on my fresh paint I should swear at him heartily, because he is one of us and what I say to him does not matter. But suppose Robert had just come from a hateful school and his mud-slinging was an attempt to get his own back against authority. I should join in his mud-slinging because his salvation is more important than a door.'

The most striking illustration of this approach is seen in Neill's reaction to stealing. Compulsive stealing he always regarded as a symbolic stealing of love, the staking out of a claim for love, based on, and justified by, the expectation that the real thing would be denied. Indeed the expectation is that the act of theft will meet with parental disapproval (hate) which in turn provided the motive for the subsequent act. The problem was to break the vicious cycle of need and adverse expectation. Neill reasoned that if approval (love) were substituted for disapproval (hate) as the adult reaction to the act of theft the motive for stealing would disappear. Hence he developed the psychological trick of rewarding the act of theft, the reward symbolizing approval. It shattered the child's picture of reality which justified his stealing, and thus opened the way to a cure.

When I give a boy money for stealing my tobacco I am aiming at his unconscious feeling, not his conscious thought. He may think I am a fool, but what he thinks does not matter much; it's what he feels that matters, and he feels that I am his friend, his approver. . . . Sooner or later the stealing ceases, for the love that was symbolically stolen in the form of money or goods is now given freely and therefore need not be stolen.

People misunderstood the therapeutic purpose of these methods and thought that the 'do-as-you-like' schools encouraged the children to all kinds of immorality and licence – a belief reinforced by the reporting of the sensational press.

But Neill always made a clear distinction between freedom and licence. Licence might be necessary for a cure; destruction (of the complex) must precede construction. But for ordinary children liberty must be bounded by the rights of others – a point which enthusiastically-minded 'progressive' parents who watch with doting admiration their children hammer nails into their grand piano have been slow to grasp.

The view that children, when freed from the civilizing influences of adults, revert to barbarism has been powerfully expressed in William Golding's novel *Lord of the Flies*. It might seem that Summerhill bears out Golding's thesis. As Neill himself admits, children who come there from disaplined schools become almost savage in their behaviour, confirming it would seem the verdict of the Freudian Ernest Jones that without the reforming influence of education the individual would remain 'a selfish, jealous, impulsive, aggressive, dirty, immodest, cruel, egocentric and conceited animal, inconsiderate of the needs of others....' Neill strongly challenges this interpretation. He does not dispute that boys freed from 'barrack' schools would behave in much the way Golding describes. But whereas Golding believes that this is the behaviour of children in their 'natural' state, Neill sees it as an extreme reaction to imposed discipline: Golding's boys are expressing the hate, created and bottled-up within them, by moralizing and hating parents and schoolmasters. Neill's 'cure' consisted in releasing that hate, by tolerating and supporting extremes of anti-social behaviour in the short-term, and then channelling the energy which had supported it into social paths. Golding's children are left only with their 'starved emotions' and 'perverted imaginations' to work out their own salvations. 'To me,' writes Neill, 'the book is proof that our way of training children is wrong and dangerous. His sick island is, in miniature, the sick island we call Great Britain.'

Summerhill (at least in its day of prosperity) has provided the full range of 'Arts and Crafts' and other sublimations one speciality was weekly plays written and acted by the children themselves. The fact that in his books Neill has not stressed these sublimations overmuch stems from his suspicion that many ostensibly progressive people encourage them as alternatives to real freedom, like the enlightened sex instructors who tell boys that it is much better to play games than to masturbate. This may well be true: the point that Neill makes is that unless the boy has been encouraged to 'live out' his interest in masturbation without guilt or reproach, the sublimation will not work: the symptom will merely be displaced.

The Private Lesson (P.L.) was a miniature psycho-analysis intended to 'hasten the child's adaptation to freedom'. It was generally used only with difficult children; but often younger children would come in spontaneously if something was worrying them. The following example is characteristic:

A girl of six comes into his room and says, 'I want a P. L.'

'Righto,' I say.

She sits down in an easy chair.

'What Is a P.L.?' she asks,

'It isn't anything to eat,' I say, 'but somewhere in this pocket I have a caramel. Ah, here it is.' And I give her the sweet.

'Why do you want a P.L.?' I ask.

'Evelyn had one, and I want one too.'

'Good. You begin it. What do you want to talk about?'

'I've got a dolly. (Pause.) Where did you get that thing on the mantelpiece?' (She obviously does not want to wait for an answer.)

'Who was in this house before you came?'

Her questions point to a desire to know some vital truth, and I have a good suspicion that it is the truth about birth.

'Where do babies come from?' I ask suddenly.

Margaret gets up and marches to the door.

'I hate P.L.s' she says, and departs. But a few days later, she asks for another P.L. – and so we progress.

Neill made it clear that he gave P.L.s only for emotional release, not to 'adjust' the child to learning arithmetic or history. This point is fundamental to an understanding of his aims. In *Discipline Without Punishment*, Oskar Spiel, an Adlerian, gives an account of the application of psychological techniques in a big school in Vienna. He divides children into those who have adopted 'useful' and those who have adopted 'useless' ways of life. The teacher's task is to make the child who has adopted a 'useless' way of life realize the 'fundamental error' of his ways and persuade it to 'adopt the positive aim presented to it'. The teacher must recognize – and this is where psychology comes in – that laziness, stupidity, truancy, are not 'given' qualities which are 'unchangeable'; on the contrary they have specific psychic 'aims' which must be regarded 'dynamically'. 'If we want to turn laziness into industry ... first of all we must try to understand the mistaken outlook of the child; we must try to discover the point at which the child's mistake began.' But the purpose of the therapy was always the same: 'to educate the child in fulfilling the demands which the community makes upon him.' This kind of mechanical 'adjustment to society' approach of normal psychiatry is one that Neill has always detested. Indeed, given the choice between the understanding 'adjuster' and the whacking schoolmaster, there is little doubt he would choose the latter. 'The child of spirit,' he writes, 'can rebel against the hard boss, but the soft boss merely makes him impotently soft himself.' With his growing suspicion of psycho-analysis, Neill gradually abandoned the P.L. in favour of complete non-interference.

However, the main ingredient in the cure was the approving and permissive atmosphere. The chief formal expressions of this were voluntary classes and self-government. The therapeutic value of voluntary classes was clear. Laziness, truancy, dullness, day-dreaming, were often neurotic 'escape' mechanisms. To force a boy to attend class when his libido was locked up in 'unprofitable investments' was not only futile, but positively harmful, in so far as it intensified his troubles. It was only when emotional anxieties had been eased that a child could bring his full libido to bear on class work.

However, even with normal children, Neill has always been against the 'play-way' approach, the attempt to make boring subjects 'artificially' interesting. Laziness or lack of interest was not, to him, primarily 'neurotic' (though it might be): it expressed a perfectly natural and healthy aversion on the part of the child to boredom. Believing, as he did, that the child is the best judge of his own interests, he considered it a 'crime' to force children to attend classes against their inclinations: they would come when they were ready. This view, as it stands, seems somewhat naïve. The child is enormously influenced by his environment. The Summerhill environment has always been anti-classroom; understandably, when the emphasis was on curing problem children. 'I wish I could take more interest in school subjects,' Neill once wrote. 'They bore me, and it is evident that they bore children.' Susan Isaacs on the other hand found children interested in quite abstract mental problems. Whether the environment is 'pro-learning' or 'anti-learning' must have a great deal to do with the child's attitude to classwork, so the child's 'instinct' is not a fair test.

Neill's dislike of learning dated from the period when he was forced to cram the pupils' minds with matter that had no relevance whatever to their lives. But his belief that learning 'touched nothing fundamental' owes a great deal to Freud's discovery of the unconscious. If all conscious processes are merely rationalizations of deep, and generally forbidden, unconscious urges, then 'training the mind', developing 'reasoning' power, is an illusion – it simply makes the mind more skilful in defending prejudices inherited from the unconscious. Indeed if the aim of psycho-analysis is to strip away the individual's false consciousness of himself, then the fact that his defensive strategies are skilfully deployed as a result of mental training increases the difficulties of successful treatment. Neill often seems to imply that learned and intellectual persons are more prone to self-deception than others; that freedom from neurosis is characterized by 'spontaneous' enthusiasms and woolly thinking. This irrationalist reduction of the conscious mental processes to the secondary and trivial is perhaps the least fortunate legacy of Freudian psychology.

Self-government, like voluntary classes, grew up with the school. Neill retained responsibility for diet, health, staff appointments, finance and general administration. He forbade sex and alcohol, the latter on health grounds, the former in deference to public opinion. For the rest the pupils governed themselves, meeting weekly in the main hall to discuss their rules and to enforce the law against offenders. Everyone above eight had one vote; the chairman and officers were selected by rotation, all over eleven being eligible. Discussion usually revolved around bed-time rules, smoking, conduct in the village and how to deal with anti-social behaviour such as bullying. Punishment was usually a fine. The headmaster, like anyone else, was fined if he spoke out of turn, and his vote counted equal to that of the eight-year-old, though his opinion counted for considerably more. Everyone was encouraged to speak his own mind and most children did. Visitors marvelled at the children's tolerance and sense of fair-play.

There are several advantages of self-government. Firstly, it is therapeutic: it releases tensions through honest discussion. Secondly, communal authority seems to give rise to much less resentment than adult authority, even if it is equally onerous. One explanation is that if the children have hammered out the rules for themselves, they are presumably agreed on their necessity, even though they may break them; the same rules, imposed by adults, might well be ascribed to 'prejudice'. Neill suggests the further reason that the individual is free to 'hate' the group and 'live out' his hatred, whereas he is forced to 'repress' his hatred for the adult rule-maker. Third, self-government avoids associating the present teachers with previous disciplining adults. Discipline is transferred from the teacher to the group, thus leaving teacher and child free to be friends. This desire by the progressive teacher to avoid identification with previous suppressing authority largely accounts for the rather ridiculous importance attached to Christian names. As David Wills says, 'Sir' is associated with the 'bogus' respect which adults have demanded in the past. 'We must, then, however presumptuously, try to give the impression that *we* are different.' Finally, self-government may be regarded as experimental civics, a means by which children may find out through social experience the necessity for some rules; and thus learn to distinguish between rules that are 'necessary' and rules that are based on 'irrelevant' moral considerations. For example, until the cancer scare, it was possible to argue that the prohibition of child smoking, like the prohibition of masturbation, was based on entirely spurious health arguments, used as a cover for a moral *Verbot*. In his *Problem* books Neill tended to view smoking as a mild neurotic symptom which if encouraged would be 'lived through' and then dropped. This ignored both its physical addictiveness and its tremendous social popularity.

Of the therapeutic value of self-government there can be little doubt. We have earlier pointed to its utility in exposing bullying and letting off steam.* Neill believes that 'the school that has no self-government should not be called a progressive school.' He admits, though, that 'good self-government' is only possible when there is a minority of older children; for although children in the gangster stage (eight to twelve) are all for making rules, they are all for breaking them also. On the other hand, David Wills, who follows Neill closely in his own school for maladjusted children, writes: 'In fact, and in practice, [self-government] is a terrible bore, its importance as an instrument is not primary, and as a system of discipline it is not efficient.'

*See above, pp. 64–67.

14 · The Influence of Wilhelm Reich

Mrs Lins liked to travel; so generally after the end of the summer term she and Neill would take a cruise – to South Africa or Scandinavia. One such trip – in 1937 – brought them to Oslo, and there Neill met, for the first time, the psycho-analyst Wilhelm Reich, destined to be the second great influence on his life. Three weeks of therapy with Reich did him more good, he recounts, than all the years of 'talky' analysis he had had with Lane, Stekel and others. Equally important, Reich's ideas added a whole new dimension to his thinking.

Reich, the most brilliant disciple of Freud, broke with his master in 1933 and from 1934 to 1939 worked at Oslo University. In America he continued his work at a special institute he himself created. In 1954 the Federal Food and Drug Administration began proceedings against him; and an injunction issued by the court ordered his books and equipment to be destroyed. Jailed for refusing to comply, Reich died in prison in November 1957. To his followers Reich is a Christ-like figure who was destroyed because he offered a fundamental challenge to an evil social morality; his opponents see him as a dangerous charlatan, who suffered from persecution mania. A more balanced view acknowledges the great contribution of his earlier work, while remaining highly sceptical (to put it mildly) of his later research into 'orgones', and the development of the 'orgone box'.

Reich's work can most helpfully be seen as an attempt to assimilate Freudian psychology to Marx's analysis of society. To Marx the 'objective' social fact was the exploitation of the masses by a small ruling class. This was 'social reality'. It followed that if the exploited could be got to recognize this fact the existing social order would disappear, since the exploited far outnumbered the exploiters. However the exploiters had somehow managed to persuade the masses that a continuance of the existing order was in their own best interests. In other words, they had persuaded the masses to accept a capitalist ideology. Thus 'mystified' about their own true interests the masses had continued to support, albeit at times rebelliously, the rule of their oppressors. For Marx the problem was essentially one of intellectual emancipation: of developing or heightening the 'consciousness' of the masses concerning their own true interests. The masses however remained obstinately wedded to their chains, so that even when actual conditions (such as in a depression) furnished the most striking confirmation of the reality of oppression, they refused to strike a blow for their own freedom.

Now the point on which Marx offered little illumination was on how precisely the transfer of capitalist ideology to the workers took place, what was the exact mechanism by which it was accomplished. Here Freud was directly relevant. He regarded the patriarchal family as the social institution through which the child was brought into contact with 'reality'. The family, with its demands for obedience and morality, represented the reality of the outside world. The child's need for parental affection and approval forced it to 'internalize' parental suppression of its natural instincts, in other words, to adopt the parents' own attitudes to itself as its own. Thus external suppression becomes internal repression; the child develops a conscience or an anxiety about doing wrong; crime becomes sin, and the original conflict between infantile desires and parental prohibitions is perpetuated as an internal conflict between instinct and morals. To Freud the development of this conscience was a necessary condition for the growth and maintenance of 'culture', for it enabled repressed desires to flow into intellectual, aesthetic and productive 'sublimations'.

Reich was highly critical of this formulation. 'If one studies the history of sexual suppression,' he wrote, 'one finds that it does not exist in the early stages of culture formation. Therefore it cannot be the prerequisite of culture.' 'The question,' Reich concluded, 'is not one of culture but of social order.' How this repressive social order developed is never made quite clear. He implies that originally a patriarchal family structure may have developed in response to real economic and military needs, but that the individual character thus formed and the social ideology of that period survived long after the 'objective' situation had changed. The reason why the ideology changed so much more slowly than the 'socio-economic basis' is that the 'character structure' is acquired early in childhood and undergoes little change, being passed down through the family from generation to generation so that in the end it becomes quite inappropriate to the new conditions.

Instinctual repression, from a Marxist psychological standpoint, was thus seen as an internal adaptation to a view of reality designed to perpetuate the existing social order; the family, and later the church and the school, were the institutions which 'socialized' the child in the interests of the ruling groups. The purpose of this socialization was to 'castrate' the worker psychologically, by making the child feel apprehensive, shy, afraid of authority, 'good' and 'adjusted'; by loading any rebellion with anxiety and inhibiting the critical and thinking faculties. 'In brief,' says Reich, 'the goal of ... suppression is that of producing an individual who is adjusted to the authoritarian order and who will submit to it in spite of all misery and degradation.'

Stated in these terms many would find Reich's theory quite plausible. But for Reich the 'castration' of the worker was more than just a metaphor: his social impotence stemmed directly from his sexual impotence. This can be illustrated by his theory of the genesis of neurosis.

To Reich the psychic disturbance was merely the superstructure of the neurosis: the real neurosis was the economic disfunctioning of the libido. Like Freud, Reich saw the libido as a closed energy system consisting of the human drive for instinctual, and especially sexual, gratification. But unlike Freud he regarded libidinal energy as physical energy, though of a new and hitherto undiscovered type. He called it the orgone energy, a 'primordial cosmic energy, universally present and demonstrable visually, thermically, electroscopically and by means of Geiger-Mueller counters'. Reich 'discovered' this energy between 1936 and 1940, but it apparently remains unknown to physicists, biologists and other scientists. Neurosis was caused by a damning-up or 'stasis' of this orgone energy, thus preventing it from achieving its natural outlet: sexual gratification. The capacity for sexual gratification was regarded as more than just 'erective and ejaculative potency' but rather the capacity for complete fulfilment in the sexual act, 'for complete surrender to the involuntary convulsion of the organism and complete discharge of the excitation at the acme of the genital embrace.' This blocked-up sexual energy is used to build up and sustain a neurotic character which Reich regarded as typical of Western society, deriving its satisfactions from 'secondary drives' which, in extreme cases, manifest themselves in destructive social activity, in less extreme ones, in irrational fears and anxieties which lead to moralizing and religious-escapist ways of life. The difficulty about changing the character structure or character armour of the neurotic individual was that it was not just 'psychic' but physical. The neurotic character was characterized by muscular rigidity: the organism physically 'expresses the fact that it is holding back. The shoulders are pulled back, the thorax pulled up, the chin is held rigid, respiration is shallow, the lower back is arched, the pelvis is retracted and "dead", the legs are stretched out stiffly. . . .' These muscular armourings were supposed to be segmented – in rings at right angles to the spine. Their function was to inhibit the flow of sexual energy to the natural source of its release – the genitals. The process may be represented diagramatically:

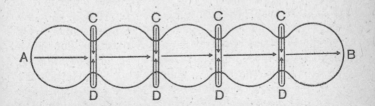

A–B   represents the natural flow of orgone energy.

C–D   represents the 'muscular armourings' which trap this energy, producing 'stasis'. The character structure is the psychic 'superstructure' of this biophysical development.

The twin purposes of Reich's therapy were, therefore, first to dissolve the muscular armourings by/ what was called 'vegetotherapy' and secondly, to restore orgastic potency, which in his later work, involved the use of an 'orgone' box or accumulator which was supposed in some way to be able to trap 'bions' or particles of this orgone energy. 'Sexual gratification,' he wrote, 'by eliminating the actual neurosis (stasis neurosis), the somatic core of the neurosis ... also eliminates the psycho-neurotic superstructure.'

The fact that the aim of Reich's analysis was to restore sexual potency rather than effect 'sublimations' as in Freudian therapy probably accounts for his imprisonment and the destruction of his writings especially as, in the heyday of MacCarthyism, he could also be plausibly represented as an agent of the Communist world conspiracy, subtly seeking to achieve its end by encouraging 'filthy' and 'degenerate' practices. The American general in the film *Dr Strangelove* who thought that his 'sexual fluids' were being polluted by Communist agents is not an altogether fanciful illustration of the widespread reaction to Reich's work.

Reich's work affected Neill's in two main areas. Firstly, it cleared up his doubts about the death instinct. It will be recalled that after 1920 Freud postulated a primary masochism, a 'biological striving for unpleasure'. Before, he had argued that neurosis resulted from the conflict between instinct and the outer world (libido – fear of punishment); now he claimed that neurosis resulted from the conflict between instinct and the need for punishment (libido – wish for punishment). The significance of the frustrating and punishing outer world was pushed right into the background. If this split in the human psyche, expressed theologically as the conflict between the 'lower' and 'higher' self, or between the Devil and God, was self-imposed – that is, not primarily due to external suppression – then there was little or nothing that education or social change could do to remove feelings of guilt and anxiety. Reich summarized the consequences of abolishing the death instinct:

> The answer given to the question, Where does suffering come from? was now 'from the biological will to suffer, from the death instinct and the need for punishment'. This made one conveniently forget the correct answer which was: from the outer world, from frustrating society. This formulation blocked the avenue of approach to sociology, an avenue which the original formulation of the psychic conflict had opened wide. The theory of the death instinct ... leads to a cultural philosophy ... which asserts that human suffering is inevitable because the self-destructive tendencies cannot be mastered. Conversely, the original formulation of the psychic conflict leads inevitably to a criticism of the social order.*

The intellectual (and emotional) resolution of his doubts about the death instinct freed Neill from his need to work with 'problem' children. Reich had observed that 'we distribute our attention very poorly if we turn 98 per cent of it to analytic detail work and only 2 per cent to the gross damages which are inflicted on the children *by the parents*.' Hitherto Neill had been concentrating primarily on cure; from now on the emphasis gradually shifted to prophylaxis; he realized he was 'wasting his time' trying to patch up children almost irreparably damaged by parental mishandling; that the more fundamental aim was to save them from that mishandling. Indeed his reaction against 'problem children' went further than that. 'Years of living and dealing with all sorts of crooks and swindlers and liars showed me that they were one and all inferiors.'

But Reich's theories, if correct, involved a far more radical attack on the existing social order than Neill had hitherto been prepared to make. His work with delinquent children was a kind of escape from the logical consequences of his own developing views. But there was no intellectual escape from Reich's alternatives. 'Sex education,' Reich wrote in his book *The Sexual Revolution,*

raises serious problems of much greater consequence than most sex reformers ever dream of. ... We are up against a powerful social

*W. Reich, *Character-Analysis*, p. 214.

apparatus which for the time being offers passive resistance but which will proceed to active resistance with the first serious practical endeavour on our part. All indecision and tendency to compromise in questions of sex education can be traced not only to our own sexual repressions but ... to the fear of getting into serious trouble with the conservative social order.

The key question was whether the educator was prepared to let 'sexuality take its natural course', which implied approval not only of infantile sexuality but also of sexual intercourse between teenagers following puberty.

Neill, for all his unorthodoxy, is not of the stuff of which martyrs are made: nor would he deny this. In his writings from the late 1930s onwards he came out strongly in favour of a sex life for adolescents. 'I know of no argument against youth's love life that holds water.... None answers the question why nature or God gave man a strong sex instinct, if youth is forbidden to use it unless sanctioned by the elders of society.' But he has never officially allowed the boys and girls of Summerhill to sleep with each other, nor has he issued them with contraceptives. Part of the reason was probably his own early sex repression: he admits to a 'vestige of Paulinity' in his system; more important was the fear that the school would be closed, or that parents would be frightened off. Summerhill was his personal creation, he was proud of it and he wanted it to continue. 'Being a human person,' he wrote in 1948, 'Summerhill means more to me than does society, and I shall remain an islander.'

What he did do, in his books *The Problem Family* (1948) and *The Free Child* (1953), was to attack with great verve and anger conventional parental responses to infantile sexuality. All the early methods of training or 'socializing' – feeding timetables, cleanliness training, nakedness and masturbation taboos – are designed to give the child a guilty attitude towards his own body and his own desires. 'It is almost incredible,' Neill wrote, 'that ignorant doctors and parents should dare to interfere with a baby's natural impulses and behaviour, destroying joy and spontaneity with their absurd ideas of guiding and moulding. These guides begin the universal sickness of mankind, psychical and somatic, and later school and church continue the process of an education that is anti-pleasure and anti-freedom.' And in another passage: 'A child left to touch its genitals has every chance of growing up with a sincere, happy attitude to sex.'

Is Reich correct in seeing sexual revolution as the key to social revolution? Eric Hobsbawm has written of 'a persistent affinity between revolution and puritanism.'* On this view, *all* achievement stems from instinctual repression, whether it be making a revolution, money or a work of art. On the other hand, it could be argued that sexually liberated adults will no longer accept the disciplines necessary to work capitalist society, leading to its spiritual disintegration, rather than to its capture by frontal assault as on the old revolutionary model. Whatever the truth of the matter, it is clear that Neill has deliberately stepped outside the argument. He sees his task as an educator is to make children happy: the revolution can look after itself.

Where Neill can be criticised is in his account of full human development. Following Reich, he believes that all sexual repression is bad. He fails to recognize that a certain degree of repression, by breaking the compulsion of the sexual drive, might make for more intense and satisfying forms of 'sublimated' pleasure. He fails, in other words, to make Marcuse's distinction between 'basic repression' enabling artistic, intellectual, and other pleasures, and 'surplus repression' which is demanded by a particular economic or social order. The need for this basic repression, arises, according to Marcuse, from the 'fusion' of the 'sex instincts' with the 'destructive impulses'; in short, from the existence of the death instinct which Reich had tried to abolish.†

This darker picture of the human psyche, with its echoes of Original Sin, is not one that Neill can accept. As he passed eighty and shed, one by one, his hopes and illusions, the primary affirmation of his life remained unshakeable – complete belief in the child as a good, not an evil, being. For almost forty years, this belief in the goodness of the child has never wavered; rather it has become a final faith.

New Society, 22 May 1969.

†*Eros and Civilization* (Sphere Books) 1969, pp. 44, 58n. 190-1.

PART FOUR

Hahn
of
Gordonstoun

15 · Beginnings

In the summer of 1903 three Abbotsholme schoolboys planned a summer walking tour in southern Germany. 'Marcan's friend Hahn (a German) ...' wrote one of them to his father, 'would also join us, and also an uncle of his, a well-known bacteriologist.'

Kurt Hahn was then sixteen. Little is known of his early life. He was born of Jewish parents and brought up as a Jew. His father's family were wealthy middle-class industrialists, but there was also a strong pedagogic tradition: Kurt Hahn was the fourth generation in which the son became a teacher. His mother's family were Polish, with a strong musical talent which, however, was not inherited by Kurt Hahn. Hahn was the second of four boys: an adored elder brother had died at the age of eleven.

The walking tour was a great success. 'Professor Hahn has been awfully kind to us. We have had excellent weather and the last three days or so among the Dolomites were grand. ... Please send some money.' The Abbotsholmians were fired with enthusiasm for their school, its principles and its extraordinary headmaster, Cecil Reddie. They communicated their enthusiasm to their romantic young companion. From them he learnt of education as a training of character rather than of intellect. He was impressed by the prefect system, which in its Abbotsholme form emphasized the responsibility of elder boys for the welfare of younger ones. The idea of the school as a community in which each contributed to the well-being of the whole was virtually unknown in Germany* and Hahn there and then conceived the purpose of pioneering it in his own country. The example of Dr Herman Lietz, whose book *Emlohstobba*, which his companions presented to him, confirmed

*There were, however, a few traditional boarding schools run by religious orders.

their own account, convinced him that it was a practicable project. On reading it, he 'felt that his fate cried out'.

Between 1904 and 1914 Kurt Hahn studied at a number of universities: Berlin, Heidelberg, Göttingen and Oxford. He could work only intermittently owing to sunstroke, which made him ill every summer: it took three decompressing operations to cure him. One result of this was that while at Oxford between 1910 and 1914 he was obliged to spend his summers in the cooler climate of North Scotland. 'This necessity,' writes H. L. Brereton, 'brought him to Morayshire where he lived on the banks of one of the most romantic rivers in Europe, imbibing at once its beauty and its legends.' In exile from Germany in 1934, he returned to Morayshire to found Gordonstoun.

He went on to Oxford on the advice of one of his professors, who told him: 'If you are interested in the old in order to help the new, it is not the German universities that can help you, but Oxford.' His residence there coincided with the brief dominance of idealism in English philosophy, represented in the person of F. H. Bradley.

Bradley's philosophy has been described as 'Hegelianism modified by Anglo-Saxon caution'. Idealism was concerned with the truth about the 'whole' universe, not with separate truths about its more or less superficial aspects. The idealists believed in absolute reality. They sought to reveal the 'intrinsic connections' of the apparently disjointed and fragmented plurality of objects in the world of sense. The apparently accidental conjunction of matter, viewed by the eye of reason, could be seen as part of a divine plan, exhibiting logic, order and harmony. Moral behaviour was to be measured by the degree of 'insight' achieved into the divine plan. It consisted in men fulfilling their function or purpose.

At Oxford Hahn studied this world under Professor J. A. Stewart, the leading Platonist of his day; and from Plato he took several leading ideas which were to be fundamental to his educational schemes. The first was the doctrine of ideals, which we have already mentioned in connection with Reddie. Plato believed that there was a 'perfect form' of every material substance, and that the purpose of life consisted in achieving ever closer approximations to these perfect forms. The pre-determined movement of life (as in the unfolding from the seed into the fully developed plant) became intelligible only if the process were conceived as being governed by the end to-wards which it moved: what in nature was unconscious, be-came in man a conscious striving towards a 'pattern of perfection' in the heavens.

The second idea which Hahn assimilated was Plato's notion that the principle of this perfection was harmony and balance. The perfection of the body, he held, depends upon a harmony of its material elements; and Greek medicine was governed by the principle that healing is the restoration of balance disloca-ted by disease. Virtue (the health of the soul) is the harmony or balance between the various faculties of the psyche: reason, the appetites and spirit. Virtue in the state is the harmony between its constituent, functional elements: thinkers, sol-diers and artisans. The same principle can be extended indefi-nitely – to relations between men, relations between states, and so on.

Plato was a political reformer who sought to recall the Athenians to the old civic virtues eroded, as he saw it, by democratic enthusiasm and soft living. His aim was to educate a class of leaders in a 'healthy pasture' remote from the cor-rupting environment, whose task it would be to regenerate society. Hahn must have been haunted by similar visions of decay as, inspired by these ideas, he drew up in 1913 plans for a school modelled on Platonic principles. The war that broke out a year later and ended in the collapse of Germany was to give them a new urgency; to convert what might have re-mained a purely academic speculation into an active campaign for social and political regeneration.

Hahn himself was important in the German politics of the First World War as the adviser, inspirer and stiffener of a group of persons who stood for a 'peace of understanding'. His moderate stand was to gain him the golden opinions of English liberals, which was to prove a great help in his educa-tional projects when he finally settled in England in 1934. But it is important to note, for this was to be a source of much subsequent confusion, that his liberalism was not really of the true English variety, though possibly its nearest German equivalent.

Hahn and his friends never opposed the war, either in public or in private. On the whole they confined their activities to 'behind the scenes' attempts to improve war aims. There was, of course, in Germany, much less of a tradition of political dissent, especially in wartime. Hahn took the view that in war the ranks were closed, and that to oppose the war was unpatriotic. In England, the Liberal dissenters were forced into the Labour Party, or at least into alliance with the anti-war Left. Hahn disliked the Left. Instead, his chief allies were a hereditary Prince – Max of Baden – and the political adviser to Ludendorff – Colonel Haeften. Few English Liberals would have looked to the aristocracy and army for allies in an anti-war cause.

But the most important divergence from English liberal opinion occurs in respect of war aims. Golo Mann, in his illuminating essay *Kurt Hahn's Political Activities,* argues that Hahn stood simply for 'peace', what is more a 'negotiated peace ... leaving the powers more or less where they were'. This is not so. He certainly stood for a return to the *status quo* in the West, and in particular for a renunciation of any claims on Belgium. But in the East he proposed to deprive Russia of substantial chunks of territory. This aim he shared with the militarists, Pan-Germans, and other expansionist groups. He called this policy *Ethical Imperialism*. German Liberals regarded the Russian Empire very much as English Liberals had regarded the Ottoman Empire: as a corrupt despotism, holding subject peoples in thrall. They wanted to 'liberate' the Poles, Finns and other non-Russian peoples very much as the English had helped to liberate the Greeks in the 1820s. However, the achievement of such aims involved a decisive alteration of the balance of power in Germany's favour, since they could only be achieved by German victories, leading to the dismemberment of the Russian empire, which the Western allies regarded as an essential counterpoise to German continental hegemony. Moreover in practice they could be carried out only by the German army, which, far from sharing the liberal ideal, thought mainly of conquest and future security. Nor were other groups lacking who had very unethical ideas about what to do with the liberated territories. Pan-Germans and *Mitteleuropeans* thought essentially in terms of establishing a German economic and political hegemony over Eastern Europe. The Western allies were not prepared to concede German expansion in the East in whatever language it was dressed up in; and upon this rock Hahn's peace-making plans were wrecked.

Hahn's reliance on German force to obtain his ethical objectives meant that his moral position was compromised from the outset. His was the familiar 'crisis of conscience' of the German liberal which was to recur in aggravated form in the 1930s. Because the army was the essential instrument of his designs he had to support the war policy; and his 'moral stands' were directed largely towards improving the 'image' of Germany's war aims; as his friend Colonel Haeften put it: 'the German sword cuts sharper when it is clean.' Thus he protested against unrestricted submarine warfare because it would bring America into the war; the attempt to hold on to Belgium because it would strengthen England's war resolve; atrocities because they would weaken Germany's position at the bargaining table. Even Ethical Imperialism was advanced as a policy to strengthen popular support for the war – to get the Socialists on the war side. At the same time he opposed a 'democratic' peace because it would leave Germany's 'mission' unfulfilled; and as late as October 1918 was urging Prince Max, who had become Chancellor, to fight on to save Germany's 'honour'. Strangely enough, Hahn, who in his educational writings picked out 'self-deception' as the greatest of all weaknesses, had an almost infinite capacity to deceive himself, not only about his own motives, but also about those of the people round him. Perhaps Golo Mann's charitable explanation is the right one: he simply did not believe in human evil.

What educational conclusions did Hahn draw from the war?

The *Memoirs* of Prince Max are a scathing commentary on German political leadership. Hahn blamed the politicians for their acquiescence in policies which they knew to be both immoral and disastrous – the disastrous side being stressed more than the immoral: atrocities, unrestricted submarine warfare, evasion of the Belgian question, the settlement in the East which was to furnish a model for Versailles. He attributed these misjudgements to character defects. This is a little unfair. Bethmann-Hollweg, Hertling and Michaelis were admittedly men of mediocre capacities, but they had responsibility without power. Only popular backing could have given them the authority to stand up to the militarists; instead they were Court appointees who could be replaced at will. But Hahn was not interested in making the system more responsible. Instinctively he mistrusted the *demos*. War showed the *demos* at its worst – hateful, hysterical, vindictive, willing to condone every excess in the intoxication of victory, drowning the voice of calm and reason. The revolution which broke out in 1918 provided another instance of its violence. It was then that the sociologist Max Weber provided him with an alternative model of civic courage. Facing a howling Socialist mob in the Rheingold Hall of Berlin in December 1918, Weber declared: 'All my life I have never crawled to Emperors and Kings, and I am not going to crawl to the mob now.' 'The crowd retired,' Hahn recalls, and 'we cheered him to the echo.' Effective leadership for Hahn then came to consist in the possession of certain personal attributes – courage, humanity, resolution, moral strength. These qualities alone would carry conviction; these were the 'aristocratic' qualities 'wherewith the democracy shall be salted'.

It was to the creation of this kind of person that Hahn now turned his attention.

To my mind [Prince Max declares in his *Memoirs*] there is no contradiction between aristocracy and democracy. The majority principle ... exercises a wholesome restraint on the aristocrat who claims to be fitted for leadership by birth or education or his own merits, forcing him to find the way of approach to his fellow citizens, from whose 'crowd profane' it has always been the chief temptation of the elect to keep aloof. . . . It is important, moreover, in its own interest to free the nobility of intellect or birth from the enervating sense of privilege.

It was to train this 'elect' and at the same time free it from its 'enervating sense of privilege' that Salem was established.

16 · Salem, Gordonstoun and Atlantic College

In a B.B.C. broadcast, delivered soon after his arrival in England, Kurt Hahn spoke of Prince Max's ambition 'to set in motion, by education, the cure of Germany's international and domestic troubles'. How much of this programme was Max's and how much of it was Hahn's it is difficult to say. Certainly the aim of bridging the gulf between insight and action, of producing 'whole men', appears to be Hahn's. Aristocratic leadership was obviously congenial to the heir to the Margravate of Baden; leadership by an 'aristocracy of talent', more likely to appeal to his private secretary. The emphasis on traditional values, too, was largely Max's: Erich Meissner has written of Max's fear of 'moral anarchy'. To Hahn, though, we must attribute the attempt to adapt traditional values to modern circumstances. The desire to save the privileged orders from the 'enervating' effects of luxury was probably suggested to Hahn by the English public-school system, especially in its Abbotsholme form of cold showers and hardy open-air pursuits.

The Wandervogel contributed a characteristic motif. It was a rebellion of the young – against adults, but more important against modern industrial civilization. These youthful wanderers, heirs to the Romantic *Sturm und Drang* tradition,* forsook the towns and roamed the fields, forests and lanes in quest of – what? They never knew – but they knew what they did not like – modern life in all its forms. The lines of the poet Hölderlin, their guide, express their idealism, sadness, and innocence:

*The *Stürmer und Dränger*, the 'men of stress and strain', were eighteenth-century university students who were deeply influenced by Rousseau and expressed their revolt against tradition and convention by throwing off their powdered wigs and walking round in their 'natural' hair! Schiller's play *The Robbers* (1781) dramatizes the conflict between 'natural' man and 'artificial' society, between elemental, spontaneous and generous impulses and the cold, dead and artificial conventions of society.

But, my friend, we have come too late. True, the gods are living,
But over our heads, above in a different world.
Endlessly there they act and – see how the heavenly spare us! –
Care very little, it seems, whether or not we exist.
For not always, indeed, a feeble vessel can hold them,
Only at times can mankind bear the full weight of the gods.
Only a dream about them is life henceforth. But to wander bewildered
Helps, like slumber, and need and night make us strong.

Here was the psychological basis of Salem, Gordonstoun and later of Outward Bound – a youthful rejection, heroic and futile, of industrialization and its consequences, a quest for an ideal, undefined, which Hahn believed could be turned to constructive purpose.

There were borrowings from Goethe too. In the *Wander-jahre* of *Wilhelm Meister,* Goethe suggested a Pedagogical Province to prepare pupils for life by simulating as closely as possible the conditions of peasant society. 'The province,' writes Sir John Adams, 'is ... a great world school.... it is planned on a magnificent scale, with towns and villages instead of class-rooms, territories for play-grounds, populations for staff, and trades and industries with their equipments for apparatus.' Training was to be both intellectual and cultural and physical and practical, both indispensable to the whole man.*

Salem School was housed in Salem Castle, hereditary home of the Margrave of Baden, overlooking Lake Constance. It opened with four boarders in 1919. The boarding element was indispensable: like all true moulders of character Hahn wanted to gain control of as much of the environment as possible. Besides he saw all too clearly that tendencies in the world outside did not altogether favour the kind of education he sought to give. Already in the Salem days, the school is seen as a 'countervailing' force, or in Hahnian terminology, as a 'protecting' and 'healing' pasture. Hahn, like Reddie, chose to work mainly with adolescent boys,† and here he was

---

*Sir J. Adams, *Evolution of Educational Theory*, pp. 277–8.

†Salem in fact had a form of coeducation, but girls are very rarely mentioned in Hahn's educational writings. Someone who knew Hahn well writes: 'Believing so strongly in coeducation I was distressed by his attitude

confronted by an immediate problem: how to overcome the 'deformities of puberty' (unspecified). The general remedy, borrowed from the public schools, was the programme of invigorating activities which Salem provided; but Hahn developed two special 'protective' techniques. The first was the training plan. This was a personal list of Do's and Don'ts, to which each boy was expected to append daily ticks or crosses, depending upon whether he had fulfilled or failed to fulfil its requirements. This was hailed as an indispensable training in 'self-honesty'; it was more likely to create a sense of guilt by giving a boy an exaggerated conscience about his own failings. Most of the items (cold showers, brushing teeth) were directed to physical, rather than moral, cleanliness, but

Sometimes certain points are entered under a cypher X, the meaning of which is only known to the boy or possibly to his Mentor if he has confided in him. These points may touch important and subtle issues of self-discipline. The entry is not a confession to a stranger, it is a confession to himself and his 'conscience'.*

The aid to conscience was the *grande passion,* the 'guardian angel of the years of adolescence'. Hahn believed that every boy had latent in him a consuming interest, which would divert energy from the 'poisonous passions'; and so, on Saturday afternoons, 'guilds' of explorers, farmers and heralds (art lovers) would set out, in the Wandervogel spirit, in pursuit of the *grande passion* that would cool their inflamed desires. The results of this prophylactic were acknowledged to be remarkable. Salem boys were noted, Hahn says, for the 'gleam' in their eye and the clear texture of their skins. Their expressions, he was to tell a somewhat astonished visitor to Gordonstoun,

to girls and when I asked him why he denied them the same opportunities as boys he would reply that he would include them in his schools if he felt they would enrich the education of boys. We had many tough talks but fundamentally I am sure he believes in the subservience of women' (letter to the author).

*Dr Hahn comments: 'The purpose of the training plan is misunderstood. It is meant to substitute self-supervision for supervision and above all to ensure the observation of health rules.'

were 'crystalline and pure'. 'You see such eyes in two kinds of people . . . ze hunter from ze hill and ze sailor from ze sea.'*

The training in leadership was a cross between the public-school prefect system and the idea of service to others: more accurately it was an attempt to revive the original Arnoldian prefect system which had degenerated into a pampered athletocracy. The prefects' function was indicated by their titles: Guardians and Helpers. Each prefect was assigned a definite responsibility for a communal service: there was a Prefect of Works, a Prefect of Juniors (charged somewhat improbably with the task of safeguarding 'the interests of the Juniors against Masters and Seniors'), a Prefect of Outposts, a Prefect of Organization and so on. The Prefects were elected from a body of Colour-Bearers which comprised a quarter of the school. There were two grades of 'dignity' a boy had to reach before he could aspire to be a Colour-Bearer: (i) after a term's trial he was given a uniform – grey shirts and shorts designed, like Reddie's, to expose as much of the body as was decent, and (ii) after a year he received the 'privilege and burden of a training plan'.

The self-electing prefectorial cadre was a somewhat wooden adaptation of the self-electing Etonian 'Pop' Society. But there the resemblance ended. Like Reddie, Hahn displayed an obsession with classification of the 'elements' of character. The school report commented on the boy's 'public spirit, sense of justice, ability to give precise evidence, power to pursue what he thinks right when facing discomforts, dangers, boredom, his own scepticism, a hostile public opinion.' With Max Weber's defiance of the Spartacists ringing in his ears, Kurt Hahn had constructed a model of 'civic courage' to resist and enlighten the 'people'.

Hahn followed Plato in defining virtue in the individual as a harmony or balance between the various faculties of the psyche, more simply expressed in public-school jargon as the ideal of the 'all-rounder'. 'What do you do with the extrovert?' Hahn was asked. 'I turn him outside in,' was the reply.

*T. C. Worsley, *Flannelled Fool*, p. 187.

'And with the introvert?' 'I turn him inside out.' 'Bookworms' should be encouraged into practical activities; practical children introduced to the joys of the intellect (though this side was less prominent). 'Success in the sphere of one's weakness,' Hahn observed, 'is often as great a source of satisfaction as triumph in the sphere of one's talents.' Here was one way in which the 'gap' between thought and action could be eliminated. For the extrovert too Hahn provided 'periods of aloneness' to enable the child 'to glean the harvest from his manifold experiences'. Thus Colour-Bearers were required to walk by themselves for two hours every Sunday 'to engender a protective habit against the exhausting and distracting civilization of today'.

Unfortunately both bookworms and athletes suffered from a lack of physical fitness, resulting from the 'easy means of locomotion' and sedentary habits. Physical fitness ranked very high in Hahn's order of priorities, not only because a healthy body denoted a healthy mind, but also because physical exercises provided opportunities for 'overcoming', for 'defeating defeatism'. In this model of challenge and response, the hurdle in athletics equalled the hurdle in life: its conquest strengthened the will by giving the boy confidence and by providing him with an experience of success. 'We have cured a stammerer by the high jump,' Hahn declared in 1934. Public-school games which attracted only the 'gifted athlete' were therefore dethroned and limited to two afternoons a week; and in their stead each boy was made to run round the garden before breakfast; the school mornings were interrupted by a forty-minute break for sprinting, jumping and throwing. Expeditions, too, were encouraged to build up physical endurance: in 1925 eighteen boys went to Finland, bought their own boat, hunted and fished for their food, and no doubt returned with a 'gleam' in their eye. But boys' experiences, Hahn argued, should not be exclusively triumphant, for that puffed up pride. They should also be confronted with defeat in order to encourage humility and a proper sense of the limitation of human powers.

The enervating sense of privilege was to be attacked in two

ways. First, Hahn advocated that 30 per cent of the pupils at Salem should come from poorer homes, 'bringing with them a definitely critical attitude' to counter self-deception and complacency. He was a great believer in the stimulating effects of 'creative tension', and an attractive characteristic was his tendency to appoint staff whose views differed violently, if not too violently, from his own, in a praiseworthy, if largely unsuccessful, attempt to provide opposition to his own dominating personality. (Here he differed from Cecil Reddie, who could brook no opposition.) Erich Meissner, to whom we shall refer later, is perhaps the best example of a permanent member of Hahn's entourage who fulfilled this function; the fact that Hahn failed more often than he succeeded is illustrated by the comment of an early visitor to Gordonstoun who noted that Hahn's staff 'worshipped him, followed him around obsequiously, and delighted to fill one up with tales of the Great Man's sayings and doings'.* The second way in which Hahn tried to break down privilege was by plunging his boys into the activities of the neighbourhood. Goethe saw the staff of his Pedagogic Province as no less than the 'population' of the surrounding countryside, and similarly Hahn attempted to make the local artisans a part of school life. 'We sent our boys,' he recalled, 'to their workshops in the villages: to the bookbinder, the builder, the joiner, the locksmith, the smith and the woodcarver. These artisans proved often real educators; they showed a greater horror of half-finished work than the schoolmaster.' Reciprocally, he and Prince Max saw the school as the centre of 'healing' forces in the neighbourhood. Here Hahn was greatly influenced by the ideals of the Cistercian monks who lived at Salem up to 1804. They believed in serving the community, not just spiritually, but by offering active help wherever it was needed. The Cistercians, Max told Hahn, 'were the road-builders, the farmers, the foresters, the doctors, the consolers and the teachers of this district.' In Salem, then, we have the development of the 'ideal of service' which was later to become the greatest of Hahn's *grandes passions*.

*Dr Hahn comments: 'You do injustice to my partners in responsibility. They were always critical but helpfully critical.'

The patronage of Prince Max made the success of the school certain, as did that of Prince Philip and Prince Charles the later success of Gordonstoun. Already Hahn was showing his shrewd appreciation of the value of titles, and, more importantly, his extraordinary ability to stimulate the 'uneasy conscience' of the well-to-do. Salem grew from four boys in 1919 to 420 in 1933. An Old Boys Group (the Salem Union) was established whose members spent much of their time 'in training' for the call to service.

The call fell on deaf ears. 'Kurt Hahn,' writes Golo Mann, 'wanted to educate young people to master modern life without damage to their souls. . . .' But he offered them very little experience of modern life, its attitudes and style. He abhorred the big city and all it stood for, and failed to distinguish between what was avoidable and what was inseparable from the life of a modern industrial society. The great enemy of escapism was himself an escapist: and the escapism of the Master was easily communicated to his pupils. 'It was no accident,' Mann observes, 'that an unusually large proportion of Salem's Old Boys withdrew into that particular outlet for innocence and chivalry, the Reichswehr' – at the precise moment, too, when Germany needed 'active citizens' to stand up to Nazism.*

Hahn's political interests continued after the war. 'Speeches were made on special occasions, letters written to British newspapers and British politicians and sometimes an article in a German paper.' The object of all this was still to achieve the 'peace of understanding' missed in 1919. Versailles would have to be revised, by peaceful means if possible, but 'if all else was of no avail, then the German sword, which must be kept unsullied, would have to speak once again.' This, as Golo Mann rightly notes, was the note of the twenties, given in Salem an additional colouring of 'ethical imperialism'. Hahn tended to reject the Weimar republic and all its works. Its

---

*Dr Hahn comments: 'You ignore the fact that active opposition was to be found in the services more than in other domains of society. All the same, if it is true that there were many young men who escaped into the army to avoid becoming a Nazi or going into concentration camps I refuse to criticize them . . .'

style was not to his liking: neither dignified, self-respecting, nor patriotic. It represented the apotheosis of 'parliament-arism'. It was the product of a 'slaves' revolt' and this in itself was sufficient to condemn it in his eyes. He tended to connect Germany's defeat with the November revolution, and thus helped to give currency to the legend of the 'stab in the back'. In all these matters, Hahn contributed, in his own small way, towards undermining the legitimacy of the Weimar settlement, which in turn paved the way for Hitlerism.

He watched the rise of Hitler with mingled admiration, hope and alarm. In echo of his 1914 sentiments, he felt Hitler's cause 'could be good or made good'. In every delinquent individual or group there is something potentially justified. If only these misguided delinquents had had the opportunity of a Salem education! Some of them had. A Hitler Youth Group was formed at school. Hahn tried to teach them the difference between a Platonic élite and a Hitlerian élite: they remained delinquents. He took the same attitude to the national move-ment. Hitler was the symbol of Germany's intention to revise Versailles; the 1932 version of the Fatherland Party. He would have his uses in a wider movement of a less melodramatic kind. It was the illusion of the Right that Hitler was really a good, old-fashioned Nationalist at heart, who could be purged, both of his undesirable followers, and of his own 'high spirits'. The Left knew better, but 'in all the statements made or in-fluenced by Hahn during the year of crisis there is no mention of the "other Germany" that was to be found among the decent, loyal people, millions of them, who voted socialist to the end despite the mediocrity of their leaders.'*

For much of his life Hahn did not believe in the reality of evil: his eyes were opened by the Potempa incident. In the autumn of 1932 five S.A. men were imprisoned and tried for trampling a Communist youth to death in front of his mother. Hitler sent them a telegram of appreciation and praise – the Beuthen telegram – calling them his comrades. Finally Hahn spoke out. In a clear and courageous message he called upon his old boys to choose between Salem and Hitler: compromise

*Golo Mann, op. cit.

had become impossible. 'Germany,' he declared, 'is at stake, her Christian civilization, her reputation, her military honour.' 'This was the moment,' Brereton writes, 'for good Europeans inside Germany to strike. His lead was not followed ...' But how could it be? There had been no preparation. And even given all the predisposing factors – the humiliations of Versailles, certain traditions in German political and intellectual thought – would the Third Reich ever have been established but for the economic collapse, the six million unemployed? Hahn said nothing about that. Vigilance, to be effective, had to start much earlier than October 1932: within three months Hitler was Chancellor. The Potempa stand illustrates both the strength and weakness of Hahn's politics: the line is drawn at murder, but the social despair that led up to it is either ignored or misunderstood.

Nor, as it turned out, had compromise really become impossible. Even after his arrest by the Nazis in March 1933 – he was released through the intercession of the British Prime Minister, Ramsay MacDonald – he continued to hope that a better Hitler would emerge, tamed and purified, his instincts suitably redirected towards the policy of Ethical Imperialism. This 'arch-Freemason and Jew' (as the Nazis described him), according to one account, begged to be allowed to stay on in Salem.* Only when it was made impossible for him to work and live in Germany did he go into exile, with an assurance from Hitler's government 'that the Salem system will not be changed'. Hahn himself denies that he asked to be allowed to stay. But, in fact, his attitude to Nazism was as ambiguous as that of any anti-Socialist German of his class and background. Had he not been Jewish, it is very doubtful whether he would have left Germany, though it is quite likely that he would eventually have joined in some conspiracy like the Goerderler one. In Germany, he would no doubt have continued to try, behind the scenes, to modify the excesses of Nazi policy; and perhaps earlier in the war, to strive for the 'just' treatment of the conquered peoples as in 1914–18. What made him unequivocally anti-Nazi was a change of environment. In this he is

*Worsley, op. cit., p. 192.

by no means unique: Nazi officials in Denmark became reluctant to enforce the anti-Jewish policy. And indeed, Hahn's own change in attitude is striking witness to his educational stress on the 'healthy pasture'. His own conscience was a mixture of individual and social. In Germany he would have endured a perpeual 'crisis of conscience', as he strove to reconcile his hatred of murder with his love of country and his belief in Germany's destiny. In England this conflict largely disappeared.

Once he had given up hope of returning to Germany, Hahn set about re-establishing Salem in England. This Jewish educator and refugee, expelled for his 'anti-Nazi activities', already well known to prominent liberals, who saw him as their German counterpart, was assured of a warm welcome from progressive circles. Hahn, a great publicist, did not disdain any platform, and thus we find him early in 1934 lecturing under the somewhat inappropriate auspices of Mrs Beatrice Ensor and the New Education Fellowship. His effect on one observer was characteristic of the impression he made on his listeners and explains his extraordinary success in recruiting adherents:

He instantly struck me as in a different category from the others [the other members of the N.E.F.]. They were enthusiastic, charming, rather dotty and somewhat amateur . . . while he was grave, serious and profound. His lectures made a considerable stir, less I think for what they said, than for what he was. For whatever you might think of Hahn as an educator, you could hardly deny that he had many of the attributes of a Great Man. He gave off personality in thick waves, and the personality had a solid Germanic weight behind it. He had a full, wide face with a small resolute chin, jutting firmly out. His pronouncements had a ring of both wisdom and authority; they were aphoristic and seemed to dig deep. I can't, for the life of me, remember any of them now, but I still remember the flavour of them, and the aroma of profundity with which he invested them.

A distinguished group of academics, politicians and public figures encouraged him in his educational projects; men like Lord Allen of Hurtwood, William Temple, George Trevelyan, William Arnold-Forster, G. P. Gooch, Philip Noel-Baker.

Many of them had opposed the First World War and were anxious for friendship with Germany. They represented the liberal enlightenment, believed that reason and conciliation would settle most problems, both domestic and international; they had an air of high moral seriousness. To them Hahn was a distinguished German who seemed to stand for most of the things they did; he could interpret Germany's position in a way which they understood and sympathized with. As an educationist he appeared to stand for a version of the moderate progressivism which nearly all of them shared. William Temple was greatly interested in the problem of youth; Allen of Hurtwood himself was connected through his wife Marjory, an Old Bedalian, with the main currents within the English progressive school movement, and had even founded a school of his own.

They therefore gave Hahn every encouragement. As a first step, Allen arranged a meeting between Hahn and a number of educationists, including Badley of Bedales, W. B. Curry, headmaster of Dartington Hall, and Geoffrey Winthrop Young, Reader of Education at London University, who was already a firm Hahn supporter. Hahn expounded his ideas, but Curry was not impressed. The German seemed disturbingly authoritarian:

He holds, quite rightly [Curry wrote to Allen], that children should not devote to athletics practically the whole of the time spent out of doors and out of class. He suggests that two afternoons a week devoted to Games is probably sufficient, and in this I concur. But what happens now? He says that to play Games on a third afternoon is declared to be a punishable offence, and he actually instanced in the meeting, in his reply to Mr Badley, an illegitimate game of Hockey as one of the offences for which punishment would be necessary....

The training-plan came in for a good deal of criticism:

Or again, take this punishment as expiation business. People like Hahn ... are so tormented themselves by their moral fanaticism that they set up a sense of guilt in any community in which they are important. Having created the sense of guilt, they then use it as an excuse for punishment....

The final paragraph in Curry's letter was especially telling:

Fundamentally what worries me about the whole business is that people like yourself, Arnold-Forster and others, whom I had thought of as Liberals, are converted by Hahn. Unless I am very profoundly mistaken ... the education which Hahn advocates is incompatible with a really liberal civilization. It seems to me ... to be the product of the tortured German soul. As Toller says in a book just published, most Germans at present are incapable of even understanding the meaning of personal liberty, so strong have been the traditions of the last generation. I can understand that Hahn's views might seem liberal in Germany. What shocks me is that they are thought liberal in England. I grant that he is a man of immense power and vitality and of considerable intellectual ability. I also insist that his psychology has far more roots in his own emotional nature than in the nature of other human beings....

Allen, characteristically, sprang to Hahn's defence.

... it strikes me as very singular [he wrote to Curry] how first the right and then the left go over the deep end in thinking certain educationalists are dangerous people. Eighteen months ago I was watching jealously to prevent the right in the New Schools Association trying to exclude Dora Russell and Neill on the ground that they were terrible and dangerous people. Now I have to watch equally jealously lest this accusation of being a dangerous person should be applied by the left to Kurt Hahn.

Besides, Allen went on,

I am sceptical of freedom for growing persons carried quite to the lengths which, so far as I can make out, would be favoured in different degrees by Neill, you and Dora. ... I am fairly confident that he is more likely to produce children of the dynamic outlook on life and a high standard of value than the more extreme freedom of some of the other schools.*

Gordonstoun started in April 1934. Hahn chose a site in his beloved Morayshire, close to Elgin and Lossiemouth and half a mile from the coast of the Firth of Moray. There were thirteen boys, but expansion was rapid. Forty-five boys were enrolled for September 1935, of which fifteen were from Salem. Certainly the prospectus was sufficiently imposing. Heading the Board of Governors was William Temple, Archbishop of York. Other prominent persons were Allen of Hurt-

*This correspondence is taken from Arthur Marwick's *Clifford Allen: Open Conspirator*, pp. 142–44.

wood, Mark Arnold-Forster, R. M. Barrington-Ward, later editor of *The Times,* John Buchan, the novelist, J. R. M. Butler, Fellow of Trinity College, Cambridge, Claude Elliott, head-master of Eton, G. P. Gooch, Sir Percy Nunn, famous educa-tionist, G. M. Trevelyan, the historian, John Wheeler-Bennett, and Geoffrey Winthrop Young – not to mention the more conventional collection of generals and admirals. Arnold-Forster and Winthrop Young entered their sons, Mark and Jocelin; the former edited the school magazine with Francis Noel-Baker. Prince Philip arrived from Salem, as did Major Chew, who took over the 'character-building' side of the programme: Chew was later to be Prince Charles's head master.

Erich Meissner came from Germany after two tough years trying to run Salem under the Nazis. This artist and romantic provided in some ways a counter-balance to Hahn's obsession with physical fitness. 'In the field of education, the needs of the body are well grasped by now. We must not carry coals to Newcastle. It is the mind that should be given care ...', he wrote in 1954. His gentler, more reflective, approach provided sustained criticism of the 'other Gordonstoun' embodied in Hahn's restless energy and overpowering will to action.

Certainly Hahn made a striking impression on both boys and parents who came to look over the school. 'With an inspired knowledge of young people, Kurt Hahn had shown me the secret passages and the priest's hole,' recalled Adam Arnold-Brown. 'I had noticed, too, that [he] included me in the con-versation, he did not talk exclusively with my parents.' Fin-ally, he showed the fascinated youth the dungeons. After looking at the cross-beams upon which the prisoners had perched, feet dangling in water into which they might fall and drown if they fell asleep, he hesitated no longer: he begged his parents to let him come to Gordonstoun.

It was quite unlike any other progressive school. The time-table, almost identical with Salem's, was crowded with acti-vities, leaving little free time. The day started at 6.30 with a cold shower and invigorating run. Between 10.30 and 11.15 there was a break for running, jumping, javelin throwing and seamanship. Lunch at 1.30 was followed by a rest period during which the boys were read to 'lying flat on their backs'. One afternoon a week was devoted to games, two to seamanship, two to a 'common task' and one to the Project: gardening, building, music, art, natural history and so on. A warm wash and cold shower at 4.30 was followed by tea and 'prep'. After supper two hours later (no meat was eaten at night) there was 'tennis for senior boys'. Hahn used to join this session with great enthusiasm, if little skill. So keen was he to win that boys had to be instructed to lose gracefully. A quarter of an hour's silence at 9.15, to enable the boy to 'glean the harvest from his manifold experiences', was followed by lights out.

Levity was not encouraged. 'Do you wish to be funny only, or do you wish to make your magazine a contribution to the building of Gordonstoun?' Hahn sternly inquired of Mark Arnold-Forster and Francis Noel-Baker in a letter of nearly a thousand words. In this case the editors reacted with spirit: 'If readers aspire to having letters of this length published, they are doomed to disappointment.' Nor were other duties to be taken lightly. The annual Shakespeare production was invested with great solemnity. Hahn was determined that life should resemble the best in art, and when one youthful Hamlet spent a week with his girl-friend, instead of returning for rehearsals, he was ignominiously discharged.

Don't you see! It's like this [the headmaster explained to T. C. Worsley]. Hamlet was a Prince, a fine character, a good character, a noble character. Now, we have playing him a sneak-thief of time, a boy who deceives us all, his parents and us, by stealing a whole week from his tasks, a feeble fellow who prefers . . . spending his hours with a . . . a . . ., trollop in Edinburgh. How can we expect a true performance of Hamlet from such a weakling . . . ?

If Hahn lacked humour, he had enormous enthusiasm. It was desperately important to him that boys should accomplish what they had set their minds to, or what he had decided that they should set their minds to. It did not really matter which: what did matter was that they should have the experience of 'defeating defeatism'. He pursued them with exhortation and encouragement, bombarded their defences, exposed their

rationalizations, striving all the while to inject into their fal-
tering efforts his own immense courage and will-power. There
was, certainly no question of leaving them alone, of waiting
for the flower of personality to blossom in its own good time.
Whether he brought them permanent gains, or only transient
successes, is something that cannot be answered.

Progress on the character-building side was encouraging.
In his annual report to his Governors Hahn noted, with some
pride: 'Already we have been able to cure, through the training plan, habits like the biting of nails.' Responsibility, too,
worked wonders: 'The nineteen year old Helper still radiates
the freshness of childhood,' and the headmaster was able to
record such pleasing sights as the 'clearness of the boys' skin'
and the 'absence of the slouch'. The moral tone apparently
still left something to be desired. 'Someone has been talking
dirt in this room. I can smell it,' Hahn was liable to exclaim as
he walked into an empty class-room. 'Is it possible in modern
surroundings ... to kindle on the threshold of puberty non-
poisonous passions which act as guardian angels during the
dangerous years?' he inquired in 1935. Clearly the fresh sea
breezes blowing in from the Firth of Moray were not in themselves sufficient to dispel either the odour or the practice of
corruption.

Hahn returned to the same subject three years later. 'Can a
community of adolescent males be kept spiritually healthy?'
he asked his governing body in November 1938. 'I can confi-
dently say today: It can, on condition that such a community
gives up its isolation and renders public service to the district
in which it is located.'

The discovery of suitable means of service came by chance.
Salem had been inspired by the Cistercian ideal. Now Hahn
came to hear of an eighth-century monk called Gernadius who
on stormy nights used to walk along the coast opposite Gordonstoun waving a lantern to warn fishermen of rocks and
shoals. Initial attempts to get the boys to emulate the efforts
of this worthy man foundered. 'They suspected me,' Hahn
wrote, 'of trying to improve their souls.' But it was different
when two leading Captains of H.M. Coastguards visited the

school. 'You are needed,' they said. If the boys would build a coastguard hut themselves, the coastguards would install a telephone and provide life-saving equipment. The response was apparently enthusiastic and thus the Gordonstoun Watchers were born, sitting in their watchtower 'looking into the darkness in patient readiness lest a stranded vessel should burn an inefficient flare'. Later fire service and mountain rescue were added, and each boy was required to join one of the three, and undergo the requisite training. In 1936 a further opportunity for service presented itself when Hahn declared that 'the boarding-school can become the core of a health-giving movement for the district in which it is placed, thereby giving health to itself.' This new 'health-giving' task took the form of offering opportunities for athletic training to the boys of Hopeman village, and a special cinder track was built with money provided by the King George V Jubilee Fund on which the sons of the local fishermen were invited to train for the Moray Badge, under the supervision of the Gordonstoun boys.* In all these ways Hahn strove to keep the 'poisonous passions' at bay, thus preserving the 'spiritual strengths' of childhood into early manhood and beyond.

As the numbers of Gordonstoun crept up beyond the hundred mark, Hitler's menacing gestures recalled Hahn to more immediate realities. Even after his ejection from Germany he still seems to have cherished the belief that Hitler would settle down if only he purged himself of his self-deceit; at the end of 1933 he was writing:

Hitler has a warm, even a soft heart, which makes him over-sensitive to suggestions that he is not hard enough. . . . The man feels he ought to keep his faith in his mission intact lest he become 'as sounding brass and tinkling cymbals'. This is his mission: cure the hereditary curse of Germany – discord; sweep class war away; and make Germany respected again in the world. . . . He does not want war, but he wants a peace in freedom, not a peace from impotence.†

*For the Moray Badge, see below, p. 220.
†In his book *The Roots of Appeasement*, Martin Gilbert dates this memorandum incorrectly in 1935 (pp. 145–6). Gilbert's suggestion (p. 145) that Lord Lothian was guided by Hahn on German matters is denied by Hahn.

Thus might Hahn have written about one of his difficult pupils. In a letter to the author Hahn comments:

> In the first year of my exile I was under the influence of home sickness, a powerful source of error. ... I indulged in wishful thinking. I thought it possible that Hitler would clean up his party. ... Many an honourable young Nazi kept on hoping that humanity and justice would one day prevail and by remaining in the party they could help to defeat the criminals in the struggle for ascendancy. All my illusions were shattered on 30 June 1934.

The Roehm purges profoundly changed Hahn's attitude towards the regime. Thereafter he became a passionate advocate of what Lord Salter called 'the dual policy', the aim of which was to separate the German people from Hitler by offering Germany a peaceful revision of the Versailles Treaty provided the Nazi menace were removed. Just as he and his German friends had tried to keep Hindenburg informed of Nazi atrocities, so now he tried to use his influence with Barrington-Ward, assistant editor of *The Times* and a Governor of Gordonstoun, to get *The Times* to publicize the concentration camps. Barrington-Ward argued that 'we cannot bring out a Bradshaw of atrocities'. Hahn wrote to him:

> You say this at a time when tortures are no longer the acts of cruel individuals but efficiently and bureaucratically built into a system. ... You do not allow yourself to know what would interfere with the sureness of your appeasing touch. The Commandants of Dachau and Buchenwald operated knowing that public opinion was well controlled. ... Unintentionally the appeasers have transmitted to Germany, to your allies of tomorrow, to the Arab world, to India, the belief that the Devil is invincible.

In 1937 he tried to get Lord Lothian to intervene with Hitler to save the eminent left-wing lawyer Hans Litten, who was being ill-treated in a concentration camp: Lothian, in effect, refused. In the Munich crisis of 1938 he urged Chamberlain to offer the Sudeten Germans a plebiscite after one year, with the choice of either joining Germany or remaining autonomous within the Czech state, the area to be governed in the meantime by peace-keeping contingents composed of Dutch, Swedish and Swiss units.

Hitler would probably remonstrate, but opinion in Germany will consider the proposed settlement just, or at least, one which does not justify war. Hitler will be under the greatest possible pressure to accept. Should Hitler say No, he will, in the eyes of Germany, bear the responsibility for the coming war. The people would enter it with a broken morale.

This analysis stands up particularly well in the light of the later discovery that the Army did not consider Germany ready for war in 1938 and that the anti-Nazi generals had prepared a plan to arrest Hitler on the first day of mobilization.

After the outbreak of war he persisted with the dual policy. In an article published in the *Spectator* of 5 December 1939, called 'A Christian Peace Procedure', he argued that an acknowledgement by the allies that Versailles was wrong, a declaration of their willingness to discuss disputed points in a friendly manner, a promise to concede Germany a share in the mandate system for colonial territories, would be of decisive help to the moderate and non-Nazis forces in Germany in their struggle against Hitler. It was on these grounds too that he opposed unconditional surrender for most of the war; and it was to do justice to the 'good' Germans that he urged in 1946 that a distinction should be made between 'Nazis' and 'Nazi criminals' in the treatment of post-war Germany.

There is a striking similarity between Hahn's attitudes and procedure in the 1930s and 1940s and those of the period 1914-18 – with the difference that he was now on the other side. There is the same emphasis on weakening the enemy's home front by isolating the extremists (in 1914-18 the extremists were Lloyd George and Northcliffe), leading to their overthrow and the possibility of a negotiated settlement; and there is the same element of naivety in the hope that the passions unloosed by war could be controlled by men of courage and humanity. Just as in 1918 he and Prince Max had decided to place their trust in Woodrow Wilson and the Fourteen Points, so now in 1945 Hahn 'had the illusion that Churchill and Roosevelt would have the will and the power to honour the pledge of the Atlantic Charter even if they had to deal with a prostrate and helpless Germany' (Hahn's letter to the author).

Underlying Hahn's approach was a basic belief in human goodness which not even two world wars could entirely shatter. There was also a pride and faith in Germany which was equally long-lived. Hahn is a symbol of the tragedy of his class, of his generation, of his nation. His idealism was the Greater German idealism of 1848, perpetually damned up by geography and frontiers, perverted by the violence that was its only means of expression, obsolete before it had had the chance to play itself out on the stage of history.

The evacuation of Gordonstoun to Wales in the war caused less disruption than might have been anticipated, and Hahn was already planning his post-war school on the grandiose lines of Goethe's Pedagogical Province. Gordonstoun would itself remain the 'core' of the 'school city'. Round it would be grouped 'vocational houses' where boys would receive technical training in accord with the profession of their choice from the ages of fifteen or sixteen. Boys from the College would eat together with the 'vocational' boys in a huge refectory. Instruction in citizenship would be given to all. The Gordonstoun Round Square, a kind of quadrangle surrounded by what had originally been stables, would be used for studies by boys from all houses privileged to work alone – each study decorated in the style and with the emblems of different European countries 'disunited today, united tomorrow'. The 'Greater Gordonstoun' would be held together by a 'brotherhood of adventure'.

Although this plan never matured, the theme of the Atlantic Community became increasingly a reconciling concept for a man separated from the country he loved by the burden of national dishonour, a stranger yet in his adopted land, whose attempts for a 'peace of understanding' had foundered in two world wars of unprecedented horror. Its pursuit became a full-time activity once a recurrence of his old sunstroke had forced his resignation from Gordonstoun in 1953. Now, in his mid-sixties, he threw the full weight of his still formidable powers behind the concept of the Atlantic College, an international school for leaders which would create through education the understanding that politics had failed to win.

The plan, born in Paris in 1955, was inspired by the experience of Air Marshall Sir Lawrence Darvall, Commandant of the N.A.T.O. Staff College, in welding many different nationalities into a single community. If these results could be attained among mature men, 'how much deeper are the roots we could sink into the youth of the Atlantic Community, if at their most impressionable period we could gather them together in residential colleges, making them members of a self-governing community'. The aim was to establish eventually six international sixth-form colleges, one each in Canada, France, Great Britain, Greece, Germany and the United States. Great Britain was selected as the appropriate launching pad for the first.

Hahn set about winning support with his usual enthusiasm and energy. Industrialists, politicians and academics were approached. 'It became clear that there was widespread support for such a project. . . .' M. Antoine Besse, the French millionaire, contributed £65,000 and with this money St Donat's Castle, overlooking the Bristol Channel and twenty miles from Cardiff, was purchased. Admiral D. J. Hoare, a naval officer with a special interest in boys' clubs, was appointed headmaster-designate, and the first Atlantic College opened with fifty-six pupils in 1962.

It has been described by its headmaster as a cross between a staff college and a residential university. Most of the boys – so far mainly from England, America, Germany and Scandinavia – have their fees paid for by their governments, by industrial scholarships, and in England by local authorities. (The Government also made a capital grant of £80,000.) The boys are selected for a two-year course leading to university entrance in their various countries, and much of the early years of the College was spent in negotiating 'equivalents' which would be accepted as qualifications for national universities. (So far these negotiations have failed to produce any understanding with France.) Eventually the aim is to establish an International Baccalaureat.

The philosophy of the College may be summarized in the following statement made by the headmaster:

The countries of Europe, and throughout the world, are still divided. Nevertheless, there are strong forces tending to draw them together and, for the first time, the energies and many-sided genius of the nations could be combined in peace instead of being wasted in conflict. Education cannot stand aside from this great creative movement. For commercial reasons alone, education must become more of an integrating and less of a disrupting force. ... Change by political means is uncertain and slow. The force of example is needed. ... The Atlantic College project is aimed at setting this example. The second aim of the College is more fundamental in nature: to provide a pattern of education suited to the special needs of our time. It is in this area that the experience and wisdom of Dr Hahn have played a most significant part. ... We need to show in a convincing manner that the educational needs of modern society do not have to be met at the expense of the more important human characteristics. The heart of the matter is the need to demonstrate that self-discipline, devotion, imagination, courage and response to challenge can be developed in materially prosperous societies.

As Kurt Hahn passed his eightieth year he still continued to keep a benevolent watch over his many and far-flung projects. To Outward Bound he preaches the importance of life-saving with added urgency; he remains active in raising fresh funds for the Atlantic College project; he returns periodically to Gordonstoun. For the rest he commutes between Salem, Brown's Hotel, London, and his sister-in-law's house near Oxford – a benign and courteous old gentleman, in a big black hat.

Note

Since the above was written, Cristopher Sykes has produced a biography of Adam von Trott, *Troubled Loyalty*, which sheds much light on the 'crisis of conscience' of a non-Nazi nationalist in much the same political position as Kurt Hahn. Like Hahn, Trott stood for the policy of encouraging the German Right to overthrow Hitler by offering to settle 'legitimate' German claims with a non-Nazi government. For an indictment of the British refusal to take the 'dual policy' seriously see David Astor, *Encounter*, June 1969.

17 · Outward Bound

Kurt Hahn may justly be called the founder of the Outward Bound Movement; but like his other ventures, it represented no new departure of principle, being heir to a tradition of philanthropic and evangelical youth service stretching back into the early nineteenth century. Its novelties may be found in a particular adaptation of method to the needs of a rather older age group, and to the extraordinary success achieved by its founder in enlisting funds for its development.

The problem of youth to which the Outward Bound Movement was addressed is a sub-species of the larger cultural and social problem created by industrialization and by the breakdown of a common system of values and beliefs. It was a problem in its own right, separate from the problem of adults. Adults were regarded as completed human beings, for better or worse. Youth however was an age of potential and growth, one moreover which was very imperfectly catered for by the educational system: compulsory schooling was not instituted until 1876 and even then only up to the age of eleven, at which point youth was turned over to the temptations of street-corner, gin-palace and lewd music-hall, such as London's Penny Gaff, 'the foulest, dingiest place of public entertainment I can conceive', as one observer wrote in 1870. This was not only a poor preparation for citizenship in the dawning age of democracy, which most enlightened persons openly welcomed but secretly feared (there was a strong tendency to identify moral laxness with sedition), it was also seen as sapping the soldierly qualities of the people at a time when the imperialist tide flowed strongly. Finally, the age of self-help believed firmly that social and economic problems were at root moral problems: that habits of piety and discipline, inculcated early, would happily ensure not only individual virtue but social peace as well.

Working-class youth certainly presented a daunting challenge to the earnest and high-minded philanthropists of the nineteenth century. Their physical state was appalling. As one commentator has observed:

In 1895 of every thousand children in a typical poor area, at least 750 were 'dirty' and 100 were 'very dirty', i.e., lousy, bug-bitten and flea-infested; from 700 to 800 had decayed teeth and 150 to 180 diseases of the nose and throat.... Nearly all were undernourished, visibly suffering from the results of rickets and adenoids.

Juvenile delinquency was widespread and fearsome gangs roamed the towns:

Ragamuffins and Hooligans ... the Scuttlers and Ikes of Manchester; the Peaky-Blinders of Birmingham; the Forty Gang, the Bengal Tigers, the Dockhead Slashers and the Bermondsey Yoboes, all the racily local gangs of roughs and toughs with studded belts and bell-bottomed trousers and ... razors.

Philanthropy stepped in where the state feared to tread. Organizations were set up to reclaim the disease-infested urchins for God and State. The Y.M.C.A. was formed in 1844 to 'win young men for Christ', aiming at their 'mutual edification and evangelization'. How was this edification to be accomplished? People had only the haziest notions about the psychology of the child and relied mainly on moral exhortation, coupled with extensive readings from the Bible. But youth, as Kurt Hahn was later to point out, is tenaciously resistant to 'manifest improvers'.

The nature of the solution was determined by the type of person attracted into youth service in the nineteenth century – a type that has continued to figure prominently in youth organizations down to the present day: the public-school type and the military type. Both brought with them largely complementary notions on how to 'handle' boys. The public-school man believed that games were the answer to sin. By keeping boys happily occupied and at the same time encouraging positive qualities such as courage and the team-spirit, they brought the errant youth, somewhat obscurely, closer to God. This ideal has been called 'muscular Christianity'. The service ideal was more muscular and less Christian. The Army man believed in the supreme educative value of drill and uniform. The former created discipline and fitness; the latter, *esprit de corps*. Both the public-school and army types believed that at root youth's problems were moral ones. Adolescent 'deformities' were blamed on sin: smoking, drinking and impurity. Demon Drink was a symptom not a cause: but youth workers were much influenced by temperance agitation and sought to tempt the adolescent away from the public-house by offering him cocoa in the boys' club. People like Seebohm Rowntree were not lacking to proclaim the novel doctrine that youth's problems could only be solved by state action to improve diet, housing and welfare; but such views had little influence on the youth workers. Although it may be thought that their diagnosis was wildly inappropriate, they undoubtedly had the knack of appealing to boys. At a time when hardly any teachers dreamt of educating a child 'through his own interests', both the public schools and the army and navy were using boyish enthusiasms and impulses, suitably purged and re-directed, in the service of their educational designs.

This utilization of youthful instincts for Higher Things lay at the basis both of the Boys Brigade, founded by William Smith in 1883, and the Boy Scouts, established by Baden-Powell in 1908. William Smith

loved boyishness; he thought it right and good that boys should be bursting with energy and brimming over with high spirits, and he took ... the unorthodox view that high spirits and love of fun directed to true manliness was a better thing than prize-rewarded good conduct which might signify, and result in, mere dullness and lack of spirit. To him the only possible pattern of manliness was Christ.*

He banded Sunday schoolboys into a Brigade in which they would be taught drill, physical exercises, punctuality, obedience and cleanliness. 'Tone' would be preserved by *esprit de corps* rather than by punishment. The Boys Brigade, described as 'play-soldiering for Christ', aimed at 'the advancement of Christ's Kingdom among Boys, and the promotion of habits of Reverence, Discipline, Self-Respect and all that tends

*W. McG. Eager, *Making Men*, pp. 320–1.

towards true Christian Manliness'. An enthusiastic observer noted a 'paradox' in William Smith's methods:

Call these boys 'boys' which they are, and ask them to sit up in a Sunday class and no power on earth will make them do it; but put a five penny cap on them and call them soldiers, which they are not, and you can order them about till midnight.*

'Play-Soldiering for Christ' in fact turned out to have a somewhat limited appeal; Baden-Powell saw that in order to capture additional boys for Christ, a more diversified range of activities would have to be provided. Eager waxes lyrical over his larger insights. B.-P.

saw that boys in an industrialized environment were starved of something essential to their growth. He discovered intuitively that the passionate interest of boys in Red Indian yarns and cowboy tales was significant of repressed energies and frustrated instincts, and indicated a force which, if released, would work with education, not against it. He gave boys the chance of imaginative action and practical romance; he gave them back their lost heritage of field and wood and hill and stream; he gave them a comradeship attested by secret signs, wide interests ... absorbing techniques, attainable standards, pride-rousing awards. Heavens! What an educationist the man was.

The Boy Scout Movement was essentially an attempt to utilize the pre-adolescent's play spirit for educational purposes. Conversations with Thompson Seton, an American who had developed a Woodcraft Organisation in the United States based on a highly romanticized view of Red Indian life, confirmed Baden-Powell in his view that 'in the work and attributes of backwoodsmen, explorers and frontiersmen' he had found a universal type 'that could satisfy a boy's romantic longings'. The need to capture youth for Higher Things was rendered more imperative by the threat of national degeneration. 'The same causes which brought about the downfall of the great Roman Empire are working today in Great Britain,' B.-P. declared in 1907, citing 'the decline of good citizenship ... due to want of energetic patriotism, the growth of luxury and idleness, and the exaggerated importance of party politics. . . .'

*ibid., p. 332.

He listed these decays and their remedies with military precision (see pages 215–16).

The Boy Scout Movement was designed as a training in discipline and obedience, observation, woodcraft, health and endurance; chivalry (the knights and their code); patriotism (history and geography of Britain and her colonies; the Flag; H.M. Services; deeds that won the empire); and saving life (ambulance work, accidents, etc.). Under health, B.-P. listed 'Physical Development, Exercises and Games, Cleanliness, Non-smoking, Continence, Sobriety, Sanitation and Food'. The Scoutmaster was to form boys into Patrols of six to eight, named after fierce animals: Wolves, Bulls, Ravens and so on. The Patrol, the educational equivalent of the gang, was to be the 'character school of the Individual'. The boys were clothed in uniforms based on B.-P.'s own dress in Kashmir. They were given insignia, flags, badges and poles. In his earliest camps, B.-P. roused them from their slumbers with a Koodoo horn captured in the Matabele campaign; and round the camp fires he encouraged them to sing Zulu war-songs. He was especially impressed by Zulu methods of education, which involved sending a boy into the bush with an assegai when he arrived at the 'age of manhood', in order to 'prove himself'; and went on to lament in *Rovering to Success*:

> For the ordinary boy in civilized countries, there is nothing of this kind. We badly need some such training for our lads if we are to keep up manliness in our race, instead of lapsing into a nation of soft, sloppy, cigarette suckers.*

The pattern of remedial education so far described rested on the view that national inefficiencies were caused by moral inefficiencies. It did not pause to consider whether the moral inefficiencies might not be caused by the national inefficiencies. The nation, its social and economic structure, was taken as given. The sole problem was to get youth to adapt to it. The youth leaders took as their model the army which welded recruits from diverse backgrounds into an 'organic unity'. Why should not civilian society do the same? The analogy breaks

*Quoted in Harold Stovin, *Totem – The Exploitation of Youth*, p. 105.

National inefficiencies	Causes	Origin	Preventive	Scout training as remedy: a systematized development of
Irreligion Indiscipline Want of patriotism Selfishness Corruption Disregard of others Cruelty	Indifference to higher conscience	Want of self-discipline	Education in character	1. Character through good environment Sense of honour Sense of duty Self-discipline Responsibility Resourcefulness Handicrafts God through nature Religion in practice Fair play Helpfulness to others Personal service for country
Crimes of violence Lunacy Thriftlessness Poverty	Drink			
Show off Loafing and shirking Low moral standards Gambling Illegitimacy Disease	Self-indulgence			
Ill health Squalor Infant mortality Mental deficiency Physical deficiency	Irresponsibility of parents	Want of hygienic knowledge	Physical health	2. Health through outdoor practices Responsibility for own physical development up to standard Health and hygiene in practice

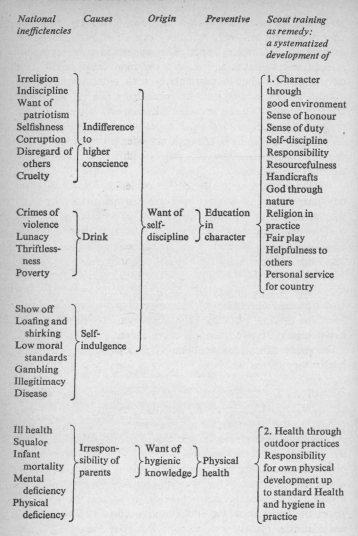

down for an obvious reason: the army exists for one purpose – to fight efficiently. Society exists for many purposes, often mutually incompatible. The appeal to submerge self-interest and self-satisfaction in a common cause could have only a limited appeal, particularly with older working-class youths, for the cause could be made 'common' only by abstracting from it all the problems that in real life give rise to contention – economic problems, power problems and so on. No doubt the youth movements did offer a wonderful escape from a drab environment: but whether they solved any national problems is far more dubious.

The inter-war period ushered in problems of unprecedented magnitude, such as continuing mass unemployment, coupled with governments of quite outstanding incompetence, such as the National Government formed in 1931; a combination well calculated to revive philanthropic concern with the problem of youth – a concern reinforced by the arrival of the cinema, with a 'corrupting' power more potent, because infinitely more widespread, than that of its predecessor, the Penny Gaff. The National Government itself, bereft of any constructive ideas for dealing with the youth problem, such as creating a better school system and providing decent recreational facilities, gladly turned the problem over to philanthropists, who busied themselves with recruiting prominent persons to their cause.

The Prince of Wales, in a speech in the Albert Hall in 1932, declared himself 'concerned for children, particularly with respect to that gap in their lives from the time they leave school until they reach the age of eighteen'. Eminent contributors to *The Times*, including William Temple, Archbishop of York, were much exercised by the decline in physical fitness, which they attributed largely to an enervating environment of luxury rather than to the miserably low wages upon which youth had to subsist. Central Councils for Physical Welfare and National Fitness were set up; a Jubilee Fund was established to distribute money among 'juvenile organisations' of 'approved worth' concerned with 'helping boys and girls to grow up with the idea and ideals that make a nation great';

the Duke of York's summer camps provided the occasion for an embarrassed mingling of working-class and public-school boys in a programme of invigorating activities; finally a Miss Majendie opened a centre at Hedingham Castle to train unemployed Rovers (Senior Scouts) for domestic service and hairdressing.

Indeed the one thing that the 'juvenile organizations' of 'approved worth' had signally failed to do was to plug the Prince of Wales's gap: the age-group fourteen to eighteen remained relatively immune to the blandishments of the Boys Brigade, the Boy Scouts and the numerous boys' clubs established to promote their physical and moral welfare. The ideal of personal service to the poor and underprivileged might well appeal to romantic junior schoolboys and also to older public-schoolboys with a conscience about their advantages: it was obviously not calculated to appeal to the poor and under-privileged themselves. Nor was the ritual of the Rover Scouts, based on the King Arthur cult, likely to appeal to the working-class adolescent: the quest for the Holy Grail was more than likely to end at the back of the unemployment queue. In their peak year – 1933 – the Rovers only attracted 38,000 members (of a total Scouting population in Great Britain of nearly 700,000): and Scouting as a whole went into decline in this decade, attributed by its leaders to 'the slackening of moral standards, and the general lack of belief in the good life'.

It was at this juncture that Kurt Hahn established his residence in England; and he immediately began to display a lively interest in the nation's youth.

He recalls that he brought with him to England two lessons gleaned from his experience at Salem: that purposeful athletic training contributed towards 'vital health', enabling a boy to 'defeat defeatism' and that the 'deformities of puberty' could be overcome by kindling the *grandes passions*. He felt he had discovered 'preventive cures' for some of the 'diseases' of modern life: the decline of initiative, of skill and care. But now he faced a further problem: should this 'cure' be limited only to the few hundred boys who could pass through Gordonstoun? Was it not Gordonstoun's mission to fulfil Prince Max's ideal of 'Cistercian service' by spreading the good news abroad, placing the possibility of 'preventive cure' within the reach of every boy, thus setting an example of active citizenship? Hahn's attention was drawn to this possibility by the deplorable 'deterioration' which set in among fishermen's sons at Hopeman village, many of whom grew up to be 'either lawless or listless'. 'Who could witness this decline,' Hahn wrote, 'without feeling guilty that certain healing experiences were witheld from the underprivileged youth of this country?' This 'uneasy conscience', so familiar a vein in philanthropy, was the start of the Outward Bound Movement.

In one respect Hahn may rightly claim to be an innovator, at least with regard to civilian youth work. The Boy Scout Movement was founded on play and fun – which appealed to younger children but less so to older ones. Public-school 'character training' was based on games: gifted athletes might benefit, but there was much less appeal to the 'ordinary' boy. Reddie and a number of other progressive pioneers like Badley diversified the environment by adding farm and estate work, crafts, building and construction, to appeal to the 'practical' side of the boy's nature, his desire to use his hands. Herbert Read stressed education through art and the imagination. Hahn's contribution was education through adventure. The love of adventure, of danger, of challenge, was the greatest of the *grandes passions* that would 'protect' youth, and the one most widespread in its appeal to the adolescent nature. Sailing across dangerous seas, going on difficult expeditions, climbing mountains – these were men's activities, not boys', and during their currency ideals would be implanted, achievements experienced and friendships formed which would have the power to transform a boy's outlook on life.

Hahn is not someone who waits upon events, though he is adept at exploiting favourable opportunities. Within a year of his arrival in the north of Scotland he was negotiating with the nearby Elgin Academy, a large day-school, for the creation of a Moray Badge, which would be awarded to all over fourteen in Morayshire who had passed certain tests or standards in jumping, running, throwing and swimming (Athletics), walk-ing, climbing and sailing (Expedition), and life-saving (Service). A feature of the scheme was a promise demanded from the participant that he would observe 'training conditions' (no smoking or drinking) while working for the award. Hahn un-doubtedly hoped, and still hopes, that such badge schemes might become an integral part of the country's educational system, to be demanded equally with academic results as qualifications for jobs or university places. At that time (1936) there was the perennial revival of agitation about the state of youth's physical fitness, and Hahn considered the moment opportune to write a letter to *The Times* announcing the institution of the Moray Badge and calling for its general adoption. 'Public schools,' he declared,' should build themselves into strong-holds of fitness for the counties in which they are placed.' The proposal was premature. Hahn received only one letter of support 'but I treasure it. It came from Lord Baden-Powell.' However, the Regional Committee of the National Fitness Council did finance three fortnightly residential courses in North Scotland in 1938 and 1939 based on training for the Moray Badge which convinced Hahn of the validity of his claims. 'There could no longer be any doubt about the healing effects which could be brought about ... There was therefore a duty to continue our campaign.'

War brought influential support and numerous frustrations. Hahn has an unerring instinct for spotting potential allies in high places and his enthusiasm and personal force generally wins over the waverers. Now Boyd-Orr, William Temple, A. C. Lindsay, Master of Balliol, Lord Dawson of Penn (the King's physician) all wrote to *The Times* advocating the large-scale adoption of the Moray Badge programme as a kind of pre-paratory toughening for the armed forces. In the House of Commons, Philip Noel-Baker and Henry Brooke lent their voices. Soon Lindsay formed a committee to bring pressure on the Board of Education on which served a galaxy of notables: Robert Birley, Walter Oakeshott, Julian Huxley and others.

Meanwhile, Gordonstoun, transferred to Wales for the dur-ation of the war, sponsored a three-week summer camp in

1940 for youths from various backgrounds, including twenty young soldiers. Hahn was alarmed by the physical condition of the soldiers: they were 'healthy but not fit. The majority had little spring, only a few had proper powers of acceleration. . . . No wonder. . . . Most of them were smoking up to twenty-five cigarettes a day.' Following this experience he offered to train 1,000 boys a year in monthly courses of 200, the 'boy-leaders' to be provided by Gordonstoun. The President of the Board of Education, more alive perhaps than Hahn to social realities, rejected this proposal as 'irrelevant to the conditions which I have got to meet'. This proved conclusive: although the army adopted many of its principles in special schools for officer and Commando training, the Moray Badge programme, as far as the nation's schools were concerned, was dead for the time being.

Once again philanthropy stepped in, this time in the person of Lawrence Holt, chairman of the Blue Funnel Line, who offered to finance a short-term sea school at Aberdovey on condition that a proportion of places were reserved for Merchant Service apprentices. But Holt saw it as more than simply offering vocational training: it was to be a training for citizenship 'through the sea' and he invented for it the title Outward Bound. The first school for 'short-term character-training' was opened in October 1941.

The Master of Balliol had insisted that the 'Service' element should be stressed in the Moray Badge programme, and here the Gordonstoun programme of training in rescue work proved apposite, J. F. Fuller, the school's second Warden, being convinced that nothing attracts the young more than the call 'you are needed'. The eminent Liberal historian G. M. Trevelyan came down to Aberdovey to baptize the new sailing ketch, appropriately named *Garibaldi*: 'Without the instinct for adventure in young men,' he declared, 'any civilization, however enlightened, any state, however well ordered, must wilt and wither.'

The need to get the first Outward Bound school firmly established in peace-time led to the formation in 1946 of the Outward Bound Trust. The first president was Seebohm Rowntree who, in old age, returned to the philanthropy that he had spent so much of his youth in denouncing. There was really only one possible source of funds and recruitment to a course of this kind and that was from industry. Sir Spencer Summers, director of the steel firm, John Summers and Son Ltd, and Conservative M.P. for Aylesbury, became the Trust's secretary and 'wrote to business friends who explained how much they would like to help were it not for sceptical reports submitted to them by their personnel managers'. Colonel Spencer Chapman, the Trust's first paid executive, toured factories to persuade employers to send their apprentices. Slowly the money came in: first a cheque of £500 from United Steel; then £1,200 following a letter in *The Times* from Trevelyan and Rowntree. Field Marshal Montgomery was persuaded to launch an appeal for £100,000 in 1948, realized four years later; a dinner attended by Prince Philip in 1949 produced £3,000 and led to an interest-free loan of £15,000 which enabled a Mountain Outward Bound School to be started at Eskdale in the Lake District in 1950. Its first Warden, Adam Arnold-Brown, was an ex-Gordonstoun pupil. George Tomlinson, Labour Minister of Education, opening it, told employers that to send boys there 'would not be an expenditure but an investment'. Oliver Lyttelton, later Lord Chandos, chairman of A.E.I. and director of I.C.I., became another enthusiastic supporter, and by the end of the 1950s with two more schools – at Moray and Ullswater – opened, over 700 firms were sending their apprentices for 'short-term character-training'. Abroad, Outward Bound schools were established in Germany, Nigeria and Malaya, in the latter country under the auspices of the High Commissioner, Sir Gerald Templer, who was much encouraged by the support of the Chairmen of British Companies with interests out there'. An old school tie – a yellow knot against a blue background to represent the twin educative forces of mountain and sea – set the seal on the success achieved.

By 1957 Outward Bound schools were training 3,000 boys and 150 girls every year: the target figure for boys, 5,000 has since been comfortably achieved. In addition a Duke of

Edinburgh Award scheme – a kind of 'do-it-yourself' Outward Bound course – was started in 1958. Boys were sent to the schools mainly by firms with 'well-established training schemes, personnel officers and the like; who also tend to have apprentices attending night schools or day release classes' – in short, a youthful industrial élite, though Outward Bound schools today take a small proportion of Borstal boys. Industry's motives in supporting the new ventures were expressed by J. Parsons, Director of Personnel at Guest, Keen and Nettlefolds Ltd, in a speech to the Conference of the Outward Bound Trust held at Harrogate in 1965:

We also have very strong obligations to our shareholders ... and in order to fulfil these obligations, we need a fair day's work for a fair day's pay; we need responsible attitudes ... we need ... honest Shop Stewards with the guts to fight a case forthrightly when there is a case to fight, and to tell their constituents forthrightly when there is not a case; we need supervision, and management and leadership with much the same qualities ... we need integrity, fairness, self-discipline, highly developed senses of responsibility. We believe that even a month at an Outward Bound School can arouse in some, and develop in others, these qualities....

Sir Spencer Summers in explaining the widespread support for the idea of Outward Bound lists three main motives: to sustain the character of the people against the temptations and 'softness' of the Welfare State; to combat juvenile delinquency; and to heal the breach between Capital and Labour. The continuity with the older philanthropic tradition of youth service is complete.

One of the features of that tradition is that it has in this country at any rate always appealed far more to the political right than to the political left. Admittedly there was a short-lived left-wing version of the Boy Scouts called the Woodcraft Folk which was, Eager remarks distastefully, 'bisexual, pacifist and Socialist'. In the Youth Movement in England we may detect a strong vein of the Disraelian 'One Nation' rhetoric, the belief that given disinterested leadership the most varied people can be got to sink their differences in a common cause: much the same feeling lies behind the Back Britain

Movement. And indeed if one supports the *status quo* it follows that social conflict is unnecessary, or at any rate much exaggerated. To those, on the other hand, who believe it to be rooted in economic injustice, the proposal to sink differences in the 'national interest' appears as a smokescreen to hide from the underprivileged the reality of their oppression and to divert them from the pursuit of their true interests. It is a serious limitation of the English youth work tradition, of which Outward Bound is an integral part, that it ignores the element of principle in the socialist demand for equality. For justice it seeks to substitute chivalry, in much the same way as the Victorian husband did. Like Reddie's Abbotsholme it is frankly élitist and believes that social strife can best be avoided by imbuing the élite with a high moral seriousness. It is not clear that this is wrong: whether it is practicable is quite a different matter.

What exactly was the training offered? Each residential school, lasting four weeks, consisted of approximately a hundred boys, aged fifteen to nineteen, divided into Patrols or Watches of ten to twelve boys each. These units were functional both as regards activities and 'character-training'. They were the right size for the mountain expeditions at Eskdale or to form the crews of the sailing ships at Aberdovey. They were large enough to get a good 'mixture' of personalities, to avoid becoming cliques of a few boys cut off from the rest of the course; and small enough to develop a common loyalty and 'collective soul', to provide each boy with a task, in short, to prevent 'shirking'. Near the beginning of the course, Patrol Captains and Vice-Captains were appointed from among the 'natural' leaders, whose tasks it would be not only to give orders but to maintain 'tone' and morale.

Psychologically there was nothing new or interesting about any of these principles of organization, which were merely the efficient utilization of well-known social capacities (gregariousness, cooperativeness, emulation, friendship, pride, loyalty) for the achievement of certain specific objects. The ideological bias may perhaps be detected in the notion of the 'natural' leader inherited from the army and public schools, and the emphasis on activities which stressed team-work and obedience rather than individuality.

It is perfectly true that the objects of the course were defined in terms of individual achievement (the gaining of Membership and Honour Badges), but with the exception of athletic 'standards' these achievements were part of the corporate activities of the group; and even in athletics they counted towards the final placing of the group. At the Eastbourne conference of 1949 a proposal for individual projects, such as local history, farming, forestry, woodwork and so on, was rejected when a leading member, Captain Bedwell, stated that 'If boys choose their own projects, far too many choose soft options.' The rationale for preferring group to individual activities was the view that citizenship 'can best be inspired by the experience of subordinating self to a greater cause'.

The object of the course was to build 'character' by putting boys through testing physical experiences. The main activities at Eskdale were: canoeing, forestry, mountaineering, including compass work and map-reading; rope work and campcraft and rock climbing; mountain rescue, including first-aid; cross-country expeditions by patrols or smaller groups; and finally athletics, which included running, jumping and throwing events, graduated according to the age of the boy, with set standards. At Aberdovey, mountaineering was replaced by seamanship, which included compass, chart and map-reading, small-boat sailing and the watches taking turns on duty.

This programme was diversified by expeditions to the mountains, generally lasting four days (at Aberdovey the boys went on a three-day cruise), camping, and various 'problems' and 'games' designed to encourage initiative and test the training. There was a sing-song and an end-of-term concert.

Daily prayers were an integral part of the routine. In addition, two services were held on Sundays, and several evenings of the course were set aside for talks on religion. The Christian purpose of Outward Bound was firmly established at the 1949 Conference. The discussion on that occasion throws light on the assumptions of the movement.

Fitzherbert Wright, a Director of the Mountain School, submitted a paper, the opening paragraph of which read as follows:

The foundation of a healthy and good social life is a genuine belief in God. This, I think, is something which all of us connected with Outward Bound believe. The question is how are we to get this belief across to a number of young men in the short period when they are under the school's influence.

There were objections to introducing a resident padre: 'The best type of personnel officer in industry or youth-leader in a boys' club introduces a strong Christian bias into his work, and done this way his teaching and example are often accepted more readily than they would be if he was a padre'. The following curriculum was suggested:

... not stereotyped prayers out of books but spontaneous ones dealing with matters close to the boys' daily lives.... this would lead on... to a few short talks ... on the wonderful things in our daily life that would not have existed if it had not been for the actions taken by Christians.

The 'religious leader', towards the end of the course, would relate 'all that had happened in the past three weeks to a definite God whose Son Jesus Christ came down to earth and by his life and actions personified what all Christians try to do'. David James, later Conservative M.P. for Brighton, Kemptown, and a member of the Outward Bound Executive Committee, wrote:

Let the boys be taught that our knowledge of God, of Heaven, of our place in the Divine scheme of things is *not* a tale made up to make children less afraid of the dark but *fact* susceptible of proof....

More practically, he argued that 'if we don't take a specifically Christian line ... there [is] nothing at all to distinguish us from Hitler's "Strength through Joy" movement.' The Conference rejected the proposals of the more fervent Christians, concluding realistically that 'religion is caught and not taught'. The Memorandum on Religious Instruction of 1952 argued that 'example rather than precept' should form the basis of Christian instruction; nevertheless it declared the need for a 'trained theological mind' to 'satisfy the spiritual appetite we seek to create'. It would be his task to 'direct attention . . . to fundamental truths of the Christian faith; e.g., the existence of a personal God, the Divinity of Jesus Christ, Belief in the Life to Come. . . .' Short daily prayers should be supplemented by Padre's Hour once a week which the boys will be 'expected to attend'. The memorandum concluded that 'one effect of the training is to make [the boys] more spiritually susceptible'.

In the end, though, Outward Bound relies on the mountains and the sea to stimulate the boys' 'spiritual appetites'. The educative influence of Nature is a great theme of Romantic poetry. Blake's lines

> Great things are done when men and mountains meet
> These are not done by jostling in the street

are feebly echoed by the Bishop of Portsmouth: 'To climb a mountain or to sail a boat . . . is a splendid preparation for opening one's eyes to ultimate truth'. A month's experience of carrying on bracing activities amidst splendid natural settings is, on this view, an effective antidote to the soul-destroying 'materialism' of modern civilization.

Certainly the Outward Bound schools are magnificently situated. Of the mountains in the Lake District (home of the schools Eskdale and Ullswater) Wordsworth wrote:

Their *forms* are endlessly diversified, sweeping easily or boldly in simple majesty, abrupt and precipitous, or soft and elegant. In magnitude and grandeur they are individually inferior to the most celebrated of those in some other parts of this island; but in the combinations which they make, towering above each other, or lifting themselves in ridges like the waves of a tumultuous sea, and in the beauty and variety of their surfaces and colours, they are surpassed by none.

The call of the sea has traditionally been the call of adventure, especially in this country. As Geoffrey Winthrop Young remarks: 'A sea-school was the first obvious expression of the movement, in a country with historic traditions of sea power, of the Merchant Venturers, of Naval discipline and the adventure of sail, all at hand for recovery.' What exactly was the world that Outward Bound was trying to recover?

Captain J. F. Fuller, Warden of Aberdovey, writes about the traditions to which Outward Bound appeals:

This was the rough cradle of men of enterprise and determination, ready to face hazard like the indomitable men of forty led by that gifted farmer and craftsman Ezekiel Hughes, who trekked the long mountain way from Llanbrynmawr to Carmarthen and Bristol to find a ship to America. How well we should remember such expeditions, by foot and by farm cart, the trudging womenfolk with children clinging to their skirts, the oft-read Bible passages and soul-stirring hymns, the scanty baggage and spartan food, planned to carry them to the other side, in ships which provided only a few feet of 'tween deck in which to live, with rationed water and kindling wood. Truly Outward Bound. . . .

And of the impact of the sea Alan Villiers writes:

. . . the sailing ship is quiet, and real – no noise there, save of the wind and sea. All nonsense melts away. The boy – perhaps for the first time – gets the chance to feel himself as one of a worthwhile team, doing something *real* – helping the *Warspite* or the *Garibaldi* or the *Golden Valley* defeat the Irish Sea . . . making a difficult mountain climb, overcoming hardship, testing the stuff of true adventure. I have seen the Outward Bound, in a few short weeks, perform feats with boys and young men which seemed like miracles, bringing to bewildered young men the realization that, even in a world as hopelessly adrift as this. . . in the last analysis, a man's soul is his own and it will strengthen and support him anywhere, through anything – if he will only find it and nourish it.

Hahn is fond of quoting a former headmaster of Eton on mountaineering – 'conquest without the humiliation of the conquered'. In the Outward Bound ideal he believed he had discovered the 'moral equivalent to war' which, in his view, is the primary quest of our age. On the other hand it is precisely this moral aspect of Outward Bound that many people find objectionable, the 'bastard mixture of Naturalism and Puritanism' as Roland Barthes has put it. And even if it be true that mountain climbing provides the moral equivalent to war, just as people did not spend all their time fighting, so now they do not spend all their time climbing mountains. Has Outward Bound anything to contribute to preparing adolescents for life in the big city? Or is it just another flight from life masquerading as a social philosophy?

18 · Hahn's Educational Philosophy

A. J. P. Taylor, in remarking upon the commonplace quality of thought contained in Napoleon's Memoirs, observed justly that the genius and originality of such men lay in action rather than reflection. This is true of Kurt Hahn. He was not in any sense an original or systematic thinker. He borrowed freely from the most diverse sources: from Plato, from the Cistercians, from Goethe, from Reddie, from the English public school, from Baden-Powell, from Max Weber and many others. Nor can his thought, in any meaningful sense, be described as a synthesis of its various intellectual strands. Its unity was psychological: it was simply a *prolegomenu* to action. When we look for expressions of his thought, we find them almost entirely in memoranda, speeches and broadcasts: he wanted to fire individuals to action, rather than influence slowly the climate of opinion through books. The structure of the speeches, too, bears the imprint of the man of action. They are short and divided into two: diagnosis and remedy. The remedy may seem wildly inadequate to the diagnosis, but that never worried Hahn unduly. The important thing was to be doing something, rather than just talking about it. Underlying and perhaps rationalizing this temperamental craving for activity was Hahn's doctrine that a man is what he does. This belief lay at the basis of his educational thinking.

Hahn's chief educational aim was to produce citizens rather than thinkers, men of action rather than scholars; an aim which may be seen as a partial compensation for his own disqualification, through early ill-health, for a fully active political career.* For Hahn himself, despite an intense and

*Dr Hahn comments: 'Nobody who reads this sentence would have thought that the Trevelyan Scholarship Scheme had originated through Gordonstoun.'

continuing interest in affairs of state, was reduced to playing the role of an 'occasional' politician, to influencing the front-men behind the scenes. Out of his experience of the First World War, as well as his study of Greek thought, grew the conviction that every man has the duty to play an active political role when the need arises or when his conscience tells him that he must; and *in addition,* has the corollary duty of equipping himself, mentally and physically, for that task, holding himself in readiness, so to speak, for the day. Beyond this lies the conviction that the intervention of right-thinking citizens at crucial moments may exercise a decisive impact on events. 'The world,' Hahn quotes Napoleon, 'is not ruined by the wickedness of the wicked, but the weakness of the good.' In education, his object has been to eliminate that weakness.

Education as a training in citizenship becomes fully under-standable only in the light of the Greek identification between private and public virtue, between the good man and the good citizen. This identification was particularly plausible for a small community, such as the Greek city-state, where the influence of personal habits and dispositions was bound to be far-reaching. The fact that the boarding-school was a com-munity of this kind made it the obvious unit for an educa-tion in citizenship. Hahn was not so naïve as to suppose that under modern conditions politics can possibly be the chief preoccupation of normal citizens. Representative democracy has taken the place of the direct democracy of the Athenian city-state. What he aimed to do through his emphasis on citizenship was to inculcate the notion of civic duty in its widest sense – that of service to the community, in whatever role the individual was equipped to fulfil.

In choosing an active, directly helpful, ideal of service, Hahn was influenced not only by the obvious decline in the opportunities for political service, but also by his belief in the educational value of action. Unlike the Freudians, he was never very interested in motives: a person may embark on an enterprise for all the wrong motives, yet the experience of doing, of attempting, will build up the character. Hence he was never worried by the 'illegitimacy' of rewards and punishments for motivation. A characteristic progressive argument has been that children should only do things for the 'right' motives: if they feel personally impelled by interest or curiosity, or achievement for its own sake. Hahn's reply is that if all activity is made to hinge on children's inclinations, they would do very little. Their own positive inclinations must be reinforced with 'subsidiary' motivations, or they will be easily discouraged and distracted. Doing things produced experiences and memories which would fortify the soul for later life. For Hahn, moral education was primarily 'experience therapy' – the implanting of impressions to 'nourish the good'.

The Cistercians were not only 'good Samaritans', they were also monks. The great distraction for adolescents, Hahn believed, was the 'sexual impulse', and thus he advocated considerable monasticism to reinforce his social purposes. Premature eroticism, too, he saw as a disease of modern society. But in addition Hahn had an ideal of adolescent innocence – especially the innocence of the adolescent boy. Like Reddie, he spoke constantly of preserving childhood's 'treasures' in a way that suited his social purposes: joy in movement, readiness for dedication, enterprising curiosity, compassion – a mixed assortment, and rather surprising, if we remember that he was talking of the 'product of the nursery' But there is little doubt that the chief 'treasure' he had in mind was that of sexual innocence.

In a report to his Governing Body in 1938 he argued that adolescent boys can be kept sexually pure if they 'serve' the surrounding community. Thus service was seen both as a training in citizenship *and* as a sublimation of sexual desires. The cultivation of the *grande passion* had a similar dual function of encouraging self-development *and* affording protection against the erotic. Although Hahn showed little sympathy for, and little understanding of, Freud, implicit in this view is the Freudian idea of the psyche as a closed energy system, in which energy absorbed by one interest is energy withdrawn from another. Whether adolescent sexual development is really as destructive of other adolescent possibilities as Hahn believes is open to question.*

Like Plato, Hahn is first and foremost a social reformer, working through the medium of education. His task was to reform a 'diseased polis'. Unlike other progressive educators, though, he does not believe the essence of reform to lie in purifying men's motives: rather in rousing them from the torpor of withdrawal. In a lecture in 1949 entitled *The Decline of Democracy* he argued that 'the people of this country were a more vigilant democracy at the time of the Rotten Boroughs than today'.

Never in the nineteenth and twentieth centuries [he went on] was there a lack of independent voices – up to this war. I will now put before you the most tragic failure in vigilance. The use of the atom bomb is an undoubted crime against humanity. . . . Who cried out in anger and shame? At the time there were some whispering protests; no warning voice was heard which the Government had reason to fear.

This decline is rooted in modern civilization:

We believe [Hahn said in 1936] that present-day civilization is diseased, often sapping the strength of the young before they are grown up, that he who is meant to serve our civilization must be fortified against it; that Education can build up protective tastes and habits likely to provide immunity.

Here, then, we have a view of education as a 'countervailing' force, deliberately acting against the pressure of a diseased society.

What are these modern diseases? Basically, Hahn identifies three. First, he cites 'soft living' in its broadest sense – the absence of challenges, the permissive environment, the widespread availability of drugs, stimulants, tranquillizers and other forms of escapism – all of which undermine physical fitness, initiative and self-discipline. Second, he points to the 'confused restlessness' of modern life which, coupled with

*Dr Hahn comments: 'Intensity must not be confused with depth. Premature monopoly exercised by sexual drives not only destroys the vitality of childhood but operates against the development of a healthy erotic passion.'

modern techniques of mass production, have undermined skill, care of craftsmanship, pride in work and various kinds of creative imagination. Thirdly, there is the impersonality of the modern state, becoming more 'rationalized' and 'bureaucratized' at every point, leading to the breakdown of any sense of community, of personal involvement (compassion). These diseases in combination erode the individual's sense of personal responsibility; typically, they produce apathy, withdrawal, cynicism, a feeling of helplessness, and social and moral callousness, which destroy citizenship, and place the management of affairs increasingly in the hands of the bureaucrat and efficiency expert, lacking in humanity and imagination. The 'withdrawal' of the individual is thus bad for two reasons: it destroys something vital in the individual himself; and it is the spiritual death of society. Increasingly as the 'best' lose interest, the 'worst' come to the fore, thus intensifying the diseases which cry out for reformation.

Modern society, Hahn insists, breeds four types of adolescents – the lawless, the listless, the angries and the 'honourable sceptics'. All four have one thing in common – a retreat from citizenship into a private world. Even the typical rebellion of adolescence – over appearance, clothes, morals – is a kind of escapism from more urgent ills crying out for cure.

Hahn particularly wants to capture the elusive 'honourable sceptics' – those made wise and cynical before their time, who 'opt out' of the battle to improve society, believing that the irrationality of the world and the iniquity of men and institutions must inevitably defeat their best efforts. He quotes the example of one of his Salem boys, who, when told by Hahn that Nazism would not last, replied, 'Mr Hahn, I do not want to shatter your illusions.' Hahn, like many other commentators on the young, identifies such vast and impersonal tragedies as the Nazi genocide programme and the constant threat of nuclear destruction as crucial in producing the cynicism and escapism of young people today. He admires such protest movements as C.N.D., though at the same time pitying their futility. Essentially he sees C.N.D. as a mass movement of escapism which, by deliberately placing itself

outside the bounds of politics, highlighted youth's disillusionment with, and rejection of, the political process.

So much for the diagnosis: the remedies inevitably sound
disappointing, even trivial. The first step in the remedial plan
is building up physical fitness. This has two purposes. First,
he sees the body as the executive instrument of the will. Hahn
believes that the flabby body will always rebel against demands made upon it, leading to the failure of enterprises
embarked upon with high hopes, a lack of staying power to
see a thing through to the end. 'If the power of overcoming
remains undeveloped in childhood, for example, through the
neglect of physical education, then girls and boys are often
soured in their dearest pursuits whenever they land in labours,
exhaustion, dangers or scorn from their fellows.' Secondly,
physical fitness produces self-confidence by enlarging the scope
of the possible. His plan of physical education marks a sharp
divergence from the public-school system: like that of Reddie
it is oriented primarily to the needs of the 'ordinary' boy
rather than the gifted athlete. Each boy was to be set physical
challenges, in athletics, in mountaineering, in camping and so
on, which, when achieved, would be rewarded by badges and
medallions, signifying certain 'standards': here as elsewhere
Hahn did not disdain competition and reward as the spur. But
he did not stop there. Maintenance of physical fitness should
become habitual, like cleaning one's teeth, so that the boy
as well as the adult would be in a constant state of readiness
for 'service'. Hence the importance in the Gordonstoun
scheme of things of the 'training plan' which on the physical side laid down a number of daily activities for which each
boy was personally responsible – such as the cold shower,
early morning run, press-ups, sixty skips a day and so on.
Hahn has testified to the fortifying properties of his own early
morning excursions, to which, no doubt, he attributes his immense octogenarian energy.

Physical fitness was merely a means, not an end. The end
was 'service to the community', in particular to the district in
which the educational establishment was located. Gordonstoun boys took over the supervision of a stretch of coastline

some short distance from their school, and Watchers in their watchtower intently scanned the horizons day after day, waiting to rescue any ships or persons in distress. As the years went by the Watchers were reinforced by Fire Guards and Mountain Rescuers, all on call to answer the cry of distress. Latterly Hahn has been increasingly impressed by the possibilities of reducing fatalities from drowning by the application of respiration and first aid by skilled laymen. The report of the Working Party of the Royal College of Surgeons on Accident Prevention and Life Saving (1963), with its revelations of accidents in the home, in industry, on the roads, in sport and adventure, has greatly expanded his horizons of service. 'In the kitchen, crossing the street, in a factory, in a boat or on a mountain we are surrounded by dangers and risks,' declared the Duke of Edinburgh. Here indeed was a noble field for Cistercian service.

The Gordonstoun programme of rescue and Samaritan work was not intended as a definitive blueprint. Gordonstoun's work was adapted to its location: eventually Hahn hopes to see a day-boarding school serving every community in the country, a great freemasonry of countervailing forces, fortifying youth against the diseases of society by inspiring them to serve that society. Of course, home life would not in all cases be conducive to the spirit the school sought to implant, but Hahn was confident that 'the boy with a training plan can carry the atmosphere of his school community to his home, as the diver carries his atmosphere to the bottom of the sea'.

The psychological basis of Hahn's remedial plan was the belief that high spirits, generous feelings, idealism, the capacity for hard work and dedication were the basic ingredients of adolescent nature. These were the ingredients that were threatened by the onset of sexual desire and by the other corrupting influences which we have noted. Like most other progressive educators Hahn thus claims that he is on the side of the 'essential' child. Unlike them, however, he sees the main threat to the child's personality coming not from the authoritarian schoolmaster or 'imposed' discipline, but from a diseased environment outside the school. In his greater emphasis on the social factors affecting attitudes and behaviour we may see the influence of Greek thought, of his own political experiences, and also of the sociologist Max Weber. Because he recognizes the power of environment he does not make the mistake of imagining that non-interference is either possible or desirable. The vacuum created by the removal from the scene of the teacher will not be filled by the child's blossoming nature, but by other pressures probably more destructive of his individuality and talents than the teacher ever was.

Hahn starts with the youthful criminal to make his point. Like Homer Lane, he believes that a 'bad boy' is an example of good qualities wrongly directed. Indeed he often characterizes the law-abiding boy as a 'low-spirited Puritan', whose obedience is the result of spiritual poverty rather than of civic or moral virtue. 'Lawless youth' on the other hand is high-spirited and adventurous. 'To prevail against the promptings of conscience,' Hahn declared in 1959, 'the baser instincts often need an ally and such an ally can be found in the longing for mastery: to outwit the constituted authorities, to gain your end by stealthy imaginative planning and resourceful daring, to experience the thrill of narrow escapes.' From this highly romanticized, though attractive, picture of delinquent youth, Hahn's remedy follows quite naturally: harness the longing for mastery, daring and adventure to 'honourable' pursuits and the 'motive power behind crime would in many cases be weakened'.

Similarly attractive is Hahn's dictum that 'every youth has in him a *grande passion*'. (He is careful to distinguish between 'passions' of the 'poisonous' and passions of the 'non-poisonous' variety.) Like Reddie, he was rebelling against the public-school neglect of the ordinary boy. He saw the public school as catering on the one hand, to the 'academic' boy, and on the other, to the natural athlete. The public schools have made some attempt to remedy this by proliferating 'hobbies', but Hahn's argument is that these activities are bound to be largely a sham unless they are thoroughly integrated into the educational purpose of the school and given 'public assent'. 'What time and nervous strength have these children to spare for their hobbies?' he asked in 1934. 'Do these hobbies occupy a place of importance and dignity in your community life? Does not the word "hobby" really preclude this?'

One of the first things which strikes one in considering the Gordonstoun system is the disparity between the aim of producing adults who think for themselves (which Hahn always maintained distinguished his system from Fascist education) and the tremendous psychological and moral pressure exerted on the boy at school. Even granted that there is a great deal of truth in Hahn's position, there is still something objectionable about the ways in which the Gordonstoun system attempts, and largely succeeds, in binding its pupils to its own particular vision. For Hahn has never attempted to win assent to his propositions by intellectual or rational means. Indeed, he is either unable, or unwilling, to partake in what is generally regarded as rational discourse. One advances an objection and receives back an aphorism. The pupils' adhesion to the truth as preached by Gordonstoun is secured by an extremely thorough system of moulding which exploits to the full the boy's susceptibility to myth, ritual and psychological suggestion. In the Gordonstoun scheme progressive and traditional public-school features are interwoven in an extremely subtle and thorough fashion, minimizing the chance to break free provided by the relative inefficiency of most systems, and by their reluctance to press their ostensible aims to their logical conclusion: most educational institutions would probably be horrified if they actually did succeed in producing the kind of pupils they assure their parents they aim to produce. Hahn, like Reddie, felt that the road to Utopia had to be thoroughly mapped out and organized: nothing should be left to chance. Thus, despite all his disclaimers, Gordonstoun boys are not remarkable for their independence of thought. Though they may well hold minority views, it is because their school does, not because they have worked them out for

Does this matter? Certainly – because no one man or one institution has a monopoly of truth. Every institution will mould to a certain extent: probably to the extent that most people who pass through it will accept most of the things it stands for. This applies to progressive as well as to other institutions: it is, after all, no coincidence that most people who go to progressive schools turn out to have progressive views. The completely free individual is the illusion of those who imagine men to be gods. Nevertheless, a very good test of an educational institution is whether it affords any real opportunity for rebellion against its aims. By that I do not mean necessarily overt opportunity. This is where many progressives went astray. They assumed that because the traditional educators beat their pupils, they beat them into the shape that they wanted. This was not so. Someone remarked rather unkindly that the sole justification of the public-school system was that it produced rebels. Certainly this was an unintended consequence, but a very valuable one. Built quite unconsciously into that system is some principle of ineffectiveness that negatives in sufficient numbers of cases the very qualities and aims that are being instilled. At Gordonstoun at present it is very difficult to find evidence of any such principle at work. In conception and psychology it is totalitarian.

Gordonstoun has to be sustained by totalitarian methods, because in the end, despite all Hahn's acuteness, its plan of education is too narrow to encompass the full 'nature' of adolescents, and its faith is inadequate to the needs of our time. This is not to deny the importance of his contribution to the modern educational debate. Indeed, in many ways, he is the most impressive (if not the most endearing) of the progressive educators. He has a social awareness which most of them lacked. He realized that the main forces acting on the growing boy emanated from outside the school, not from within it, and quite deliberately conceived of his school as a countervailing force against certain social tendencies which he abhorred. This is a much more modern formulation of the educational problem of today than that of the traditional progressives who saw the enemy as authority in general and who were therefore quite unable to conceive that school authority might have a very important function in protecting the child against, say, the authority of the teenage culture or the mass media. Indeed it was his desire to protect the finer possibilities of adolescence against the pressure of a commercialized, exploitative, culture that partly explains (though it does not justify) his extreme methods. He felt that the child had to be fortified by the school in such a way as to make him impregnable to the temptations and pressures of life 'outside'.

But this is precisely why Gordonstoun's answer is inadequate. For Hahn makes no real attempt to understand and master the forces which govern modern society; he merely evades them. His remedies are marginal to the problems he describes. His system is ultimately escapist. His products do not go out into the world with the object of changing it: they retreat into worlds of their own. It was not Salem old boys who took the lead in resisting Nazism: there is no roll call of Salem martyrs under the Hitler regime, though thousands of Germans perished in the struggle against it, just as today it is not Gordonstoun alumni whose influence is felt wherever history is being made. In a very real sense Hahn himself is the greatest, indeed the only, product of his own system.

PART FIVE

The Future of Progressive Education

19 · Progressive Theory and Social Change

Is the progressive impulse in English education advancing or declining? If we limit the query to the dozen or so small, independent, largely boarding, communities which pioneered progressive ideas in this country, the answer is not encouraging. The English progressive school movement stopped growing after 1940. The Second World War was not followed by a great outcrop of new progressive establishments as the First World War had been. With the single exception of Atlantic College, no new progressive school of any importance has established itself since the war. A number have closed down. Others, like Summerhill and Kilquhanity, have survived only with difficulty. The ones that have done well, like Bedales and Gordonstoun, have become more orthodox.

The broader picture is more encouraging. The modern school is undoubtedly more humane than its predecessor. There is much less corporal punishment. The curriculum in many schools has been widened to embrace the arts, vocational studies, travel and adventure. There is much exciting experiment in new teaching and learning techniques; soon every school worth its salt will have its language laboratory, computer centre, teaching machines, New Maths and closed-circuit television. The new school buildings are an infinite improvement on their drab Victorian ancestors.

Nor has progressive thought failed to make an impact on social attitudes. Whether all teenage repudiation of adult values can be traced back to Dr Spock is doubtful: but certainly a more permissive home and school environment has influenced the attitudes of the young to love and war, to clothes and music, to manners and style, though such influences cannot easily be separated out from others such as affluence, advertising and the advent of nuclear weapons. Whether the progressives take an unmixed pride in the revolution they helped to unleash is again doubtful: they would approve of anti-Vietnam demonstrations but not the pop and pot and promiscuous sex that often accompanies them.

Are their achievements permanent or transitory? Certainly there have been powerful tendencies working in the opposite direction. The expansion of the private sector of progressive education has come up against a financial limit, as the wealth which had created and sustained the independent sector was taxed away to pay for the Welfare State. The traditional public schools, being old and well endowed, have been able to maintain and improve their position *vis-à-vis* their progressive challengers – which at any rate seemed unlikely in the 1920s. Of course, in order to do so they have had to undergo considerable modernization – but this has by no means been in an unequivocally progressive direction. For one thing, they have paid much more attention to the examinations which all progressives loathed. The reasons are clear. Middle-class children were now being forced to compete for jobs and incomes which had before been theirs by right. Also the requirements for those jobs were changing. The idea of the amateur, of the 'good all-rounder', which the progressives inherited from the public schools was giving way to the need for the trained specialist. The progressives entirely failed to foresee this further evolution of the industrial system, with its need for a highly trained labour force and a highly skilled managerial élite. The educational system was bound to respond to this need at all levels, though in the case of Britain it has done so somewhat sluggishly.

Progressive education had little contact with working-class children whose needs have recently come to dominate educational discussion. As we have seen, the progressives chose, for a variety of reasons, to work with middle-class children. In the English context that was where their clientèle lay. If they thought at all about working-class education it was in terms of the gradual application of progressive techniques to state education. And indeed in the 1930s there *were* genuinely progressive experiments in the senior elementary schools, whose children were turned out on to the labour market at the age of fourteen without having to face any examinations. But since the war the demand has not been that every working-class child should be given the opportunity to develop his soul, but that he should be given the opportunity to become a qualified engineer earning two thousand pounds a year. The personal ideal of affluence and the social need for skills combined to give working-class education a direction very different from the one the progressives would have envisaged. Because their own clientèle was rich, they could afford to turn their backs on the scientific civilization in the name of Higher Values. For the poor, the lower value of affluence came first – and with it the training in industrial skills that alone could bring it into being and sustain it.

The problems that came to light in educating working-class children could not be dealt with by means of the traditional progressive analysis of failure, based on the experience of dealing with middle-class children. This analysis was twofold. In the first place the failure of the child to adjust to school life was seen as psychological: Johnny's attention wandered from his arithmetic lesson because he was worried by bed-wetting or had a complex about masturbation. The remedy in this case was therapy. In the second place it was seen as the result of an unnecessary clash between youth and age in which youth, on the whole, had right on its side. The remedy in this case was to make the school environment more attractive to the child, by diversifying the syllabus, making discipline more permissive and improving methods of instruction.

These insights are by no means negligible. But the attempt to educate working-class children revealed a third problem: the failure of a whole culture to adjust to the demands of school life. The anti-school attitude came not from the individual soul of the child, nor was it the product of an insufficiently interesting school syllabus. Rather it reflected a basic lack of sympathy and understanding between the school world and working-class culture. If the cultural norms of school and family were identical, as was generally the case with the middle class, then it was plausible to explain an individual child's deviation from those norms in clinical terms,

But where those norms diverged, a clinical explanation would not do. For example, the psychological explanation of truancy made little sense in a culture where truancy might be the 'normal' response, just as the psychological explanation of delinquency made little sense where the parental culture was strongly hostile to the police. The basic educational problem here was not to improve the child's behaviour and attitude by therapy, but to act upon the environment which supported them. We may call this the difference between the psychological and the sociological approach.

Similarly the old progressive solutions of making the syllabus more attractive and discipline more permissive had only a limited relevance to working-class education, though they have not been without their influential advocates, especially the recent Newsom Report (1964). The difficulties here have been partly practical, notably the control of the state system by local authorities, inhibiting experiment, and the lack of money. But an even more fundamental barrier is to be found in the purpose of working-class education. As we have seen, the progressives could afford to relegate the normal activities of school life – notably those connected with study – to a secondary role, because the economy did not then require specialized skills, and because, in any case, their children were not relying upon school achievement for their future position in life. The scope for progressive experiment came to be severely circumscribed by the evolution of the educational system into a job-allocating system. This evolution was compatible with the addition of adventure, music and art courses to the syllabus, so long as they did not displace the more 'serious' subjects from their central place. It was compatible with the proliferation of courses, because modern society required new categories of skilled manpower. It was compatible with the most sophisticated teaching and learning techniques, because society required ever higher standards of competence. It was compatible with the best psychological insights because society could not afford the wastage of talent and the wrong motivations. What it was not compatible with was an education which had no relevance to society's needs, or relevance only to the private visions of progressive pioneers.

Of course, I am overdrawing the technological side of the picture: the conception of 'society's needs' has itself been influenced by progressive thought, especially in its commitment to the idea of the self-development and self-fulfilment of the individual. Such a commitment has also been made possible by the fact that we are no longer a society threatened by danger or poverty. There has been a general relaxation from the harsh struggle for survival – prematurely, critics would say – and this has been reflected in the educational system. The point is that in so far as progressive theory has run counter to the commercial, industrial and defence needs of society it has not been able to prevail. Its old enemy Society jealously guards its interests.

Here we really approach the heart of the progressive failure. Progressive thought never outgrew the intellectual enthusiasms of the eighteenth century, when men, liberated by science from the medieval dogmas of Christianity, felt for the first time that the world was theirs to shape to their will. At all times in history men have regretted their condition. But until then tragedy had been accepted as man's lot. For the Greeks the ultimate vanity was *hubris* – the attempt to usurp the place of the Gods. In Christian thought man was condemned forever to imperfection by virtue of a defect in the will called original sin. But in the eighteenth century man replaces God as arbiter of his destiny. The chains that bind man, suggests Rousseau, are not those of God or God-given nature, but of society, a human construct, and therefore alterable by human will.

Educationally these ideas came into their own once the industrial revolution had thrown up a wealthy middle class, free from the poverty the masses and the feudal conceptions of the landed aristocracy. By the end of the nineteenth century there existed in England a prosperous rentier class which could afford to relax and cultivate the finer things in life. If the public schools were designed to turn the sons of manufacturers into gentlemen, the progressive schools were designed to turn the sons of rentiers into aesthetes. An enlightened upper class

would suffuse society with finer feelings: industrial philistinism would give way to something infinitely nobler and more
beautiful.

The vision of Prometheus Unchained took many forms in
the intellectual thought of the nineteenth century. The progressives were most influenced by its Romantic aspect. Like
the Romantics, they refused to accept the model of progress
held up by science and industrialism. For them man's liberation lay not through reason, but through love, creation, self-
expression. The Romantics sought not to bind feeling with the
chains of reason, but to liberate feeling for creative achievement.

We need not spend much time on the great debate between
Reason and Feeling except to say that both sides pushed their
theories to absurd extremes. Men of reason like Locke and
James Mill tended to view the child simply as a rational adult
in miniature; and childhood itself as a disease to be got over
as quickly as possible. John Stuart Mill gives a horrible account
of his father's ultra-rational scheme of education which led
him at eighteen to a nervous breakdown and to the discovery,
through Wordsworth, that there was a dimension to life un-
dreamt of in his father's philosophy. On the other hand, men
of feeling like Blake and Rousseau went to the opposite extreme of claiming divine status for childish impulses. Both
sides made fervent appeals to man's 'essential nature', the one
side declaring, in Bertrand Russell's words, that 'man's chief
glory is his capacity for reason'; the other side seeing it as the
capacity for artistic creation. We ought now to be able to
view the whole question with a certain detachment. The progressives, following the Romantics, were surely right in their
contention that children were not just adults in miniature, that
childhood has its own valid modes of feeling and expression,
that people do not grow up, they merely grow older and become different, and that each stage of life has to be accepted
and 'lived out'. All the progressives, from Neill to Hahn,
are united in their insistence that the 'treasures of childhood
must not be sacrificed to some conception of society's needs
or some clearly defined end product. What united them was

this common attitude rather than agreement on detail: for as we have seen they all tended to define the 'treasures of childhood' in different ways.

On the other hand, the progressives tended to neglect the fact that the foundations for the adult stage, which is marked by the greater capacity for reason, have to be laid in childhood, and that this necessarily involved some violence to purely childish impulse. They forgot that some of the greatest adult achievements are born out of childhood misery; that Darwin and Einstein, to mention just two of many cases, were both profoundly unhappy at school. They glossed over the possibility that a well-adjusted childhood may be the recipe for a well-adjusted mediocrity. So violent was their revolt against the pedantic schoolmaster that they tended to reject the methods of reason altogether, which led them into such remarkably naïve assumptions as that the world would be made better through love and that all causes of strife would be abolished if only everyone were 'fulfilled'.

It is now realized better than before that all great achievement involves some synthesis of the imaginative or intuitive and the purely rational processes. As Sir Peter Medawar recently remarked, 'All advance of scientific understanding, at every level, begins with a speculative adventure, an imaginative preconception of *what might be possible....*'* Reasoning is simply that intellectual process which may help our dreams come true – but the dreams themselves spark the endeavour. Progressive Romanticism was an over-reaction to a scientific scholasticism which prevailed in the nineteenth century. Education can revert to the classical task of holding the 'imaginative' and 'critical' elements in balance, as Reddie indeed tried to do, but which most of his successors neglected.

But to return to the main argument: both the Romantics and Rationalists, whatever their other differences, were agreed that the path to man's liberation lay in freeing some vital qualities or attributes of human nature from the chains of society which imprisoned them. They appealed in short to

* In *Encounter*, January 1969, p. 17.

some 'essential' human nature as a stick with which to beat custom, convention, all the accumulated legacy of the past, which was seen as alien, external, imposed. Freud, the last great poet of human nature, lent support to this formulation with his early doctrine of instincts versus repression. Freudian Marxists like Reich, and later Marcuse, saw this alien social reality as capitalist-industrial society. Logically this view entailed overthrowing existing society and putting something else in its place. But most English progressives, being as Eysenck would put it 'soft-hearted', did not go that far. They ignored the social dimension entirely, and limited themselves to trying to 'insulate' children from the oppressive society by putting them in boarding schools in the country, encouraging pre-industrial pursuits, and abolishing as far as possible all 'distorting' adult direction. Perhaps they hoped, like Hahn, that their products would go boldly into society and change it. In this they were disappointed. Their pupils did not, on the whole, enter politics, though Bedales has produced Malcolm MacDonald and Konni Zilliacus. They went into those professions offering a high degree of personal fulfilment – the arts, universities and increasingly the mass media. There, of course, they have not been without considerable influence in eroding traditional values. But the erosion has been gradual and partial, and to the observer, viewing things through middle-class progressive eyes, the world did not seem to be improving as it should have been.

Indeed, two world wars and the advent of nuclear weapons dealt a blow to progressive optimism from which there has been no real recovery. After the Hitler war especially, many progressives came to the conclusion that the world was not on their side. The collapse of their exaggerated hopes left them incurable pessimists. Bertrand Russell wrote in 1956: 'There is on the whole, much less liberty in the world now than there was a hundred years ago'. H. G. Wells, who in the 1920s had enthused about world government, peace and brotherhood, wrote in 1945 in *Mind at the End of Its Tether*, 'The end of everything we call life is close at hand. . . .' The climate of opinion shifted sharply away from easy progressivism. No longer did men think that there was some simple key that would open the door to a wonderful future.

One casualty of this loss of faith has been the optimistic progressive account of human nature. Are man's bad qualities implicit in human nature, or are they a response to social stress? The progressives took the latter view. Man's violence, to take one example, was a response to social terrorism imposed by the state or the ruling class, institutionalized in authoritarian systems of education and morality. If only these systems could be overthrown or circumvented, man would become peaceful. Much has been made of the fact that monkeys only fight under specific social conditions. Yet, as Lorenz* has pointed out, all monkey communities, whether peaceful or hostile, rest upon force. Again, it has been argued that the prolonged dependence in humans of children upon adults, unique in living species, creates memories of humiliation and impotence which in later life have to be erased by aggressive behaviour, by proving oneself to be better than others.†

The question whether man is 'by nature' good or bad, brutish or benign, is really unanswerable. Rousseau wrote 'Man's first instincts are always good: the why and wherefore of the entry of every vice can be traced....' Neill gives as an example the child's play instinct. What could be more 'natural' and delightful? It is the callous adult suppression of childish play, Neill suggests, that produces much of the discontent that feeds aggression in later life. Yet the play of kittens, to which Neill often refers approvingly, has a definite element of torture in it – as any mouse knows. The proposition that man is civilized by curbing his childish impulses would seem to be just as tenable as the proposition that he is civilized by giving them full play.

But even if we accept the optimistic view – that man is born full of original goodness rather than original sin – is this formulation of much help? One of the great realizations of recent times has been that man, whatever his so-called nature,

*In his book *On Aggression*.
†See Anthony Storr's review article in the *Sunday Times*, 27 October 1968.

is trapped in his history and culture much more completely than the progressives realized. The walls of Jericho, it has become plain, are not going to crumble at a blast from the progressive trumpet.

Time and time again we are forced back to this progressive lack of any social dimension. Society was seen as an oppressive monolith 'outside' human nature. There was no attempt to analyse it, to break it down into its various component parts and see which of them might be helpful to progressive projects, or which of them were necessary features of any social existence. In particular the progressives never stopped to consider whether certain uses of force or authority might not be safeguards against worse uses of it. (Hahn must be excepted from this criticism.) Thus they deliberately set about undermining the authority of teacher and parent in order to liberate the true 'nature' of the child only to discover that authority usurped by the 'peer group' or the mass media or the pop idols. Whether the changes in social habit we have been describing earlier are regarded as good or bad, it cannot be claimed that they spring from the absence of authority. Do the current cult words like 'groovey', 'trendy', and 'with it' suggest an absence of authority? The proliferation of cults and cult words, far from suggesting a rejection of authority, suggest rather a restless craving for it.

From the immensity of social change now taking place it is very difficult to discern any clear pattern, much less disentangle causes. Nowadays everyone is in theory much 'freer' to hold any opinion than before: yet most people agree that the eccentric is vanishing, that the age of the individual is giving way to the age of the combine or the group. Again, the removal of external pressures and a growing affluence have encouraged relaxation, diversity, pluralism; yet at the same time more and more people are compelled to become part of organizations which inevitably mould their opinions: Galbraith has described in frightening detail the emergence of 'corporation man' with goals and motivations set by the firm; the same theme has been treated dramatically in the recent American play, *The Latent Heterosexual*. Man has been released by education from a specialization imposed by custom – only to fall into bondage to a specialization imposed by the need for expert knowledge. What seems to be at work is almost a straight process of substitution: as soon as one set of constraints is removed another set immediately imposes itself.

Yet this very process brings about its own reaction. Modern man, it is clear, has a deep need periodically to hurl his defiance at society. His enhanced realization of human possibilities makes society, chained to habit and inertia, seem doubly oppressive. He is prepared to risk death and mass violence, the probability, indeed certainty, of an outcome very different from his hopes, in order to reassert his notion of autonomy in face of impersonal forces before which he normally feels – and is – helpless. The upheavals of the 1930s and in particular the failures of Russian Communism imposed for a time a salutary restraint on his passions: we all become good social democrats, believers in piecemeal reform, in slow and miniscule adaptations to the *status quo*. From today's vantage point it seems probable that the age of *Sturm und Drang* is returning.

The modern student movement uses much of the language of the progressive movement in education. It asserts man's right to self-fulfilment at the expense of society's claims. It asserts his right to an education – at least at the university level – geared to his own needs and purposes and not to those of an impersonal structure 'outside'. To that end it proposes changes in the curriculum and organization of university life which have a very progressive ring about them: courses which reflect the interests of contemporary youth rather than those of tired old age, an organization which gives the student 'self-government' and ends the authority of the teacher and the professor. There is the same assault on the examination system which tests only what society wants and ignores qualities to which it is opposed.

Sociologically, the postgraduate generation which leads the student revolt is the modern equivalent of the rentier class which spearheaded the first progressive revolution. Like them it has acquired the taste for wide-ranging social criticism and the income and status to support it. Both have wanted to reform education but from different perspectives. The nineteenth-century consumers of progressive ideas were parents who required a certain education for their children; their modern equivalents are those children or grandchildren grown up. They were vicarious progressives: they campaigned for a progressive world for their children; the second wave want a progressive world for themselves. They have moved from the health farm to the streets. For them the aims of educational and social revolution have achieved a unity which was impossible for their predecessors, for they are the subjects of their own demands.

In face of the new student militancy the old progressivism inevitably has a pale and worn out look. The bigger and more reputable schools like Bedales, Dartington Hall, Gordonstoun and Atlantic College are best placed for survival, especially if they succeed in attracting the patronage of the increasing number of parents likely to work in international or European organizations. The existence of the smaller schools is more precarious. Summerhill was saved by the publication of Neill's book, *Summerhill*, in the United States in 1962. Today 70 per cent of the children are American. But can the school survive after his death? Education, like industry, has to realize economies of scale if it is to make ends meet. The smaller schools can only remain small by running down their facilities and standards. This in turn diminishes their appeal. But is there that much demand? Certainly schools which cannot offer a sound academic education would seem to have little chance of surviving, at any rate at the secondary level. Even today, few children stay on at Summerhill or Kilquhanity above the ages of thirteen or fourteen. The children, having been emotionally sorted out, are whisked off by their parents to prepare for examinations.

The difficulties of the progressive schools are in part those of the independent sector as a whole. It is not surprising that a number of leading independent-school spokesmen are now making overtures for state money, much as they dislike the

principle of state control. This coincides with the Labour
Party's wish to integrate the independent sector in the
national system in order to end privilege. But how is this to be
accomplished?

The hostility of the progressive movement to the state has
already been mentioned. Partly, it stems from a natural fear
of losing its established independence. But there is a deeper
motive. It sees the national system as basically hostile to the
kind of educational innovation which it champions. The fate
of Michael Duane at Risinghill* serves as an awful warning
as to what could happen if the progressive schools came under
the control of local authority bureaucracy. The Labour Party,
in an effort to meet these objections, and largely under the
influence of Dr Michael Young, offered in 1962 'special provision for genuine experimental schools'. By giving a subsidy
or paying fees, the state or local authority might take up a
proportion of places in the schools.

But on what basis would children be chosen and what other
strings would be attached? The public schools are worried
that they may be swamped with 'need' cases, which will convert them into schools for special children. This fear is even
more strongly felt by progressive schools, which already suffer
from the stigma of catering for unusual children. For example, Summerhill and Kilquhanity, which already take a
proportion of 'difficult' children financed by the local
authorities, might find this proportion drastically increased
as a result of 'integration'; which is not something they would
welcome. Dartington and Bedales might find themselves
getting too many children from broken homes; Gordonstoun
too many 'unacademic' children. They fear, in short, that any
'bias' of the school would be greatly accentuated in the inter-

*Risinghill, a comprehensive school in Islington, catering for a racially
mixed population, including West Indians and Greek Cypriots, got a bad
reputation when its headmaster, Duane, abolished corporal punishment.
Staff friction, rumours of wild lawlessness, and local authority enmity led
to its closing in 1965 as part of a 'reorganization', despite a remarkable fall
in the probation rate, considerable parental support, and a great loyalty of
the children to the headmaster leading to a demonstration to Downing
Street, in a vain effort to avert its closure. See Leila Berg, *Risinghill*, 1968.

ests of bureaucratic tidiness. 'X is a thief – doesn't Neill deal with those cases? – Summerhill is the place for him.'

Michael Young has suggested that the progressive schools might become laboratories for educational research and experiment, attached to university departments of education. On the other hand, the progressive schools are not, as I have indicated earlier, primarily 'experimental' schools. They stood, and still stand, for something definite – a concept of education based on a certain view of the child, on a certain view of the relationship between the individual and society, on a certain view of the good society. Their system is sustained by the nature of their recruitment. Their utility for researchers is therefore bound to be limited, especially as, being small boarding schools, they have largely cut themselves off from the main lines of research and innovation in the huge, day comprehensives.

Nevertheless, many of the progressives do feel it to be something of a paradox to be ranged on the conservative side of the political debate over education. At Bedales, one was conscious of a fight between conservatives and radicals for the ownership of the word 'progressive'. Progressive in the Bedales context is traditional – Doing What Badley Did; it means 'the Bedales way of life'. But progressive also implies an attack on tradition – and should the Bedales tradition be exempt? The dilemma would be less acute if 'the Bedales way of life' was still being copied elsewhere, for then, however traditional the school itself might have become, it would still be a progressive example to others. But when the school is without disciples, when the progressive school movement as a whole has become a little isolated family affair, with staff switching from Bedales, to King Alfred's, to Frensham Heights to Dartington and then back to Bedales in a kind of incestuous merry-go-round, then progressives begin to doubt whether they stand any longer for anything of importance. Even the Outward Bound and Voluntary Service movements, which progressives see as potential links between progressive and state education, can hardly be thought of as a new radicalism for a city culture.

Perhaps, as Professor Stewart has written, the progressive schools today can be no more than 'good schools of their kind for children whose parents want to send them'; that if the voice of the '0.2 per cent' grows fainter* that is because it has had its say, made its contribution, and the torch has now passed to others.

*'The Progressive Schools and their Future', *New Society*, 13 February 1964.

Bibliography

This bibliography does not aim to be comprehensive. I include only the material which I have read and found useful.

1. General

M. Boultwood and S. Curtis, *A Short History of Educational Ideas*, (1965 edition) runs to well over 600 pages. S. Curtis, *Introduction to the Philosophy of Education* (1958), is shorter. R. Rusk, *The Doctrines of the Great Educators* (1956), is helpful. A standard work is H. Barnard, *A Short History of English Education* (1958 ed.). W. H. G. Armytage, *400 Years of English Education*, is less comprehensive, but more interesting. Cyril Norwood, *The English Tradition of Education* (1929), is a high-minded defence of the public-school tradition, while E. B. Castle, *Ancient Education and Today* (1961), traces the sources of that tradition in Greek and Jewish thought.

Some contemporary controversies: *Aims in Education – The Philosophic Approach* (ed. T. H. B. Hollins, 1965) has a number of philosophers discussing what education should be trying to do. There is a good critique of John Dewey. K. Lovell, *Educational Psychology and Children* (1963 ed.), also attacks Dewey's scientific method, as well as discussing the latest developments in this field. The best introduction to the modern literature is D. Ross, *Educational Psychology* (1964). John Vaizey's *Education in the Modern World* (1967) describes the conditions which have given rise to modern educational explosion. J. Floud, A. H. Halsey and F. M. Martin, *Social Class and Educational Opportunity* (1956), is a pioneering work on the social determinants of educability. G. H. Bantock, *Education and Values* (1965), attacks the political bias of the sociologists, as well as the methodological inadequacies of such early 'scientific' educators as Susan Isaacs. David Reisman, *The Lonely Crowd* (1956), is a classical exposition of some unintended consequences of the progressive revolution in the United States, as is Richard G. Hofstadter's *Anti-Intellectualism in American Life* (1964). Mrs Floud's 'Teaching in the Affluent Society' (*British Journal of Sociology*, December 1962) considers the role of the teacher as a 'countervailing force', as do F. R. Leavis and Denys Thompson in *Culture and Environment* (1964 ed.) On the modern public school the best accounts are: G. Snow, *The Public School in the Modern Age* (1959), John Wilson, *Public*

Schools and Private Practice (1962), J. Dancy, *The Public Schools and the Future* (1963), and Graham Kalton, *The Public Schools: A Factual Survey* (1966). For state secondary education see: *Half Our Future: A Report of the Central Advisory Council for Education* (Chairman Sir John Newsom, 1963); *British Secondary Education* (ed. Richard Gross, 1965) and John Partridge, *Middle School* (1965).

2. Progressive Education

General Background: Rousseau's *Émile* is the key text. For the best short accounts of the Enlightenment and the Romantic movement see: Alfred Cobban, *The Enlightenment*, The New Cambridge Modern History, Vol. VII, and W. Stark, *Literature and Thought: the Romantic Tendency*, ibid., Vol. 8. For a sensitive treatment of the child in Romantic literature see Peter Coveney, *The Image of Childhood* (1967 ed.). David Newsome, *Godliness and Good Learning* (1961), is an excellent account of the transformation of the nineteenth-century public school. The best literary attacks on the public school are Alec Waugh, *The Loom of Youth* (1917), written when he was only seventeen, Robert Graves, *Goodbye to All That* (1929), and Esmond and Giles Romilly, *Out of Bounds* (1935), which also has a short account of Bedales. A very comprehensive but somewhat dull intellectual background and international history is W. Boyd and W. Rawson, *The Story of the New Education* (1965). The *New Era*, the journal of the New Education Fellowship, is a great quarry of twentieth-century progressive thought (complete set in Bodleian, Oxford). There are two Penguins on Freud and Jung respectively: J. A. C. Brown, *Freud and the Post-Freudians* (1951), and Freida Fordham, *An Introduction to Jung's Psychology* (1953). A short and simple guide to Dewey's thought is John Dewey, *Education and Experience* (1938). Miss Helen Parkhurst of the Dalton Plan gives an account of its theory and practice in *Education on the Dalton Plan* (1937). E. M. Standing has written a biography of *Maria Montessori – Her Life and Work* (1957). For a contrast between Montessori and Susan Isaacs see Nathan Isaacs, 'A Critical Notice', *Journal of Child Psychology and Psychiatry* (October 1966). Bernard Wright, *Educational Heresies* (1925), is typical of progressive thought in the mid-nineteen twenties.

The Schools: *The Modern Schools Handbook* (ed. Trevor Blewitt, 1934) and *The Independent Progressive School* (ed. H. A. T. Child, 1962) contain essays written by headmasters of progressive schools in the two periods. L. B. Pekin, *Progressive Schools* (1934), is an enthusiastic account. J. H. Badley has written his *Memories and Reflections* (1955). W. B. Curry, *The School*, (1934), is a statement of his educational philosophy. *Dartington Hall: An Account of the School* (1958) was written just after he had given up his headmastership. J. H. Simpson, *Schoolmaster's Harvest* (1953), describes the educational pilgrimage of the innovator at Rencomb. Bertrand Russell's educational theories have been described by J. Park, *Bertrand Russell on Education* (1964). His own *Education and the Social Order*, and *On Education* (both published in the 1930s) are classics. Hibburd and Montgomery, *A Short History of King Alfred School*, is unpublished. There is a considerable literature on schools for maladjusted and delinquent children: Otto Shaw. *Maladjusted Boys* (1965). and David Wills, *Throw Away Thy Rod* (1960), were both influenced by Neill. Michael Burn, *Mr Lyward's Answer*, (1964 ed.), is an uncritical account of Finchden Manor School. *Experiment in Education at Sevenoaks* (1965) describes some interesting experimental projects in an unprogressive school.

Contemporary Comment: The papers read to the *Dartington Hall Conference on Progressive Education* (March/April 1965, unpublished) are a valuable guide to current trends in progressive thinking. Professor W. A. C. Stewart, 'The Progressive Schools and their Future' (*New Society*, 13 February 1964), is a brief survey of history and current prospects. His monumental, two-volume *Pioneers in Education* (1967/8), came out after my manuscript was completed. There are occasional newspaper accounts: the more sensational the school, the more sensational the newspaper. Thus the *News of the World*, 14 January 1962, reported that pupils at Burgess Hill, London, aged 5–18 'are allowed to smoke, drink beer, swear, and scrawl "Ban the Bomb" slogans on the walls.' More sober recent articles have been: Colm Brogan, 'Gospel of Gordonstoun' (*Yorkshire Post*, 24 August 1962); Caroline Nicholson, three articles on Progressive Schools in the *Observer* (23 and 30 June, 7 July 1963); Leila Berg, 'Why the Caning Had to Stop', (*Guardian*, 22 January 1965) – she has since written a book, *Risinghill* (1968), on the whole of that dubious episode; 'Bedales Still Distinctive' (Special Correspondent, *Times Educational Supplement*, 19 February 1965); 'Experiments in Education', two articles on Dartington Hall (Edward Blishen) and Atlantic College (Gordon Brook-Shepherd), *Weekend Telegraph*, 22 April 1966. 'An Afternoon at Kilquhanity' (from a Correspondent, *Times Educational Supplement*, 23 September 1966.)

School magazines have been a great help. Both the *Abbotsholmian* and the *Atlantic College Magazine* are praiseworthy but dull. *The Bedales Chronicle* is witty, sophisticated, ironical; the *Gordonstoun Record* has already been described: the unofficial paper (*Outlook*) is by no means remarkable. The Kilquhanity *Broadsheet* specializes in blood-curdling tales of rebellion (imaginary) against the headmaster. The unofficial King Alfred School journals *Quintessence* and *Locus Classicus* are more imaginative and lively than the official one, *The Alfredian*. Dartington Hall and Summerhill do not produce a regular magazine; Friends and old pupils of Summerhill publish a magazine, *Id* (nineteen issues so far), mainly devoted to Neill, his ideas, and his disciples.

3. Reddie, Neill and Hahn

Reddie of Abbotsholme: the basic sources are Cecil Reddie, *Abbotsholme*, (1900), remarkable, among other things, for the author's extraordinary prose; B. M. Ward, *Reddie of Abbotsholme*, a sub-standard life; *Fifty Years of Abbotsholme: A Collection of Personal Impressions* (1939). Since this manuscript was completed Michael Holroyd has devoted a chapter of his biography of *Lytton Strachey* (1967) to describing his subject's schooldays at Abbotsholme. There are a large number of books by and about Edward Carpenter, Reddie's chief mentor. His three best: *Towards Democracy* (a long epic poem, 1883), *England's Ideal* (1887), and *My Days and Dreams* (autobiography, 1916). A. H. Moncur Syme, *Edward Carpenter: His Ideas and Ideals* (1916), is a good straightforward account. Another influential book was John Ruskin's *Unto This Last* (1862). W. Jolly, *Ruskin on Education* (1894), is commendably short. T. Carlyle, *Selected Works, Reminiscences and Letters* (ed. Julian Symons, 1955), contains his *Sartor Resartus* (1839). Of the many different texts of Walt Whitman's *Leaves of Grass*, I have used the 1860 one, published by the Cornell University Press, 1961; F. B. Freidman, *Walt Whitman Looks at the Schools* (1950), contains his educational journalism.

Neill of Summerhill: Neill is the most entertaining of all writers on education – also one of the most prolific. He has also written some (unsuccessful) children's stories His first book, *A Dominie's Log* (1915) contains his first rebellious thoughts on conventional education; *A Dominie Dismissed* (1918) is a semi-fictional dramatization of his early mental and emotional conflicts; *A Dominie in Doubt* (1920) is a transitional book: Neill has come into contact with Freud and Theosophy; *A Dominie Abroad* (1922) describes Neill's experiences at Hellerau, near Dresden, and a lot more on Freud; *The Problem Child* (1926) is the first clear statement of his belief in 'natural goodness'; there are two more *Problem* books before the war: *The Problem Parent* (1932) and *The Problem Teacher* (1939), interrupted by *That Dreadful School* (1937), the most complete statement of his pre-war position; *Hearts Not Heads in the School* (1945) has a touching memorial to his first wife, Mrs 'Lins'; *The Problem Family* (1947) is especially good on the very young child; this is continued in *The Free Child* (1953), in which Neill talks about the upbringing of his daughter, Zoe; *Summerhill: A Radical Approach to Education* (1961) is a compilation from earlier writings and introduced Neill's ideas to the United States; *Talking of Summerhill* (1967) is in relaxed question-and-answer form.

A most important source for Neill's early life is *Notes on My Life* (unpublished manuscript, 1939); a dialogue between Neill and Maria Montessori in the American magazine *Redbook* (1963) sums up the differences between their philosophies. The two people with the most influence on Neill were Homer Lane and Wilhelm Reich. Homer Lane's *Talks to Parents and Teachers* (1928) gives his ideas; E. T. Bazeley, *Homer Lane and the Little Commonwealth* (1928), is a good account of Lane's school for delinquents; W. David Wills, *Homer Lane: A Biography* (1964), is excellent. There has been no good life of Reich. There is a Penguin compilation, *The Function of the Orgasm* (1965).

Hahn of Gordonstoun: a collection of Hahn's published writings has been deposited in the Cambridge University Library. His essays and talks include: 'A German Public School' (*The Listener*, 17 January 1934); *The Practical Child and the Bookworm* (1934); *Education for Leisure* (1938); 'Christian Peace Procedure' (*Spectator*, 12 December 1939); *Two Sermons* (Liverpool Cathedral, 1943); *Ten Years of Gordonstoun* (1943); *Aims and Obstacles* (1950); 'Juvenile Irresponsibility' (*Gordonstoun Record*, 1956); 'The Atlantic Colleges' (*Time and Tide*, 8 February 1958); 'The Ruse of Conscience' (*Gordonstoun Record*, 1960); 'Unnecessary Deaths' (*The Listener*, 26 April 1962); *The Aristocracy of Service* (1962); *Education and the Crisis of Democracy* (1962); *Address to the Outward Bound Conference* (1965); *The Young and the Outcome of the War* (1965); *Remarks on Human Behaviour* (1965). In addition Hahn was largely responsible for the writing of the *Memoirs of Prince Max of Baden* (tr. Calder and Sutton, 2 vols., 1928), an apologia for their joint attitude in the First World War.

Professor Golo Mann has written a long essay entitled *Kurt Hahn's Political Activities*, translated from the German by C. Sutton, but as yet unpublished in this country; Golo Mann also gave an address at Salem on the occasion of Hahn's 80th birthday. A hostile comment on Hahn is to be found in T. C. Worsley, *Flannelled Fool* (1966). Arthur Marwick, *Clifford Allen: The Open Conspirator* (1964), includes comments on Hahn by leading progressive educationists of the 1930s; Adam Arnold-Brown, *Unfolding Character: The Impact of Gordonstoun* (1962), is a glowing tribute to Hahn and the school. Erich Meissner, *The Boy and His Needs* (1956), is the educational philosophy of Hahn's closest collaborator. For the general background to Hahn's political activities in Germany and England see A. J. P. Taylor, *The Course of*

German History (1945), and Martin Gilbert, *The Roots of Appeasement* (1966). Gilbert's *Plough My Own Furrow: The Story of Lord Allen of Hurtwood* gives some correspondence with Hahn about Hans Litten, the left-wing journalist imprisoned by Hitler.

W. McG. Eagar, *Making Men* (1953), and E. E. Reynolds, *The Scout Movement* (1950), are indispensable background to Outward Bound. A hostile and entertaining view of Youth Movements is to be found in Harold Stovin, *Totem – The Exploitation of Youth* (1935). *Outward Bound* (ed. David James, 1957) is a comprehensive account of the growth of the movement. The papers of the *Outward Bound Conference* held at Harrogate (1965) give a good idea of current trends and debates. *Accident Prevention and Life Saving* (report of a working party set up by the Royal College of Surgeons 1961–3) recommends the greater use of trained laymen in these two areas.

Index